Early Education
in the Public Schools

Penny Hauser-Cram, Donald E. Pierson, Deborah Klein Walker, Terrence Tivnan

Foreword by Craig T. Ramey

Early Education in the Public Schools

Lessons from a Comprehensive Birth-to-Kindergarten Program

 Jossey-Bass Publishers

San Francisco • Oxford • 1991

EARLY EDUCATION IN THE PUBLIC SCHOOLS
Lessons from a Comprehensive Birth-to-Kindergarten Program
by Penny Hauser-Cram, Donald E. Pierson,
Deborah Klein Walker, and Terrence Tivnan

Copyright © 1991 by: Jossey-Bass Inc., Publishers
350 Sansome Street
San Francisco, California 94104
&
Jossey-Bass Limited
Headington Hill Hall
Oxford OX3 0BW

Library of Congress Cataloging-in-Publication Data

Early education in the public schools: lessons from a comprehensive
birth-to-kindergarten program / Penny Hauser-Cram . . . [et al.].
    p.   cm. — (The Jossey-Bass education series) (Jossey-Bass social
and behavioral science series)
    "A joint publication in the Jossey-Bass education series and the
Jossey-Bass social and behavioral science series."
    Includes bibliographical references and index.
    ISBN 1-55542-328-0
    1. Early childhood education—Massachusetts—Brookline—
Longitudinal studies.   2. Brookline Early Education Project.
I. Hauser-Cram, Penny.   II. Series.   III. Series: Jossey-Bass social
and behavioral science series.
LB113.25.E27   1991
372.21'09744'7—dc20   90-22972
                                                                          CIP

Manufactured in the United States of America

The paper in this book meets the guidelines for
permanence and durability of the Committee on
Production Guidelines for Book Longevity of
the Council on Library Resources.

JACKET DESIGN BY WILLI BAUM

FIRST EDITION

Code 9128

A *joint publication in*

The Jossey-Bass
Education Series

and

The Jossey-Bass
Social and Behavioral Science Series

Contents

Foreword

American public education is the backbone of American democracy; it is also the primary means by which we preserve our competitive economic system and ensure personal choice. Yet Americans from all walks of life are increasingly dissatisfied with both the process and the results of our public educational system. Academic underachievement, particularly in literacy and mathematical skills, poses a formidable challenge to our desired way of life. Behavior problems and dropping out of school have lifelong consequences that are causing a rising tide of public alarm. Changes in the basic structures and functioning of the American family, such as nontraditional employment patterns, teenage parenting, and divorce, are also associated with calls for public education to be more supportive of contemporary families. Changes must, can, and will be made to address these complex issues.

The Brookline Early Education Project (BEEP), begun in the early 1970s in a diverse but generally affluent Boston suburb with a daring and innovative school superintendent, has resulted in useful and important insights concerning one approach to school reform. The authors of this book—Penny Hauser-Cram, Donald E. Pierson, Deborah Klein Walker, and Terrence Tivnan—are experienced leaders of that project, and they tell a balanced and hopeful story about the educational and scientific aspects of the Brookline experiment.

The central premise of the Brookline project is that high-quality, family-oriented, comprehensive education during the first five years of a child's life "can serve as a community base for primary prevention activities, ensuring that children enter kindergarten as healthy, competent learners. The BEEP study consisted of three major components—parent education and support, early childhood education for toddlers and prekindergarteners, and health and development monitoring." Each family in the study was randomly assigned to one of three levels of services, ranging from minimal additions to existing services to more intensive additions, thus allowing a powerful examination of whether the amount of preschool educational services can be associated with school readiness and subsequent scholastic progress.

The major finding is that an intensive level of intervention during the first five years positively modifies subsequent classroom behavior and academic skills. This effect was most pronounced for children from less well-educated families—the only children at significant scholastic risk in this sample. To say it another way, the children at greatest risk for school difficulties benefited from the program, but *only* if the preschool services were intensive. This conclusion is consistent with the recent finding from a similar preschool educational intervention program dealing with low-income families (Ramey and Campbell, forthcoming). The Brookline finding is particularly important considering the high level of family support and educational services generally available to all children attending Brookline public schools. While the measured effect on scholastic performance of children from highly educated families was not so great, this does not imply that such children and their families did not benefit in other ways from participating in these programs, and the mix of families across the socioeconomic spectrum is a healthy feature of the Brookline program. Also, it should be noted that the high level of services available to all children and families in Brookline probably affected a conservative estimate of program impact. The scholastic performance of children from less well-educated families, in the minimal- and moderate-intensity intervention conditions, was likely to have been at a higher base level than it would have been in a town with fewer general resources.

Early Education in the Public Schools is particularly notewor-thy for several features. First, it adds important new data to a growing national data base of the long-term positive conse-quences of high-quality preschool education. Second, it links extensive preschool experience to a reduction of observed be-havior problems later in school, thereby demonstrating a plau-sible mechanism whereby preschool effects are sustained. Thus, it makes a significant advance over the frequently cited long-term but unexplained effects from the Perry Preschool Project (Berreuta-Clement and others, 1984). Third, and perhaps most important, the project clearly demonstrates that public schools can launch and sustain large-scale, complicated preschool re-forms successfully. Parents from all backgrounds can be meaning-fully involved in better preparing their children for public edu-cation, while teams of professionals from diverse disciplines, including education, pediatrics, and psychology, can work co-operatively and productively toward goals that elude the grasp of a single disciplinary approach.

In the process of telling the reader about the successes of the Brookline approach, the authors are also refreshingly can-did about the difficulties and limitations that they encountered and about the changes in the program they would now make in the light of experience. Because this book is so clearly and forthrightly written, it can be a catalyst for continued discus-sions by educators, policymakers, researchers, and concerned citizens. It is an important and timely addition to the continu-ing debate about how to improve public education in the United States. The main conclusion that I draw from this work is that significant positive changes are made possible by foresightful and intensive efforts. Such successes will not, however, be easy, simple, or inexpensive.

February 1991   Craig T. Ramey
                         Director
                         Civitan International Research Center
                         The University of Alabama
                            at Birmingham

For the children and families of the
Brookline Early Education Project—
who by their participation, enthusiasm,
and development demonstrated the value
of early childhood education

Preface

During the last two decades, the daily lives and basic composition of American families have changed substantially. Because the majority of women with very young children are now in the work force, the care and education of young children has emerged as a significant national issue. Moreover, the percentage of children living in poverty has increased substantially. In many communities, parents and policymakers have looked to the public schools for assistance. Indeed, the mission and responsibility of the public schools in the education of young children have become a central part of the debate about public solutions to a host of social problems, including inadequate child care, disenfranchised parents, fragmented services for multineed families, and early school failure.

In this book, we tell the story of one school district's experience with developing an early education program. The Brookline Early Education Project (BEEP) was a comprehensive school-based early education program that enrolled over 200 families with children of infant through kindergarten age. Although BEEP was built on a theoretical framework and research base shared by many early childhood programs that were developed in the 1970s, the findings of this project contribute important new information to the array of outcomes demonstrated by such programs. BEEP combined several attributes that made it unique in comparison to other early childhood programs.

1. It was a school-based program, and its success required that a network of alliances link parents, school personnel, and the project's staff.
2. It was family oriented and operated from the premise that the family is the prime educator of the child.
3. It served a racially and economically heterogeneous population of children and neither focused exclusively on children from one particular group nor assumed a family deficit model.
4. It was a comprehensive health, developmental, and educational program and involved a multidisciplinary team of educators, pediatricians, psychologists, social workers, and other specialists.
5. It provided home-based support to families during children's infant and toddler years followed by a school-based prekindergarten program during the children's preschool years.
6. Its evaluation incorporated questions about the value of different levels of intensity of services as well as the value of early childhood services per se.

In several critical ways, BEEP anticipated current debates about early education policies and programs such as the merits of school-based programs for young children and families, the importance of programs that offer support to families with very young children, and the value of comprehensive and intensive services. In other ways, BEEP struggled with some issues, such as ways to develop bilingual programs for young children and their families, that have continued to elude general consensus.

Audience for This Book

In this book, we describe the experiences and findings of BEEP within the context of current educational and social issues. This book is intended for those involved in establishing policies and developing programs for public schools — educational administrators, school board members, teachers, and community leaders. But it is also intended for all individuals who have an interest in the potential value of high-quality early education programs for all young children and their families. Thus, we draw conclusions and implications that will interest many audiences: state departments of education, state legislatures, elementary and secondary schools, preschool and child-care programs, health care providers, social service agencies, federal agencies, parents, and students of child development.

Each of us was involved in BEEP in a different way. Penny Hauser-Cram was a preschool teacher in one of the BEEP classrooms, later becoming a member of its evaluation team, and focused primarily on the impact of BEEP on parents. Donald E. Pierson was the director of the program from its inception through its evaluation. Deborah Klein Walker was a consultant to the evaluation team from its inception and, in the early days of program planning, helped to develop a battery of instruments that assessed children's competence in school. Terrence Tivnan was a member of the evaluation team at BEEP and determined the analytical strategies used in investigating the program's effectiveness.

Overview of the Contents

A variety of social forces have placed early childhood programs in the forefront of social change. Chapter One presents the reasons why schools today are grappling with the notion of providing early childhood programs. Chapter Two summarizes the extensive literature on the success of early childhood programs. Chapter Three describes the controversy about the role of the public schools in early childhood and family support programs. We consider the arguments raised by both critics and advocates of school-based early childhood programs.

Beginning with Chapter Four, we discuss the various aspects of BEEP, starting with a description of the impetus for BEEP, its origins, and the research and community base upon which it was built. Chapter Five presents an overview of the three interrelated program components — parent education and support, early childhood programs, and periodic health and development monitoring; each component is described in more detail in the chapters that follow. In Chapter Six we focus on

the parent education and support aspects of BEEP. Chapter
Seven describes the school-based early childhood programs for
children. As many early education programs in the future will
need to make decisions about culturally sensitive means of working with non-English-speaking families, we pay particular attention in Chapter Eight to the strengths and limitations of our
approach to providing a bilingual program for children from
Hispanic families. Chapter Nine describes the health and development monitoring system devised at BEEP and synthesizes
the findings about the optimal time for assessments in early childhood. Like all programs, BEEP was changed in response to problems encountered during its implementation, and in each chapter
we discuss the problems and decisions we made pertaining to
the various program components. Our intent is to make the pitfalls as well as the strengths of BEEP apparent so others can
design programs based on the lessons we learned.

The two chapters that follow the description of the program present information about its evaluation. First, in Chapter Ten, we summarize the views of parents who participated
in the program, emphasizing the program components they
found most and least valuable. In addition, we describe a study
we conducted on the effects of BEEP on parent participation
in the public schools. In Chapter Eleven, we present the findings
from the evaluation of BEEP based on its impact on children's
functioning in kindergarten and second grade. We outline the
difficulties encountered in evaluating a multifaceted program
like BEEP, and the decisions we made to cope with these problems. Also, we present data on the impact of BEEP on children
but summarize the results for readers unfamiliar with statistical techniques. In the final chapter, Chapter Twelve, we consider the experience of BEEP in light of current discussions about
the merits and drawbacks of school-based early childhood programs and delineate components critical to the future success
of programs for young children in public school settings.

We also have included several appendixes to assist readers
interested in implementing early education programs or want-
ing to refer to the evaluation data presented in Chapter Eleven.
Appendix A details the type of questions parents asked us about

the program in general and about their child's development in particular. Appendix B describes the questions BEEP staff used to generate discussions with parents during home visits. Appendix C is a table of assessment measures, and Appendix D is composed of a series of tables presenting evaluation data. Finally, Appendix E includes a policy statement on early education adopted by the Brookline Public Schools (Brookline, Massachusetts) as an example of the type of document that school districts can develop as part of their policy formulation on early education.

February 1991

Penny Hauser-Cram
Worcester, Massachusetts

Donald E. Pierson
Lowell, Massachusetts

Deborah Klein Walker
Boston, Massachusetts

Terrence Tivnan
Cambridge, Massachusetts

Acknowledgments

This book was made possible by the generous support of two private foundations, Carnegie Corporation of New York and The Robert Wood Johnson Foundation. We are especially grateful and indebted to Barbara Finberg, executive vice-president of Carnegie Corporation of New York, for her enduring interest, guidance, and encouragement from the outset to the completion of this project. We also thank Margaret Mahoney and Ruby Hearn of The Robert Wood Johnson Foundation for their consistent support of the comprehensive health-related aspects of the project.

Robert Sperber, superintendent of schools for the public schools of Brookline, Massachusetts, had the foresight to see the potential significance of early education in the public schools; he put together the team that launched BEEP, and he demonstrated the strong leadership that is essential for the survival of innovative projects. Burton White, director of the Harvard Preschool Project, provided much of the initial impetus for the project. Behind the scenes, the late Francis McKenzie, Brookline's director of Pupil Personnel Services, and Larry Dougherty, coordinator of language arts, worked untold hours generating school, community, and funding support for the fledgling project. Elizabeth Nicol, project historian, compiled mountains of meeting notes, wrote reports that served as essential documentation, and kept the project on course with reminders of the stated goals and priorities. Pamela McClain was instrumental in shaping the project's standards and spirit of inclusiveness.

Much of the project's uniqueness derived from its collaboration with Children's Hospital Medical Center in Boston. Initial support and guidance were offered by Julius Richmond, Robert Haggerty, and George Lamb. Melvin Levine was the driving force who expanded the scope and significance of the project. He led the medical team, developed instruments that have oriented pediatricians to an improved understanding of both normal development and learning disorders, and published many papers that have presented the work of BEEP in medical journals. Pediatricians Judith Palfrey and Frank Oberklaid and Nurse Margaret Hanson modeled the practitioner styles that fostered parental trust and interdisciplinary collaboration, and they have also analyzed and reported on the extensive medical data base.

Diana Kronstadt, Ruth Wolman, and Catherine Buttonweiser served as diagnostic program supervisor, psychologist, and social worker, respectively, through the major share of the project. Their expertise and insights were vital to the effective delivery of services and their careful documentation assisted the project's systematic record keeping. They were assisted in their efforts by the psychological testing skills of Joan Grenzeback, Martha Markowitz, Thomas Perez, and Diane Schodlatz and by the social work skills of Joan Gordon and Angela Polk.

BEEP's education staff personified the ideals of the project. They helped make this book possible in several respects: by their expert work with children and parents, by their development of resource documents, and by their keeping of extensive records that went far beyond the ordinary teaching role. We especially wish to acknowledge the contribution of the *Infant Toddler Curriculum of the Brookline Early Education Project,* written by Mary Jane Yurchak, education program supervisor, with assistance from Barbara Curry, Selma Klein, Marianne Kohn, Alison Lavin, Pamela McClain, Martha Niebanck, Marsha Rogers, Maureen Rooney, Anne Tuzman-Isaza, and Gail Wolfson. (Appendixes A and B are excerpted from this guide.) Yurchak, Rogers, and Wolfson also drafted the Prekindergarten Profile of Goals, which Barbara Murphy, prekindergarten coordinator, extended and conscientiously implemented. We also wish to acknowledge that many other teachers made significant contributions with their planning and dedicated delivery of "the BEEP model." Those who participated over several years included: Karen Amado, Judith Black, Milagros Cordero, Cynthia Lawrence, Una McGeough-Nugent, Felicita Perez, Jeanette Reynolds, Judith Rodriquez, Margaret Simon, Carole Thomson, Su-Ing Tsoi, and Sandra White.

This book benefits enormously from the data base that was collected, coded, analyzed, and reported over the years by the research staff. Those who made important contributions included: Cary Aufseeser, Susan Boltansky, Martha Bronson, Anthony Bryk, Barbara Carroll, Elizabeth Dromey, Virginia Evans, Thomas Ferb, Jane Fort, Patricia McLaughlin, Michelene Malson, Martha Markowitz, Lynn Meltzer, Kevin Nugent, John O'Brien, Kathleen O'Leary, Brant Robey, Maureen Spofford, Kathleen Sullivan, Maureen Sullivan, Janet Swartz, and Heather Weiss.

The support staff created a welcoming climate for the families and prepared numerous position papers, manuals, and manuscripts. Roxana Caminos, Kathleen Carspecken, Jean Ehrenberg, Shoshanna Fine, Maureen Rooney, Sue Ryan, Barbara Scotto, Linda Solomon, and Cheryl Whitfield all deserve special mention for their competence, cheerfulness, and patience.

We were fortunate to benefit from the experience and counsel of many consultants at each stage of the project. Two individuals, Craig T. Ramey of the Civitan International Research Center at the University of Alabama, Birmingham, and Donald Steinwachs of the Health Services Research and Development Center at the Johns Hopkins University, were particularly helpful in planning the second grade evaluation and in guiding us through the voluminous data analyses.

The project could not have been launched or have survived without the interest and counsel of community and professional advisory groups. Those who gave extensive support included: Joan Bergstrom, John Cawthorne, Jessica Daniels, Robert Hayden, John Hubbell, Amando Martinez, Jean McGuire, Dorothy Mooney, Nettie Nathan, Joan Ottinger, Donald Polk, Lawrence Reiner, Gloria Rudisch, Michelle Seltzer, Cecilia Soriano-Bresnahan, Myra Togut, Ann Wacker, and Irving Williams.

Likewise, the many after school meetings voluntarily attended by school personnel generated ideas and policies that were essential to our plans and progress. Consistent participants over the years included: Roger Aubrey, Barbara Berns, Robert Boyd, Martha Farlow, Ruthellen Fitch, Myra Gannaway, Kathleen Gerritz, Naomi Gordon, Sondra Gotkin, Estelle King, Treva Krantz, Barbara LaPotin, Linda Larson, Mary Mokler, Priscilla Moulton, Bette Peterson, Shirley Partoll, Jeff Resnick, Patricia Ruane, Debra Schein-Gerson, Virginia Seavey, Harriet Sutfin, Louise Thompson, and Shirley Thorne.

Robert Sperber's successors as superintendent of schools, Charles Slater, William Sheridan, and James Walsh, have maintained the commitment to early education in Brookline. They and the Brookline school committee members, now including parents who participated in BEEP, have found ways to continue key aspects of the BEEP model through an early education office, transition to kindergarten, bilingual prekindergarten, home visiting, a drop-in center, and adult education programs.

We are indebted to Linda V. Beardsley for her compilation of references and conscientious proofreading. Marty Wyngaarden Krauss offered many helpful suggestions and reactions to chapter drafts.

Finally, we express appreciation to Allen Jossey-Bass for his initial interest in this book and to Lesley Iura for her undying support and guidance that saw us through to publication.

Since we have received so much help and support, we worry that we have overlooked or given inadequate attention to many important contributions. For this, we apologize. And we alone take full responsibility for any errors, omissions, inaccurate interpretations, or insensitivities that appear in the following pages.

P.H.-C.
D.E.P.
D.K.W.
T.T.

The Authors

Penny Hauser-Cram is a senior research associate in developmental and behavioral pediatrics at the University of Massachusetts Medical School. She received her B.S. degree (1968) from Denison University in psychology, her M.A. degree (1976) from Tufts University in child study, and her Ed.D. degree (1983) from Harvard University Graduate School of Education in human development. Her research interests include aspects of research design and measures of child development applicable to longitudinal studies of normally developing and atypical children and families. Her published work includes *Essays on Educational Research: Methodology, Testing and Application* (1983, with F. Martin). Before assuming her current position, she was a faculty member of the Eliot-Pearson Department of Child Study at Tufts University and director of the Eliot-Pearson Children's School.

Donald E. Pierson is professor of education and dean of the College of Education at the University of Lowell in Lowell, Massachusetts. He received his B.A. degree cum laude (1964) from Princeton University in psychology, his Ed.M. degree (1965) from Harvard University in research in instruction, and his Ph.D. degree (1970) from Harvard University in education. His current interests include an early childhood demonstration school and school-college partnership programs. Pierson was director of the Brookline Early Education Project from 1972 to 1984. Previously, he was an elementary school principal in Weston, Massachusetts.

Deborah Klein Walker is the assistant commissioner for the Bureau of Parent, Child and Adolescent Health in the Massachusetts Department of Public Health. She received her B.A. degree magna cum laude (1965) from Mount Holyoke College in psychology and her Ed.M. degree (1975) and Ed.D. degree (1978) from the Harvard Graduate School of Education in human development. Walker's current research focuses on the social functioning of children with disabilities and chronically ill children in schools and on evaluations of secondary prevention programs for pregnant teenagers and teenage parents. Her past work included studies of the assessment of social and emotional factors in the development of young children and early intervention programs and policies. Her published work includes *Socioemotional Measures for Preschool and Kindergarten Children* (1973) and *Monitoring Child Health in the United States* (1984, with J. B. Richmond). Before assuming her current position, she was associate professor of human development at the Harvard School of Public Health (1976–1988).

Terrence Tivnan is a lecturer on education at the Harvard Graduate School of Education. He received his A.B. degree (1969) from Harvard College and his M.A.T. (1970) and Ed.D. (1980) degrees from the Harvard Graduate School of Education. His teaching and research interests have concentrated on research methodology and applications of statistics in educational and social science research settings. He is currently involved in several projects focusing on developmental studies of children with special needs, and he has been a participant in the Harvard University Seminar on Assessment.

The Movement Toward Earlier Education

Chapter 1

The Need for Early Childhood Programs: Changing Social Realities for Families

The birth of a baby is often a time of great celebration. Family and friends gather to share their joy and to support the mother and father. In the hospital, nurses and physicians often give advice about bathing and feeding the baby. But soon, the parents and the baby begin their life together at home. And the parents begin to ask questions: Should I pick her up whenever she cries? What can he see? Does her fussiness mean she'll be overly active? Why does he spit up so much? As the baby gets older, the parents have new questions: When should we begin toilet training? Should we let her watch television? He has a funny way of saying many words — is that a problem?

Where do parents get answers to their questions? Perhaps they turn to family, friends, or a pediatrician. Until recently, it was unlikely that parents would think of the public school as a resource for information about child development. But, increasingly, parents are considering public schools to be places where they can ask questions about their child's development and where their child can join an educational program before kindergarten.

This book presents the story of one such educational project in the public schools. The Brookline Early Education

Project (BEEP) was a comprehensive program for all parents and for their children from the time of the children's birth until they entered kindergarten. It provided health and developmental monitoring, home visits, and preschool services along with parent education and support services. Initially developed in 1972, BEEP was the first program of its kind in this country. It was established as a model program from which other programs could develop and was explicitly designed to test policy questions about the extent of services required to affect children's competence in elementary school.

Currently, school-based programs like BEEP for children under traditional school age (five or six years old) exist in only a few states. Such programs are increasing in number, however, and interest in early education programs is widespread. School committees, school administrators, and state departments of education are anxious to learn about early education programs. Given the myriad of concerns schools face today, such as low test scores, high dropout rates, illiteracy, and inadequate funds, why is early education becoming such a prominent part of the school agenda?

Today's advocates for early education come from diverse arenas. Business leaders, concerned with the quality of the work force, view early education as critical to improving students' sustained interest in school and, thus, to developing a work force that is adequately trained. For example, the Committee for Economic Development, a group of 225 corporate officers and university presidents, issued two reports that maintain that the United States cannot continue to compete in the global marketplace if the number of its children who are poorly educated and who live in poverty continues to escalate (1985, 1987). The reports assert that preschool education is an investment that offers a very high yield.

State governors have also recognized the benefits of early education programs (National Governors' Association, 1987). Private foundations such as Carnegie Corporation of New York have emphasized the value of developing successful early childhood programs in their funding priorities and have focused attention on "the early years of life as one of the great leverage points for the human future" (Hamburg, 1987, p. 3). Moreover, the importance of the early years of life has even been recognized in the White House. In his 1990 state of the union message, President Bush said that one of the six objectives we must meet by the year 2000 is that "every child should start school ready to learn" (Fiske, 1990, p. 22).

At a time when urban, suburban, and rural schools are confronting so many critical issues, such as crime, substance abuse, and adolescent pregnancy, it may seem surprising that they are interested in early education. Yet school administrators are considering whether they should extend their responsibility to the youngest members of our society. Several major influences on communities are pressuring schools to consider expanding their educational focus to children under five years old and their families. These forces will continue to emerge as critical influences on schools and communities during the next decade, and most school committees, school administrators, teachers, and parents will become familiar with early education.

The Need for Early Childhood Programs

Two substantial changes have occurred in the daily lives and composition of families that have affected the need for early childhood programs in the United States: the increasing number of women in the work force and the increasing number of children living in poverty. Without question, the employment of women, including women with young children, is one of the major changes in family life in the last decade. The percentage of mothers with children under six years old who are employed is now close to 63 percent (U.S. General Accounting Office, 1990), and that figure is projected to increase (Hayes, Palmer, and Zaslow, 1990).

Large numbers of women also have entered the work force at earlier points in United States history. During World War II, when women were needed in the labor pool, child-care centers were established through the Community Facilities Act of 1941 (the Lanham Act). The employment of women was viewed as a necessary part of the war effort. After the war, the nation reestablished its traditional family life, with men employed and women at home (Cahan, 1989). In contrast, women's entry into the work force today is considered a personal, rather than a national, economic necessity.

Although some families arrange for parents to work different shifts or have relatives who can care for their children, a large proportion of families rely on individuals who are not family members to care for their young children (Hayes, Palmer, and Zaslow, 1990). Because this shift in family life has occurred for families of all economic circumstances, the interest in quality care and education of young children is not relegated to only one group in our society. A pressing need for child care among families of all economic circumstances has brought child-care issues into the current political arena.

Nevertheless, the need for child care and health and social services is profoundly greater for some families than for others. The number of families living in poverty has increased substantially over the last two decades; recent estimates indicate that about one in every four children lives in poverty and that one in every two black children will live in poverty during at least part of his or her formative years (Newberger, Melnicoe, and Newberger, 1986). The rise in family poverty is partially attributable to the increase in the number of children born to adolescents (Henshaw and others, 1989), the number of households headed by women, and the number of working poor (Ellwood, 1988). Moreover, projections suggest that the number and proportion of children living in poverty and with poorly educated mothers will rise steadily over the next three decades (Pallas, Natriello, and McDill, 1989). The group of children entering school in the year 2000 will be much different than at any other time in U.S. history. More children who are Hispanic, Asian, and black, more children living in poverty, more children living in single-parent households, and more children whose home language is not English will enter school at that time than ever before (Halpern, 1987). Increasingly, many young children will grow up in environments that provide unequal opportunities even before the children begin elementary school.

Currently, favorable educational opportunities are disproportionately available to families who can afford them. This disparity has occurred in spite of the Head Start Program, which began in the 1960s and is now the largest public program providing educational and developmental services to preschool children from low-income families. Head Start enrolls only about 16 percent of eligibile families (U.S. General Accounting Office, 1990). According to the Children's Defense Fur.d (1987a), 54 percent of three-year-olds and 67 percent of four-year-olds from families with annual incomes over $35,000 attend preschool. In contrast, about 17 percent of three-year-olds and 33 percent of four-year-olds from families earning less than $10,000 annually attend preschool. Hispanic children, part of the fastest growing minority population in the United States, are the least likely of any children to attend preschool; fewer than 15 percent of Hispanic three-year-olds are enrolled in a preschool program, an enrollment rate that is half of that for whites or blacks (Pendleton, 1986). These figures indicate that children enter elementary school with immensely different experiences, some of which can be predicted by demographic features alone.

Children in poverty not only enter school at a disadvantage because they have not attended preschool but also often face disadvantages at several stages of their development. For example, children from poor families are more likely to be born prematurely and to perform more poorly at five years of age than other children with similar birth histories (Siegel, 1983). Furthermore, as risk factors such as low maternal education, inadequate social support, large family size, and stressful events accumulate, children's cognitive performance tends to decline (Sameroff and Seifer, 1983). Children who grow up in poverty face "double jeopardy," for they are exposed more often to risks such as illness and maternal depression and suffer more serious consequences from those risks than do other children (Parker, Greer, and Zuckerman, 1988). The majority of children exposed to multiple risks will demonstrate declines in intelligence quotient (IQ) scores in the absence of intervention in early childhood (Ramey and Campbell, 1984). Thus, the projected increase in the percentage of children living in poverty in this country is especially troubling. As more children enter elementary school having been exposed to multiple risks, schools are likely to find that fewer children are able to meet the basic social, emotional, and cognitive demands of the classroom.

The School Reform Movement

During the last decade, the inadequacy of the current educational system in the United States and the need for reform have been discussed widely. In 1983, the National Commission on Excellence in Education described in its report *A Nation at Risk* the failures of America's schools. A series of reports quickly followed in the wake of *A Nation at Risk,* and they received a great deal of attention in the media. These reports generated much public discussion about ways to improve the quality of public education, and numerous state and local reforms of all aspects of education, including changes in the curriculum and graduation requirements, were implemented (U.S. Department of Education, 1984).

Although seldom an integral part of initial efforts at school reform, early childhood programs were mentioned in various reports. For example, Mortimer Adler (1982) recommended in *The Paideia Proposal* that children from less than optimal home environments receive "tutelage" during the preschool years. John Goodlad (1984) suggested many changes be made in the way schools are structured, among these that children begin school when they are four years old. He maintained that enrollment in school at such an early age would result in higher levels of academic attainment and in eventual benefits to society.

Recent school reform movements have tended to include early childhood programs as a critical part of their reforms. For example, the National Association of School Boards recommends that early childhood units be instituted within all elementary schools and that state education agencies promote funding of early childhood education as an "investment" strategy (Schultz and Lombardi, 1989). From the viewpoint of school reform, early childhood programs are a means of involving parents and children in working with schools toward education goals. From an economic vantage point, such programs are critical to the development of a competent work force. From a human rights perspective, early childhood programs help equalize children's opportunity to learn from formal schooling. Early childhood education appears to have an important role to play in the future of American schools.

Recent Legislation Involving Early Childhood Programs

Another influence on current thinking about early childhood education emanates from legislation that has occurred at the national level. Two bills, in particular, have brought early childhood issues into the jurisdiction of the public schools. The first, the 1988 Elementary and Secondary School Improvement Amendments (Public Law 100-297), reauthorized Chapter I of Title I of the Elementary and Secondary Education Act of 1965 and officially extended public school services to some three- and four-year-olds. Chapter I is the largest federal program of aid to elementary and secondary schools. It allocates funds to local education agencies primarily based on the number of children from poor families in each locality, but children are selected for its programs based on their achievement, not their family's income. Public Law 100-297 authorizes a new program, called Even Start, for educationally disadvantaged parents and their young children who are between the ages of one and seven. To participate, parents must not be enrolled in school or have a high school diploma. The program provides home-based education for parents and children.

The second bill has focused on young children with disabilities. Public schools became responsible for the education and integration into the classroom of children with disabilities through the Education for All Handicapped Children Act (Public Law 94-142) passed in 1975. Preschool incentive grants to encourage states to increase educational services to preschoolers with disabilities were first funded in 1977. Since the passage of the Education of the Handicapped Children Act Amendments of 1986 (Public Law 99-457), in order to receive federal preschool funds, states have been required to provide free and appropriate education and related services for all eligible children with disabilities who are three to five years old (Hauser-Cram, Upshur, Krauss, and Shonkoff, 1988). The government thus has placed public schools firmly in charge of the education of preschool-age children with disabilities. Moreover, Title I of this legislation (referred to as Part H) encourages states to provide services for children with disabilities who are younger than three years old and their families. All states have applied for funds to provide services to preschoolers with disabilities, and about one-third have designated departments of education as the lead agency in providing these services (Garwood, Fewell, and Neisworth, 1988). Thus, in many communities, public education systems provide substantial services to children under five years of age.

Another piece of legislation creates pressure for more child care, although not directly from the public schools. The Family Support Act of 1988 (Public Law 100-485) initiated a Job Opportunities and Basic Skills Training (JOBS) program. This act mandates that states require parents with children over three years old (or at state option, over one year old) to participate in the JOBS program to receive funds from Aid for Families with Dependent Children (AFDC). Although parents with children between three and six years old are required to participate only part time, states must guarantee child care for these parents as well as for all AFDC recipients who are working or participating in approved job training programs (Smith, Blank, and Bond, 1990). The Congressional Budget Office estimates that 68 percent of eligible children under six years old will participate in some form of government-funded child care (Hayes, Palmer, and Zaslow, 1990). Such widespread participation could result in a dramatic increase in demand for child care, especially in communities where quality child care is not widely available. The public schools already house the majority of child-care programs for adolescent parents (Marx, Bailey, and Francis, 1988), and they may be the logical place for many communities to turn for the development and implementation of child-care programs.

In conclusion, the forces that have brought early education to the forefront in social and political discussions are diverse in origin and appeal. Some, such as the introduction of many women with young children into the work force and the plea for school reform, apply to the majority of families and children today. Others, such as legislative mandates, focus only on certain groups of children or families. Nevertheless, public education is clearly involved in the education of some children under the age of five years already. The critical question for policy makers is whether some form of public education should be extended to all young children and their families.

Chapter 2

The Benefits of
Early Education:
What Do We Know?

Although current enthusiasm for early education comes from diverse influences, early education programs were initially built on a history of research on child development. The foundation for such programs, which was laid before the inception of BEEP in the early 1970s, was made up of a combination of theories about early development and knowledge derived from research studies. This foundation was a critical part of the creation and development of BEEP. Indeed, BEEP was initiated during the first wave of enthusiasm for early education programs that were developed based on research evidence. Currently, a second wave of enthusiasm for early education programs, also based on research findings, exists in this country. While much interest in early education is fueled by the forces discussed in the first chapter—the changing nature of the family, interest in school reform, and legislative influences—the catalyst for such renewed enthusiasm is due largely to a confluence of findings about the effects of early childhood programs.

The history of early childhood programs in the United States is punctuated by different philosophical stances about the nature of childhood, competing psychological theories about the malleability of human development, and diverse beliefs about the benefits of programs outside of the home for young children.

Although wide ranging public support for early childhood programs in this country is fairly recent, federal funding of early childhood programs has occurred at three distinct times during U.S. history. During the Great Depression, the Federal Emergency Relief Administration was established. One of its tasks was to create nursery schools largely to provide employment for school personnel who had been laid off (Cahan, 1989). Once federal support ceased, many of the schools disbanded, although similar centers were established again during the Second World War. In 1941, the Lanham Act made federal monies available to establish child-care centers in areas with high levels of female employment. Once World War II was over, federal support for child care was withdrawn.

It was not until the 1960s, when Head Start was introduced, that the government supported early childhood programs primarily to promote the optimal development of children. The educational programs for young children that were initiated in the 1960s, in contrast to earlier programs, derived from a research base. Much of this academic research was on the effects of early experience on child development. A number of psychologists and educators studied the conditions under which children form and develop their cognitive and social skills. Evidence drawn from diverse fields of study pointed toward the important and lasting effects of children's experiences during the early stages of development.

Two investigations were particularly influential on government policy: J. McVicker Hunt's *Intelligence and Experience* (1961) and Benjamin Bloom's *Stability and Change in Human Characteristics* (1964). Hunt's book consolidated a good deal of the available work on neuropsychological development, learning theory, and Piaget's ideas about the development of intelligence. Hunt's work strongly emphasized the major effects that early experience has on later development, adding to the longstanding debate about the relative effects of environment versus heredity in determining human intelligence.

Bloom (1964) reviewed and analyzed the evidence that had been collected from an array of studies of human development. One widely cited inference of Bloom's work is that approximately 50 percent of intellectual development occurs by the age of four years. Bloom concluded that early education can profoundly affect "the child's general learning potential" (p. 110). He implied that attempts to influence the course of a child's development through education would be most effective if they occurred during this early time period.

Effects of Early Experience. Several types of evidence pointed to the conclusion that the child's first few years of life exert a disproportionate effect on later functioning. First, studies on maternal-infant bonding and its disruption (Bowlby, 1951) and on children reared in aversive, unstimulating environments (Dennis, 1960; Goldfarb, 1943; Spitz, 1945) suggested that extreme deprivation during a child's early years resulted in devastating long-term consequences. Second, studies on animals led to the conclusion that certain types of environmental deprivation cause permanent disruption in normal physiological growth. Hebb's (1949) studies on the degeneration of optic pathways in animals reared in the absence of light is often cited as evidence of the consequences of deprivation.

Although the view that the first few years of life exert critical influence on the rest of development was certainly part of the zeitgeist during the years BEEP was planned and initiated, only a few years later this view began to be questioned, at least in the academic community. Jerome Kagan, whose early work stressed the role of continuity of characteristics displayed in early life (Kagan and Moss, 1962), presented data that cast doubt on prior beliefs about the extent to which retardation in infancy and toddlerhood is predictive of later developmental delays. His studies of infants and toddlers living in a rural community in Guatemala documented substantial cognitive and social delays compared to children living in the United States (Kagan, 1980). He attributed the delays to the restrictions placed on children in the first year of life during which time they were seldom allowed to be mobile or included in social interaction. Yet he found that by the age of ten years, these Guatemalan children as well as the U.S. children demonstrated similar cognitive performance. This finding caused him to speculate that early experience may not play as great a role in development as he had assumed.

Clarke and Clarke (1976) developed a similar thesis based on a series of studies on children's later functioning after early deprivation. These researchers concluded that in many cases, children who had experienced adverse early experiences displayed unusual resiliency when placed in stimulating and nurturing environments. They hypothesized that although such resilience is greatest during early childhood, it continues throughout adulthood. Clarke and Clarke questioned the assumption that adverse early experiences always produce permanent detrimental effects but nevertheless maintained that children's early years are important and that individuals benefit from favorable environments throughout the life cycle. Even though the conclusion was drawn that early experiences may not be as powerful in determining the course of development as had been thought, the studies they reviewed pointed to the relatively strong links between the conditions under which children are raised and their status on developmental and educational tasks.

Effects of Social Class. Influential evidence also came from the studies of the effects of social class differences on children's intellectual and school performance. One of the most prominent and controversial studies discussed in the 1960s was the "Coleman Report" (Coleman and others, 1966), in which measures of social class were found to be stronger predictors of children's school achievement than such factors as school expenditures or teacher qualities. Other evidence indicated that social-class differences between middle-class and lower-class children not only appeared at the time the children began school but also often increased over time (Deutsch, 1967). These findings were disappointing for educators, for they indicated that schools did not deal successfully with the performance differences between socioeconomic groups that already were apparent when children arrived at school. Moreover, the schools' potential to overcome difficulties and discrepancies in educational achievement based on race and social class seemed to be quite limited. Apparently public schools could not overcome the differences in achievement and educational potential that emerged during the pre-school years.

Effects of Head Start. The evidence from the studies of early experience and of social class differences in educational achievement pointed toward educational programs for preschool children. A number of programs were initiated during the 1960s specifically for children from low-income families. The most prominent among these was the federally funded Head Start Program. Head Start took place in a wide variety of settings and used a number of different educational models and methods for delivering services. Despite the differences among programs, they shared a common premise that early education can make a substantial difference in the lives of children and families living in poverty (Zigler and Valentine, 1979). Head Start represented a substantial national effort to extend publicly supported education to children of an age range that had not previously received widespread educational support.

Moreover, the Head Start Program was unique in that it was intended to provide comprehensive services. Rather than focusing narrowly on educational interventions, Head Start also was designed to improve children's social, nutritional, physical, and affective development. The program's major objectives included:

1. Improving children's physical health and physical abilities
2. Helping children develop emotionally and socially by encouraging self-confidence, spontaneity, curiosity, and self-discipline
3. Improving children's mental processes and skills, in particular, conceptual and verbal skills
4. Establishing patterns and expectations of success for children that will give them confidence for future learning efforts
5. Increasing children's capacity to relate positively to their family members and others, while at the same time strengthening the family's abilities to relate positively to the children and their problems
6. Developing in children and families a responsible attitude

toward society and encouraging society to work with the
poor in solving their problems
7. Increasing the sense of dignity and self-worth within chil-
    dren and families (Richmond, Stipek, and Zigler, 1979)

When Head Start was initiated as part of President Johnson's War on Poverty, many people were enthusiastic and op-
timistic about the benefits that would ensue. Although some of
the early evaluations showed promising findings, the first formal evaluation of Head Start, the "Westinghouse Report" (Cicirelli and others, 1969), was rather discouraging. This report,
which received a good deal of attention, indicated that the effects
of Head Start throughout the country were much less promising than had been hoped for or anticipated. Gains were not evident from short-term summer programs, and even the gains
from long-term programs were more limited than expected.

The Westinghouse Report became the center of controversy and criticism (Smith and Bissell, 1970; Zigler, 1973). Some
debates centered on programmatic and political concerns related
to Head Start and other educational programs, and other debates
focused on issues of research and evaluation design (Steiner,
1976). These latter arguments were often about the definitions
of adequate comparison groups and the limitations of the instruments used, instruments that assessed cognitive domains but
not psychosocial domains. One inescapable conclusion was that
substantially improving the educational prospects of young children would be more difficult than anyone had anticipated.

The Westinghouse Report made it apparent that short-
term programs were unlikely to be effective, and full-year Head
Start programs replaced summer programs. But even the positive gains that had been evident in the evaluations of Head Start
appeared to dissipate during the children's first few years of
elementary school (Datta, 1969). Some advocates of early education argued that children needed additional services in elementary school to maintain the gains they made in Head Start. This
argument resulted in the development of Project Follow-Through
(Rivlin and Timpane, 1975). Other advocates of early education maintained that Head Start and other programs like it were

doomed to be limited in effectiveness because they were starting too late in the life of the children and that intervention efforts should begin earlier. This last line of thinking led directly to the development of BEEP.

Harvard Preschool Project. The most direct research impetus for BEEP was the work of Burton White, a psychologist who had studied the effects of children's early experiences on their subsequent development. White, with his colleagues, conducted studies of animals and human infants that demonstrated the effects of enriched and deprived environments on later behavior (White and Held, 1966). During the late 1960s, he directed the Harvard Preschool Project, in which he and his colleagues conducted a series of studies to explore the origins of the competencies and behaviors that enable children to experience success in school (White, 1971; White and Watts, 1973).

One of White's research strategies involved identifying children who appeared to be relatively successful or competent at a particular age level and comparing their behaviors in interacting with parents, teachers, and peers with the behaviors of children who were generally considered less successful (White, Kaban, Attanucci, and Shapiro, 1978). Once they had identified these differences in behavior, White and his colleagues could then look for the origins of the behaviors by studying children of a slightly younger age. A series of studies led White and his colleagues to focus on the ways in which children interacted with their mothers over the entire course of their early development (White, Kaban, and Attanucci, 1979). Thus, rather than studying children's development in isolation, the researchers focused on the interactions between mothers and their infants.

White and his colleagues concluded that the important differences in development that are easily observed among children at entry into elementary school actually begin to occur much earlier than researchers had often assumed. Their studies indicated that the key foundations for a child's later success are developed during the first three years of life — with the most crucial stage of development being the time from about eight months to twenty-four months of age. During this time period, the infant is becoming more mobile and independent and is beginning to develop more formal language skills. These language skills are very important for the child's development of cognitive and social skills that become keys to later success in school. According to White, the typical educational interventions are doomed to fail because they occur much too late. He concluded that early education should begin during infancy (White, Kaban, and Attanucci, 1979).

A second important conclusion from White's work was the central role that parents play in influencing their children's development (White, Kaban, and Attanucci, 1979). His observational studies revealed critical differences among the ways in which mothers interacted with their young infants. Many mothers that White and his colleagues observed did a superb job of interacting with their infants and providing an environment that would foster the full development of the child's emerging skills. Other mothers appeared to have much more difficulty in developing what White considered to be an effective style for fostering a child's growth. He saw this as an educational problem. Because White considered the parent as the central figure in influencing a child's development, he believed that many parents needed assistance in becoming the most effective "teachers" that they could be and that much of the educational potential of young children is wasted because we have not adequately studied or applied the principles that influence development.

BEEP was initiated in the early 1970s, a time of great belief in the value of providing support and educational services to parents and young children. Although the Westinghouse Report dampened some people's enthusiasm for early education, it also stimulated more research into the process of children's development. Studies such as those conducted by Burton White pointed to the value of understanding the effects of various aspects of a child's environment, including the mother's approach to interacting with the child. During the 1980s, a great deal of academic research focused on delineating various environmental effects on children's development and on gaining more knowledge about the development of infants and toddlers. At the same time, evaluation approaches evolved from those selected during the early studies of the effectiveness of Head Start. Some evaluators began to explore the long-term effects of early education and selected outcomes (such as school attendance and placement in special education classes) that have meaning for educators and are well understood by the general public.

Extended Research Base of Early Childhood Programs

The rekindled interest in early childhood programs in the 1990s is similar to the enthusiasm for such programs in the 1970s, although it has occurred for very different reasons. Research evidence on the success of the demonstration programs of the 1970s has grown, and media attention to these programs and public belief in the long-term benefits of such programs has flourished. Findings from both early childhood demonstration programs and the Head Start Program form a powerful research base upon which child advocates, researchers, and the public, in general, can build.

Long-Term Effects of Demonstration Programs. The Perry Preschool Project is the most widely publicized of the early childhood demonstration programs. This project, organized in 1962 by the High/Scope Educational Research Foundation, provided a preschool and home-visit program to three- and four-year-olds from economically disadvantaged families. The children were selected based on their parents' low educational and occupational status, their family's size, and the children's scores on the Stanford-Binet Intelligence Test. Children in the program and a matched comparison group were compared at multiple age points. Although findings were published for the children at several ages, the most provocative findings, presented in a report entitled *Changed Lives* (Berreuta-Clement and others, 1984), are based on analyses of outcomes collected when project children were nineteen years old.

The report presents several types of findings, among which are school outcomes and society-related outcomes. The fifty-eight children who attended the Perry Preschool Project had significantly better school careers than the sixty-five demographically similar individuals who were not program participants. Specifically, the researchers found that a higher proportion of participants were functionally literate and enrolled in postsecondary education than individuals in the comparison group and a smaller proportion of participants had been classified as mentally retarded during the school years or had dropped out of school. A higher proportion of participants were employed than individuals in the comparison group, and a lower proportion became pregnant, were arrested, or were dependent upon public assistance.

The dramatic findings of this project were further underscored and made especially appealing to policymakers by a cost-benefit analysis (Barnett, 1985). In a cost-benefit analysis, analysts place a dollar value on both the resources expended—the costs—and the effects produced—the benefits—(Barnett and Escobar, 1990). Such analyses include actual costs and also involve estimates of money saved (for example, money saved because participating children do not need special education services). They also include less measurable costs (for example, the cost of opportunity lost to parents because of the time consumed by the program). On the one hand, cost-benefit analyses involve many assumptions and estimates and, therefore, tend to be controversial. On the other hand, they yield estimates that policymakers, in particular, find beneficial. The cost-benefit analysis of the Perry Preschool Project is the most substantial economic analysis of an early education project. Barnett (1985) concluded that each dollar contributed to the project would yield a return of $5.73. This general finding of substantial savings due to early education has been cited by advocates for all types of early education programs.

The results of the Perry Preschool Project, including the cost-benefit study, have been well publicized outside of traditional academic circles. Researchers involved in the project made a deliberate attempt to make the findings known on both state and national levels (Schweinhart and others, 1986). The media responded rapidly. Undoubtedly, the researchers' use of outcomes that are readily understood and have apparent value and costs associated with them bolstered the case for the success of the Perry Preschool Project, in particular, and early childhood programs, in general.

The findings from this project were similar to those of prior reports on the potential long-term advantages of early education (Lazar and Darlington, 1982). The Consortium of Longitudinal Studies joined twelve early childhood projects in an attempt to find as many of the projects' original participants as possible and to develop a standard set of data on the participants' subsequent development. The first follow-up study (Darlington and others, 1980) revealed an interesting set of outcomes about the participants' school careers. The study found that children who had participated in early childhood projects were placed in special education classes significantly less often, had slightly lower rates of retention in grade, showed initial gains in both measures of IQ and reading and math achievement (although such gains were not sustained), and were more oriented toward achievement than nonparticipants. A second follow-up study, which included only four of the original projects, reported a similar set of findings for participating children ten years or more after they had been enrolled in early childhood projects (Royce, Darlington, and Murray, 1983). The researchers noted positive effects on participating children for school-related variables such as lower rates of placement in special education classes, lower rates of being held back a grade, and higher rates of high school graduation than nonparticipants.

Other studies have added to the array of findings about long-term outcomes for children and families who have been involved in early education programs. For example, a ten-year follow-up study of fourteen children and families who had been enrolled in the Yale Project (Provence, Naylor, and Patterson, 1977; Provence and Naylor, 1983) produced findings consistent with those of the Consortium of Longitudinal Studies and the Perry Preschool Project but also included a broader look at the effects of an early education program on parents (Seitz, Rosenbaum, and Apfel, 1985).

Families who participated in the Yale Project received services from a team of professionals, including a social worker, a pediatrician, a primary day-care worker, and a developmental examiner. The program assisted families from the time of the mother's pregnancy until the child was thirty months old. Services included a child-care program (although participation appeared to vary greatly) and a home-visit program. Unlike many previous early education programs, the Yale Project focused on family support rather than direct intervention with the child.

Seitz and her colleagues found that ten years after the project was completed, children who had been participants did not differ from nonparticipating children in their scores on an intelligence test but did differ substantially and positively on a composite index of school adjustment (Seitz, Rosenbaum, and Apfel, 1985). The index included achievement scores, rates of absenteeism, classroom behavior measures, and rates of use of school services. The evaluators also found that the project was associated with important effects on families. Almost all families that had been involved in the project were reported to be self-supporting, in comparison to only 50 percent of the nonparticipating families. Seitz and her colleagues interpreted these findings as indicative of a change in the participating mothers' visions of their own life in response to the project's intensive, personalized, and nurturant approach to the mothers.

Effects of Head Start. Head Start is more difficult to evaluate than many of the demonstration projects because it is a broad program with multiple goals. One of the most important criticisms of the initial Westinghouse Report was that it relied on too narrow a range of outcomes. Since that time, many evaluations of Head Start have attempted to apply a broader range of outcomes that match the multifaceted goals of the program.

Although recent evaluations of Head Start have not received the public attention given to the Perry Preschool Project, the Head Start Program is well known by the public. The most substantial review of Head Start to date, conducted by McKey and others (1985), involved aggregating the findings from 210 studies of Head Start. The review presents an array of findings about the extent and limitations of the effectiveness of the Head Start Program, in general. It also indicates that children participating in Head Start displayed immediate gains in both cognitive and socioemotional development and demonstrated improved health compared to nonparticipants. The findings also show a decline in the improved status of participants over nonparticipants on traditional measures of achievement over a three-year period. Despite the indication of dissipating effects, the participants in Head Start outperformed nonparticipants on long-term measures of school success such as lower rates of repeating a grade or being assigned to special education classes. Using the results of many of the studies reviewed by McKey, the Children's Defense Fund (1987b) estimated that nationally $10 billion could be saved by the reduced costs of special education, repeated grades, and delinquency if Head Start were available to all eligible children.

The evaluations of both the model demonstration programs and the Head Start Program reveal important consistent findings. Although initially elevated, achievement and cognitive test scores of participants tend to become increasingly like those of nonparticipants over time. But the school careers of children who have attended such programs appear to follow a different cycle than those of their peers. They are more likely to remain in school and to meet various expectations of the educational environment.

Some educators have speculated about the mechanism for this change in school career paths. For example, Weikart (1987) maintains that children who have attended high-quality early education programs may enter school with an image of success. Teachers may also view those children as successful because of their elevated test scores and their positive self-esteem. Even though these children may not maintain high test scores, the cycle of success may sustain the children's relation to the learning environment of the school. Debate may continue about *how* early education changes children and their families, but few will doubt that such programs have produced valuable outcomes.

The Current Debate: Should Public Schools Be Responsible for the Very Young?

Although the demand for early education programs is increasing, these programs are not consistent in the kinds of services they offer and the types of families they serve. Indeed, the most constant attribute of early education programs is their variability. For example, some programs enroll children for half a day and others provide full-day educational or custodial care. Some programs are only for children with low-income and adolescent parents, and others serve only children with disabilities. Even advocates of early childhood programs are not in consensus about the best way to respond to the increasing demand for early education. Some advocates argue that Head Start should be substantially extended and minimize the role that public schools might play (Hayes, Palmer, and Zaslow, 1990). Others maintain that the public schools offer the best option for operating early childhood programs (Zigler, 1987).

BEEP, the first comprehensive early childhood program that was available in the public schools, was initiated long before the controversy about school-based programs became so prominent. Yet, many of the same issues debated today were being discussed about the implementation of BEEP. Educators and parents asked many questions, including: Can principals and other school personnel really extend their responsibility to young children when they are overworked already? Will kindergarten teachers expect BEEP children to enter school having learned how to read? Will BEEP children be bored in traditional classrooms after having had such a stimulating early childhood experience? Will BEEP parents ask too much of teachers since they are accustomed to such a responsive staff at BEEP?

As in other discussions about designing educational solutions to social problems, the debate about the proper role of the public schools in responding to societal needs and demands for more early childhood programs touches on many fundamental issues. Values, assumptions, and views of the rightful intersection between family life and educational institutions, as well as beliefs about the limitations, promise, and accomplishments of public education, underlie many aspects of the controversy. In the first part of this chapter, we review the issues debated by advocates of school-based early childhood programs and by those people who caution against the wholesale expansion of such programs. Since much of the discussion about school-based programs has been limited to the preschool-age group, most of the arguments we present here relate to early childhood programs for three- and four-year olds. In the second part of the chapter, we review briefly the range of recent school-based early childhood programs. Although many of those programs are exclusively for the preschool-age children, a few focus on parents of infants and toddlers.

Two Views of School-Based Programs

The Advocates. The arguments in favor of school-based programs center around three themes: equity, continuity, and logistical advantage. Issues of equity form the basis for many discussions about the role of education in American life. Public education is designed to be available to all citizens, and is intended to provide equal opportunity to all citizens. Advocates of school-based early childhood programs stress the importance of universal access to schools. School-based programs represent a move away from categorical programs that offer services to specified children or families, such as children from low-income families or children with developmental disabilities. The stigma associated with such programs can drive away the very individuals the programs are attempting to serve. Unlike social service institutions, schools view education as their primary mission. All children have educational needs, but only some children require other social services. School-based programs also can enroll heterogeneous group of families. While all families can benefit from the heterogeneous mix, families from traditional risk groups such as families with multiple needs or those in which parents are exceptionally young or have low levels of education can especially benefit. Presumably, families that are functioning well can serve as child-rearing models for other families (Hausman and Weiss, 1988). Similarly, children can model positive peer interaction and approaches to learning for each other (Gresham, 1984).

Responding to heterogeneity is not a new function for the schools. As a result of federal legislation for the handicapped (Public Law 94-142) schools have had to learn how to respond to children's special needs and to find ways of integrating children with different skills and abilities into a single setting (Wang and Baker, 1985–1986).

Some advocates of school-based programs claim public schools can offer families with young children continuity. Schools have a vested interest in children being well-prepared for formal educational experiences. Questions about how best to prepare children for their later school experiences are critical and often engender controversy. (This will be discussed in more detail in the next section.) But most parents and educators agree on the need for children to enter formal schooling as well prepared as possible. Advocates of school-based early education maintain that, at the least, the coordination of early childhood and elementary programs encourages communication among teachers about the expectations, demands, and nature of learning that occurs in each setting, and at each stage of a child's development.

Another aspect of continuity concerns children's transition from preschool to the first formal school experience, which may be either kindergarten or first grade. The importance of helping children and families make successful transitions from one environment to another has been acknowledged by educators (Powell, 1988–1989), pediatricians (Shonkoff, Jarman, and Kohlenberg, 1987), and psychologists (Sarason, 1987). In one of the few studies on the transition from preschool to formal schooling, Ladd and Price (1987) found that children who attend a new school setting with a large number of familiar peers tend to view school more positively and have less anxiety about entering the new setting. If children attend preschool in the public school system in which they will continue their education, they are more likely to enter elementary school with a group of peers they know and some familiarity with the setting.

Continuity is of value for parents as well as for children. Parents who develop a productive pattern of communication with teachers (or similar service providers, such as home visitors) during their child's preschool years tend to maintain positive patterns of communication into their child's elementary school years (Seitz, Rosenbaum, and Apfel, 1985). Most studies have indicated that the relationship between the school and the parents is a powerful factor in affecting children's capacity to learn in the classroom (Bronfenbrenner, 1986). During their child's early years, parents are more likely to perceive schools as friendly, rather than formidable, places. Patterns of productive home-school communication may be more easily established during preschool programs than at a later point. Moreover, if early childhood programs are housed in the schools, parents and teachers may maintain beneficial communication patterns more easily through the elementary grades.

Advocates of school-based programs also stress the relative ease of adding these programs to the well-established delivery system of the public schools instead of developing new structures or allowing programs to be managed in the current haphazard way. The public schools already have established relationships with other community agencies and, for the most part, form a stable system that can help to coordinate the services offered by these other agencies. To a large extent, schools have been required to take on this coordinating role for young children with disabilities and their families since the passage of Public

Law 99-457. Gradually, the public schools are gaining experience with this role, and such experience places the schools in a good position to extend their expertise to programs for all children and their families.

The ability of the public schools to maintain a stable teaching staff also gives school-based programs an advantage over community-based programs. Public schools generally offer teachers higher salaries than are available in the private sector. Teachers in community-based early childhood programs typically earn lower salaries than teachers in public school kindergartens (Grubb, 1987). Low salaries are at least partially responsible for the high turnover rate found among early childhood teachers, a rate close to 40 percent annually (U.S. General Accounting Office, 1990). Yet, continuity of care is one of the most important indicators of a quality program for young children (Hayes, Palmer, and Zaslow, 1990). With the promise of higher salaries and a more professional environment than other programs, school-based programs would offer more stability of teaching staff and thus promote high-quality programs.

The Critics. Despite the arguments in favor of having public schools play a major role in the early childhood years, many people believe that the trend toward school-based early childhood programs is misguided. These critics tend to marshall their arguments around two fundamental themes: issues within the school (such as the curriculum and teacher preparation) and issues within the community (such as the needs of multicultural communities and competition with other community agencies).

The critics of school-based programs are most concerned that the content of the curricula and the process of teaching in these programs will mimic that seen in the elementary schools (Elkind, 1987, 1988; Grubb, 1987; Katz, 1987; Zimiles, 1986). Elementary school teachers and early childhood teachers often have dramatically different views of how children learn and what schooling should accomplish. Undoubtedly, some of these differences are due to the diverse ages of the children involved, but others reflect important theoretical differences about teaching children.

According to some critics, teaching in the elementary school, which tends to focus on the acquisition of knowledge in specific subjects, is largely derived from the behavioristic model of learning (Fromberg, 1989). Schools regard children as primarily responding to the stimulus, that is, subject matter, presented. Much of the instruction is didactic in approach and dominated by "teacher talk" (Sirotnik, 1983). Elementary schools emphasize practice through drills and worksheets. The schools maintain a fairly rigid timetable during the day, with specific subjects taught at designated times. Assessments are often highly formalized and include standardized tests as well as other formal mechanisms for determining grades or promotions (Grubb, 1987).

In contrast, most early childhood programs derive from a developmental model of behavior, often based on Piaget's work (1954). In this model, children are thought to learn through active interaction with aspects of their environment and to be active participants in constructing the knowledge they gain (Kamii and DeVries, 1977). In programs based on the developmental model, subjects are integrated, not discrete. For example, mathematical concepts are taught through activities such as weighing different objects, measuring quantities to cook, or figuring out how to divide equally a set number of objects among friends. Children are encouraged to work with others, and the demarcation between work and play is blurred. The teacher's role is one of observing, encouraging, mediating, and extending children's thinking and activities, rather than primarily one of dispensing information and maintaining discipline.

The National Association for the Education of Young Children (NAEYC) has developed a set of guidelines for early childhood programs. These guidelines, which have been well received by educators and developmental psychologists alike, consist of ten main points involving the curriculum (Bredekamp, 1987).

1. A developmentally appropriate curriculum provides for all areas of a child's development — physical, emotional, social, and cognitive — through an integrated approach.

2. Appropriate curriculum planning is based on a teacher's observing and recording each child's special interests and developmental progress.
3. Curriculum planning should emphasize learning as an interactive process. Teachers need to prepare an environment in which children can learn through active exploration and interaction with adults, other children, and materials.
4. Learning activities should be concrete, real, and relevant to the lives of young children.
5. Programs should provide for a wider range of developmental interests and abilities than the chronological age range of the children in the group would suggest.
6. Teachers should provide a variety of activities and materials. They should increase the difficulty, complexity, and challenge of an activity as the children increase their involvement with it and as the children develop understanding and skills.
7. Teachers should provide opportunities for children to choose from a variety of activities, materials, and equipment and the time for children to explore through active involvement. Teachers should facilitate children's engagement with materials and activities and extend the children's learning by asking questions or making suggestions that stimulate the children's thinking.
8. The program should provide multicultural and nonsexist experiences, materials, and equipment for children of all ages.
9. Teachers should provide a balance of rest and active movement for children throughout the program day.
10. The program should provide outdoor experiences for children of all ages.

Although the practices described by the NAEYC guidelines are derived from both research and theory, few studies have attempted to determine the long-term effects of different models of early childhood curricula. Perhaps this is because such studies are so difficult to undertake. One large multisite study, the Head Start Planned Variation Project, attempted to compare the effects of eleven different curriculum models on children. Overall, the researchers found few differences among models and claimed that no curriculum was a clear winner or loser (Rivlin and Timpane, 1975). Yet they also recognized that such a result was perhaps inevitable because the "model as planned" and the "model as implemented" in each site varied considerably. In contrast, Weikart and his colleagues chose to compare three discretely different approaches to teaching preschool children: the traditional nursery school approach, the developmental approach, and the behavioristic approach (Weikart, Epstein, Schweinhart, and Bond, 1978). Although they initially found few differences among the groups taught by each method, substantial differences emerged at a follow-up study conducted when the children were fifteen years old (Schweinhart, Weikart, and Larner, 1986). Children who had been enrolled in the behavioristic model had significantly higher rates of delinquent behavior and related behavior problems in contrast to their peers who had been in either a developmental or traditional nursery school setting.

How could only one or two years in a half-day preschool program have such long-term consequences? Schweinhart and his colleagues suggest that children who are enrolled in formal academic approaches at a young age fail to view themselves either as learners or as responsible for their own actions. In contrast, children who are exposed to developmental approaches become self-initiated learners and internalize societal rules through understanding the consequences of their actions on others.

Many early childhood professionals fear that if the public schools run early childhood programs, the developmental approach will be abandoned for a more academic curriculum. The tendency to formalize early childhood programs is apparent in many kindergarten programs, programs that some people claim have been pressured into adopting a curriculum resembling that of the first grade (Silvern, 1988). A survey of elementary school principals indicated that 85 percent of them placed a priority on academic achievement in the kindergarten programs in their schools (Educational Research Service, 1986). Critics of school-based prekindergarten programs maintain that since in many schools aspects of the traditional first-grade curriculum are now introduced in kindergarten, inappropriate academic demands also will be placed on children of preschool age if public schools oversee preschool programs.

Teacher preparation is another issue often raised by critics of school-based programs. Teachers of young children need to understand the development of children and the needs of families. Some people fear that as the school-age population decreases, teachers who are no longer needed for the elementary grades will be assigned to early childhood programs. Teachers who are trained to teach older children are ill prepared to understand the needs of the young child and may have inappropriate expectations of preschoolers.

In a review of state policies about kindergarten programs, Fromberg (1989) found that teachers in kindergarten programs often had been elementary school teachers or in other positions and did not have training in early childhood education. Teachers' unions are sometimes more concerned about the continued employment of teachers than the hiring of teachers with appropriate training (U.S. General Accounting Office, 1990). Even training teachers in early childhood education, however, may not ensure quality early childhood programs. Rust (1989) observed that if early childhood teachers are isolated in elementary schools, they themselves may change and become more like elementary school teachers in their views of the educational process.

Another problem of school-based early childhood programs is that not all school administrators support them. Some administrators believe that early childhood education is not a public school responsibility (Bridgeman, 1988). Others want to avoid the additional administrative work such programs may involve ("NAESP's Child Care Survey," 1988). If the government imposes such programs on schools without the strong support of the school administrators (Sarason, 1987) and teachers (Rust, 1989), the programs will most likely fail.

Critics of school-based programs are also concerned about the role of the school in the community. Although some people argue that schools are well situated to respond to local needs and multicultural diversity, others maintain that schools have done a poor job of educating children from minority groups (National Black Child Development Institute, 1985). For example, black children are three times more likely to be enrolled in classes for the educable mentally retarded than their white peers, and, in fact, they comprise almost 40 percent of such classes (National Black Child Development Institute, 1985). Such statistics exemplify the concerns of minority groups that if schools operate early childhood programs, children from minority groups will tend to be labeled as nonachievers at an early age (Moore, 1987). Moreover, parents with a modest education or from minority groups are often intimidated by the public schools (Moore, 1987) and may resist enrolling their children in programs offered by the schools. In fact, schools have not uniformly displayed a strong commitment to parent involvement (Grubb, 1987). Some people fear that early childhood programs in the public schools may intensify the separation between the home and the school (Silvern, 1988).

The National Black Child Development Institute (1987) suggests that because school-based early childhood programs have the potential of benefitting black and other minority families, the idea of such programs should not be dismissed. Instead, the institute believes that certain safeguards should be required regarding the role of parents, the curriculum, the teachers, and the school administration. These safeguards include involving parents in policy and matters of curriculum, selecting teachers from the community with experience in early childhood education, choosing or designing culturally sensitive and developmentally appropriate curriculum, moving away from a reliance on standardized testing of children, adhering to health and safety standards, and providing access to health care and nutrition programs.

Some critics of school-based programs maintain that these programs will compete with community-based programs. If school-based programs offer higher salaries for teachers than community-based programs, they are likely to attract teachers from community programs. On the one hand, higher salaries for teachers in early childhood programs are not only desirable but also critical to the maintenance of quality programs. On the other hand, if, for example, teachers are recruited from Head

Start into school-based programs and offered salary increases, Head Start is bound to suffer. Instead, salary levels for all programs need to be commensurate with those of other occupations requiring a similar range of responsibilities and skills.

A Consolidation of Views. Although advocates and critics of school-based early childhood programs appear to hold distinctly different views of the promise of such programs, these views may not be as far apart as they seem to be. The main difference between advocates and critics appears to be the extent to which each group believes programs run by the public schools can be distinct from elementary school programs, can involve parents, and can respond to the developmental needs of the young child and the cultural heritage of the child's family. Considering the hopes of the advocates and the fears of the critics, we maintain that successful school-based programs must adhere to a set of standards about the curriculum, role of parents, training and experience of teachers, and collaboration with other community resources. (We discuss these in more detail in Chapter Twelve.)

Examples of School-Based Programs

In several states, school-based programs for young children and their families have been initiated, often as part of school reform. The programs tend to be of two distinct types: prekindergarten programs (usually for four-year-olds and, sometimes, three-year-olds) and parent support programs (usually for parents of infants and toddlers). We briefly review each type of program in this section.

Prekindergarten Programs. Several surveys point out the growth in state-initiated prekindergarten programs (Day, 1988; Mitchell, Seligson, and Marx, 1989; Schweinhart and Mazur, 1987). Currently, more than twenty-seven states are funding prekindergarten programs, although the number of children participating in each state varies considerably (Mitchell, Seligson, and Marx, 1989). Alaska and Delaware, for example, provide public programs for fewer than 100 children, whereas programs in California, New York, and Texas serve thousands of children. In most cases, prekindergarten programs are newcomers to state education agencies; only four states have funded such programs for more than ten years (Day, 1988).

The most recent survey (Mitchell, Seligson, and Marx, 1989) provides an overview of the characteristics of state-supported prekindergarten programs. In general, they found that most programs are for four-year-olds, are half a day long, and are targeted for children considered to be at risk for poor school performance. Very few programs encompass the hours of a working day or provide year-round services. For the most part, staffing patterns are within the range considered acceptable to early childhood professionals, one teacher to every ten children. Texas, a notable exception, allows a ratio of one teacher to every twenty-two children. Fourteen of the states with prekindergarten programs employ teachers with training and experience in early childhood education. Although less is known about the curricula of the prekindergarten program, eighteen states require some elements of a developmental approach in their curricula, and twelve favor academic or school readiness programs. Although some programs, especially those based on the Head Start model, provide comprehensive services, including medical, nutritional, and social services, no state has a comprehensive children's policy that encompasses all types of services.

Family Support Programs. During the last decade, researchers and educators have emphasized family support programs. The term *family support* has different meanings in different fields, however. For example, in the health and social services, family support programs help parents to raise children who are at risk or who have disabilities at home, rather than place them in foster care or institutions. In the field of education, family support programs offer services that aim to enhance parents' child-rearing abilities, empower families to act on their own behalf (Weissbourd and Kagan, 1989), and foster families' informal support networks (Bronfenbrenner and Weiss, 1983). In general, family support programs have derived from an ecological perspective described by Bronfenbrenner (1979) and stress the importance of the family and the community in the nurturing and optimal development of children (Weiss, 1989). Although family support programs can be designed for families with specific characteristics, such as adolescent parents, several models of these programs offer services to all families. These models have the advantage of a nondeficit and nonstigmatizing orientation (Weiss, 1989); that is, they do not assume that participating parents have poor parenting skills but build on the needs of all parents to learn about parenting. The activities that such programs provide vary widely but often include parent discussion groups, parent-child activity groups, information and referral services, and home visits.

Both grass-roots and university-affiliated family support programs have begun to offer services during the last decade (Zigler and Black, 1989). Many different agencies are involved in operating and coordinating the programs for a variety of population subgroups, and, in most cases, the specific agencies involved vary from one community to another. In contrast to the programs that are initiated locally, both Minnesota and Missouri have statewide family support programs operated by their departments of education.

The program in Minnesota, entitled Early Childhood Family Education, began its pilot phase in 1974. In 1989, it was operating in over 60 percent of the 435 school districts in the state (Hughes, 1989). Its goal is to "strengthen families by enhancing and supporting parents' ability to provide for children's learning and development" (Engstrom, 1988, p. 16). Although the program itself varies from one community to the next, in most sites, parents and their child (from birth to five years old) attend a parent-child class approximately one and one-half to two hours a week (Seppanen and Heifetz, 1988).

In Missouri, the New Parents as Teachers program began in 1982 and was designed for all first-time parents (White, 1988). At first, it operated in only four communities; now it operates statewide. The purpose of this program is to "create a sensible and comprehensive educational system to help parents guide the learning process of their children from birth to the third birthday" (White, 1988, p. 10). In monthly home visits and group meetings, parents can ask questions about child rearing and learn about their children's development. At least initially, program leaders actively discouraged parents from enrolling their children in full-time child care (White, 1988). The program has recently been integrated with comprehensive child-care services in some sites (Zigler and Ennis, 1988). An evaluation of this program indicated that children of participating parents consistently had higher scores on a range of ability and achievement measures than either national norms or the scores of a comparison group of nonparticipants. Moreover, participating parents were more knowledgeable in some areas of child development than comparison parents (Pfannenstiel and Seltzer, 1989).

The family support programs in Minnesota and Missouri are based in the public school system. Seppanen and Heifetz (1988) speculated that parents prefer having the public schools, as opposed to other agencies, operate such programs. They reason that most parents view education as the purpose of the schools, whereas parents view other agencies as having a more problem-oriented focus. Programs based in the public schools, therefore, benefit from these views.

In conclusion, the array of school-based early childhood programs in the United States is small but growing. Two types of programs exist. In general, one type of program is aimed at children from specific risk groups and usually involves prekindergarten services to children the year (or two) before they begin kindergarten. This type of program may include additional health and social services to families. A second type of program is available to all families but focuses on the infant and toddler years and provides few services to the child apart from the parent. Although both are valuable, neither model satisfies the current need for comprehensive early childhood programs from birth through the preschool years.

PART TWO

The Brookline
Early Education Project
(BEEP)

The Origins of BEEP

The Brookline Early Education Project (BEEP) was begun in 1972 as an integral part of the public school system. In contrast to other demonstration programs in early education, which generally had their roots in the child development research community, BEEP was initiated by public school personnel. Although public interest in preschool programs was increasing in the 1970s — the Head Start Program was well underway — the commitment by a public school system to undertake a program of the magnitude of BEEP was most unusual.

In this chapter, we discuss the motivations for early education in the community of Brookline, the development of BEEP, and the key features of the program that emerged from the planning period. In general, BEEP was developed to help parents and their children from a child's infancy through a child's entrance into kindergarten. The goal of the program was to develop a combination of education and health care services that would enable each child to fully realize his or her abilities. The aim was for children who participated in BEEP to be able to perform well in all of the areas that are related to success in school, including the important areas of social interactions with other children and adults as well as the traditional academic areas of the early years in elementary school. The success of these children in school, it was reasoned, would help to reduce the need for special services once the children reached school age. At the time BEEP was begun, such a program was considered a most unusual undertaking for a school system, and many factors were instrumental in its development.

The Impetus for BEEP

The initial force behind the development of BEEP was the Brookline superintendent of schools, Robert I. Sperber. He reasoned that if schools paid more attention to children at a young age, the schools could reduce the extent of remedial resources required for students during their later school years. Sperber and his school staff put together a team of people from different fields and agencies who would work together over many years in planning and carrying out this large-scale and long-term educational innovation. Two of us became members of this planning team.

As with any innovation, a number of factors were critical in fostering BEEP's development. Three interrelated concerns of Brookline teachers, guidance counselors, and other school personnel were factors in the development of BEEP.

1. School personnel reported that many children were entering school with previously undetected developmental and learning disabilities. Moreover, some disabilities were not detected until students had been in school for several years.
2. Teachers and counselors voiced their impression that, despite extensive and expensive remediation efforts, some children were not achieving their full potential during their school years because schools and parents failed to collaborate sufficiently.
3. School personnel were becoming increasingly aware of the mounting evidence that children's cognitive processes are well formed by five or six years of age, the time they ordinarily enter into formal education. Teachers and other school personnel expressed concern that schools enter the lives of children and families too late to make a difference.

BEEP was initiated at a time of great enthusiasm and belief in the value of early childhood education. Various research studies (discussed in Chapter Two), which were becoming better known at this time, stressed the importance of the first few years of a child's life in forming a child's cognitive abilities. For example, the work of Hunt (1961), which emphasized the major effects early development has on later development, was known to the education community. Similarly, the interpretation of Bloom's (1964) work on the importance of early indicators of intelligence had certainly filtered into the general mainstream of educators' knowledge. The initial evaluations of Head Start had been published, and these evaluations led to much discussion among educators about the need for some children to receive an even earlier start with home-based programs during the infant and toddler years. Most educators were also aware of the findings from the Harvard Preschool Project that emphasized the importance of the child's home environment, and especially the mother-child relationship, on the child's later development (White and Watts, 1973).

This combination of influences — a leader in education with a clear vision about the value of early education, a community of school personnel who desired new approaches to problems in education, and scholarly research that pointed to the importance of development during the early childhood years — created a climate that was receptive to the notion of a new early education program. Moreover, early education was not a new concept in Brookline. In 1968, in response to interests of teachers and parents who desired a preschool but could not afford the private school rates, the Brookline schools initiated an experimental nursery school for four-year-olds. Located at the high school in conjunction with a kindergarten class, the nursery school actively involved high school students and prompted further interest in early childhood education. The program was free to participating families, with enrollment on a first-come first-serve basis.

In 1969, Sperber appointed a task force on early childhood education. The task force developed suggestions about the way in which the schools could expand services to young children and their families. Educating parents, from the birth of their child until the child entered school, was prominent among these ideas. A report generated that same year by guidance counselors, social workers, psychologists, learning disability specialists, nurses, and a physician (all of whom comprised the Pupil Personnel Services of the schools) made a similar suggestion. This report stressed the importance of early detection of potential disabilities in very young children and proposed an extension of public education to children below five years old. In summary, when BEEP was first being considered by Superintendent Sperber, the schools in Brookline had already had some positive experience with operating an early education program, and personnel in the schools viewed early education as a potential solution to the educational problems brought about by undetected learning and developmental disabilities.

As indicated by the wide range of professions represented in the report made by the Pupil Personnel Services, Brookline was a school system that relished collaboration with professionals in many fields. The Brookline schools had collaborative agreements with many area colleges and universities for interns and staff development programs. Furthermore, the Children's Hospital Medical Center of Boston had agreed to provide the schools with medical services by physicians and other consultants. The notion that good education requires support from professionals in diverse fields such as social work and medicine was clearly a part of the philosophy of the school system. Collaborative efforts became a natural part of the schools' vision of an early education program.

No school system operates productively unless it reflects the values and interests of the area it serves. The Brookline Public Schools were no exception to this rule. The town of Brookline, Massachusetts, located adjacent to and surrounded on three sides by the city of Boston, has a long tradition not only of commitment to excellence in education but also of interest in early education. The Brookline school department's expenditures per pupil rank consistently in the top 10 percent among the 351 Massachusetts cities and towns. The town introduced a kindergarten program in 1936, forty years before the state department of education made kindergarten programs mandatory.

According to the national census of 1970, Brookline's

population of almost 60,000 had taken on increasingly urban characteristics at the time BEEP was initiated. For example, almost 33 percent of Brookline's residents reported during the census that their primary language was a language other than English. Almost 20 percent of families were headed by single parents. Over 75 percent of the school-age children attended the public schools, and most of the remaining children attended parochial schools. Unlike Boston, however, the average level of education of adults in Brookline was fairly high; the median years of schooling for adult males was reported to be almost fourteen years.

In the 1970s, eight neighborhood school districts, each housing grades K–8, fed into one central high school. The neighborhoods varied widely in socioeconomic characteristics, with those closest to Boston generally being the poorest. Census results from 1970 indicated that nearly every family in which the parents were college graduates sent their preschool-age children to a private preschool for one to three years. In families where the parents were not so highly educated, less than 50 percent of the preschool-age children attended a private preschool, a day-care center, or Head Start. Most of the latter families relied on friends, relatives, and the town recreation program for informal child care.

As people grew concerned in the 1960s about the effects of racial segregation in the Boston schools, Brookline's superintendent of schools became a founder and Brookline became a charter member of the Metropolitan Council for Educational Opportunity (METCO). METCO is the busing program funded initially by the Ford Foundation and later by the state of Massachusetts to reduce racial isolation and encourage integration of Boston children into surrounding suburban districts, all of which had few black children. Parents of minority children in Boston could request that their children attend Brookline or other participating public schools if space was available. Children from Boston were provided with free transportation to and from the suburban schools. The Brookline school system's commitment to this program set a precedent for inclusion of Boston minority families in Brookline's early education programs.

Thus, when educators and others began to think of forming an early education program in Brookline, many favorable conditions already existed:

- A superintendent of schools convinced of the need for schools to reach children before they were five years old
- A school staff concerned about the number of undetected learning problems exhibited by their students
- A general climate of knowledge about the importance of the early years of life in determining future development
- A school system with a history of involvement with early education programs
- A school system that believed education could not be considered in isolation from other critical services such as health care and social services
- A town that valued education and ethnic diversity

The Process of Developing BEEP

BEEP grew quickly from somewhat humble beginnings to become very ambitious. Plans for the program at first included relatively modest ideas about providing some form of prekindergarten program for four-year-olds. Eventually, these plans for BEEP expanded into a research and demonstration project that included services to children and families from the time of the children's birth until their entry into kindergarten.

The expansion of the project to the infant and toddler years was a direct result of the influence of Burton White, who served as a consultant to the superintendent of schools. Based on his research at the Harvard Preschool Project, White stressed the importance of a child's development before the age of three in establishing the framework for the child's later competencies (White, Kaban, and Attanucci, 1979). He convinced the school staff that children and families needed educational services during the children's infant and toddler years.

The project grew in scope as well. School personnel were convinced that if the project focused narrowly on education, children with other concerns such as health or social service needs might not benefit as fully from BEEP as they should. Members of the school staff who were committed to the notion of a comprehensive early education program sought help from medical personnel at the Children's Hospital, and several pediatricians became quite enthusiastic about the promise of such collaboration.

After much discussion, it was determined that the basic purpose of the program — to facilitate children's competence in school — would best be achieved by offering a program to parents that would begin at their child's birth and extend up to their child's entry into kindergarten. The program would be comprehensive in focusing on health and educational issues. It would place the parents at the center of the educational process. Rather than replacing the parents with experts or consultants or teachers, the goal of the program would be to build upon the knowledge that parents are in fact the most important teachers of their children, and the focus of the program would be on helping parents be as effective in child rearing as possible.

BEEP was planned to be a demonstration of an early education model in which a public school system took responsibility for coordinating programs and services to families during their children's preschool years. The involvement of a public school system did not mean that professionals were to take charge of raising the children. Thus, one of the main objectives of BEEP was to encourage parents to assume informed responsibility and effective advocacy for the quality of their child's education and health care.

We want to emphasize that the purpose of BEEP was not to accelerate or force children's development. Instead, the project's activities were designed to facilitate children's competence in school by arranging for each child a school, home, and health care environment rich in resources and opportunities. The notion of school competence, which served as the central focus of BEEP, is complex and requires some elaboration.

Psychologist Robert White (1959) defined competence broadly as the capacity to interact effectively with the environment. Over the years, this concept has been applied by psychologists and educators (for example, Harter, 1978) to explain

the highly motivated mastery and self-initiated learning behaviors of animals and humans. Two aspects of competence have
become prominent in the child development literature: (1) social skills, such as the ability to make friends and work and play
with others, and (2) self-regulatory skills, such as the ability to
select and complete tasks (Hauser-Cram and Shonkoff, 1988).
Many early childhood experts have proposed that indexes of
competence would be more appropriate measures of early education's impact than relatively narrow measures of intelligence
(Scarr, 1981; Walker, 1973; Zigler and Trickett, 1978).

Despite its appeal and its accepted validity, competence
is a difficult construct to define. Our early attempts at BEEP
to generate a simple framework for describing the various components of school competence were, ultimately, not very helpful. The areas traditionally considered in definitions of school
competence — intelligence, achievement, problem-solving ability, language skills, coping style, and socioemotional skills —
are interrelated and overlap. We decided that teachers and
other school personnel who worked with children could best determine the characteristics of children whom they perceived as
competent in the classroom. Therefore, a group of school staff
members, assisted by child development experts, met to define
school competence. The group determined that in kindergarten a competent child does the following:

1. Selects activities and tasks that are consistent with his or
   her abilities
2. Focuses and maintains attention
3. Displays organized behavior in the classroom by selecting
   and planning tasks, choosing appropriate materials to accomplish the tasks, and completing the tasks successfully
   with minimal distraction
4. Perceives the many relationships between objects and actions such as size, function, order, position, and time
5. Understands and uses language effectively
6. Performs age-appropriate motor activities and fine motor
   tasks
7. Plays alone and with others
8. Interacts successfully with adults and other children

These were the skills and abilities — the competencies — that BEEP was designed to promote. The educational and family support program for children and parents, described in the chapters that follow, evolved with this focus on competence.

BEEP was developed not only to assist the families participating in the program but also to be a demonstration program that would provide information on the strengths and weaknesses of a wide variety of possible services for young children and their families. We hoped that other communities and agencies would learn from BEEP and would develop approaches to preschool education that would best suit their local needs. But, as the plans for BEEP were being made, it became apparent that BEEP would be a costly program, perhaps too costly for many communities to implement. We began to consider which component could be eliminated, yet without knowledge of the effects of any component, it was difficult to determine which components were least important. We simply did not know if a program as intensive as BEEP was necessary for all types of families. Therefore, variations in the intensity of various service components provided to families were built into the research design of BEEP. Rather than focusing only on one global question about the effect of BEEP on participants, BEEP's components were designed to answer three basic questions about the effects of services: In general, did BEEP reduce the number of chidren who fail to demonstrate competence in elementary school? Did the effects of BEEP differ for children from families who received more or less service? Did children from certain types of families benefit more than children from other types of families?

These questions were critical to the design of both the program's components and the program's evaluation. Three levels of service were devised to provide systematically different amounts of service to families: extensive amounts of service (A level), moderate amounts of service (B level), and minimal amounts of service (C level). Families were randomly assigned to one of the three levels. Although the levels varied in intensity (and, therefore, cost), they did not differ in philosophy or goals. Nevertheless, parents assigned to the minimal level of service did not have a home visitor and, therefore, had a less personal link to BEEP. (We discuss the differences in level of service in more detail in Chapter Five.) The decision to expand BEEP from simply a program to an "experiment" with random assignment required a strong commitment by everyone involved in running the program to objective and systematic program evaluation.

In conclusion, the chief characteristics of the program included the following:

1. It would be based in the public schools. This would allow exploration of the role that the public school system could play in coordinating and providing early childhood services and provide continuity of educational experiences and support for children and families from the children's early years onward.

2. It would be a birth-to-kindergarten program. This time span would avoid the possible shortcomings of starting a program too late in a child's life or ending it too soon.

3. It would be strongly family centered. The main premise of the program was that the family is the primary educational influence on the child, and thus the program would attempt to build on this idea by helping to support the parents and family as much as possible.

4. It would be multidisciplinary in approach, involving educators, psychologists, pediatricians, social workers, and others in providing services to families.

5. It would be ethnically and economically heterogeneous in its enrollment. Unlike many other programs that had been proposed and developed during the 1960s and early 1970s, BEEP would have no special eligibility restrictions. Families from diverse backgrounds would be recruited. This was an important difference from many other programs, but it was consistent with the notion of a preschool program that would be run under the egis of a local public school system.

6. It would include a substantial investment in research and evaluation. We hoped that the project would produce results

of use and interest to researchers and program planners throughout the country.

Since declining enrollments were projected for elementary schools, initial plans called for Early Education Centers to be located in the elementary schools. At the outset of the project, however, enrollment did not decline as rapidly as anticipated and it was necessary to rent space for the project. As the project grew, we moved to Wheelock College, located on the Brookline-Boston border. By the project's third year of operation, school enrollment had declined sufficiently to allow space for the prekindergarten programs in each elementary school. By the time the children entered kindergarten, one small school closed, and the entire building was made available to house our research efforts.

Beyond an initial planning grant from the Bureau of Education for the Handicapped, our efforts to obtain federal funding were unsuccessful because BEEP was not intended to serve only one type of child, such as a child with disabilities, or one type of family, such as low-income families. Federal agencies generally were restricted to funding categorical programs (that is, programs that serve one type of client), and BEEP's comprehensive approach cut across categories. Two private foundations ultimately supported the project. Carnegie Corporation of New York was particularly interested in the potential of the project for reforming or redirecting educational policies involving young children and the public schools. The Robert Wood Johnson Foundation was particularly interested in the contribution that such a project might make in changing health care systems and involving pediatricians with issues related to educational development. Working in concert, Carnegie Corporation of New York agreed to fund BEEP's education-related components, while The Robert Wood Johnson Foundation funded health-related components.

In conclusion, the critical ingredients for a project such as BEEP were all in place in the early 1970s. A great deal of research had been done in both theoretical and empirical issues related to children's development during the preschool years.

The federal government had a strong interest in and commitment to early education. Brookline was a fertile setting for such a program. The community had a longstanding commitment to high-quality education. It already had a reputation for excellent schools, and it had a capable and committed staff, with easy access to expertise and innovative ideas from the universities, hospitals, and other agencies in the Boston area. Fortunately, two foundations were willing to invest substantial amounts of their money, time, and expertise in supporting the project over many years.

Chapter 5

An Overview of the Program and Its Participants

Enrolling in BEEP was my initiation, so to speak, into child development and education. It was my way of learning. I mean, I had this little baby. "Gee, I kind of like him, but I'm afraid to pick him up." And then my friend told me about BEEP and I thought, "Well, maybe I can learn more about mothering and child development and things like that."

At the time I joined I didn't know anything about having children and I thought it would be nice to join a group of other mothers in my situation, who had things in common to discuss. It was sort of like feeling all by myself out in the wilderness. It was a way to get to talk to people about babies.

Just having even a small contact with other children and adults of every race—when they get into kindergarten it won't be foreign to them. They'll be used to being with groups of kids, used to latching onto other adults besides me. Hopefully, it will make the transition easier.

An Overview of the Program Components

The components of BEEP were chosen to demonstrate that a school system can serve as a community base for primary

Table 1. Array and Timing of BEEP Program Components.

| Timing | | Child Assessment | Parent Education | Child Programs |
Program Phase	Child's Age			
	Birth	Neurological exam (2 weeks)	Orientation discussions	
Infant		Physical, sensory, and developmental exam (3½ months)		
	1 year	Physical, sensory, and developmental exam (6½ months)	Home visits[a]	
			Center visits •Toy library •Book library	Drop-in center: •Playrooms
		Physical, sensory, and developmental exam (11½ months)	Parent groups[a]	Respite child care[a]
Toddler	2 years	Physical, sensory, and developmental exam (14½ months)	Home visits[a]	
			Center visits	
		Physical, sensory, and developmental exam (24 months)	Parent groups[a]	Weekly playgroups
		Dental screening	Parent-teacher conferences	Respite child care[a]

3 years	Physical, sensory, and developmental exam (30 months)	Center visits
	Health history (36 months)	Parent groups[a]
4 years Prekindergarten	Physical, sensory, and developmental exam (42 months)	Parent-teacher conferences
	Dental screening	Guided classroom observations[a]
	Lead and anemia screening	
5 years	Entry into kindergarten exam	Final conference
		Daily prekindergarten, with optional extended day care

[a]These components were avaiable only to those in the moderate and extensive levels of program participation.

prevention activities, ensuring that children enter kindergarten as healthy, competent learners. The program consisted of three major components — parent education and support, early education programs for toddlers and prekindergarteners, and health and developmental monitoring of the children. Each of these three components (described in detail in Chapters Six, Seven, Eight, and Nine) were based on a similar philosophy about child development and parenting.

BEEP provided several different types of services at different ages throughout the children's first five years of life. The timing and array of the aspects of BEEP for each program components are displayed in Table 1. The combination of health and developmental assessments, parent education, and programs for children within BEEP provided a comprehensive and rich array of services for parents and children.

As we mentioned in Chapter Four, the full set of services listed in Table 1 was not offered to all parents participating in BEEP. Instead, a range in extent of service was intentionally designed as part of the research aspect of BEEP. Children's programs and health and developmental assessments were offered to all families, as was access to the toy and book-lending libraries and the BEEP playroom. The parent education and support services, however, varied according to the family's service level assignment. Families assigned to the minimal level of service (C level) did not receive home visits nor were they offered parent groups. In general, families in the C level needed to initiate their contacts with BEEP, except for the health and developmental assessments.

When families were given an orientation to the BEEP program, they received an explanation of the complexity of the service levels offered to parents. Program staff made clear that some families would receive frequent home visits (once every three to four weeks) and could attend parent groups, whereas others would receive fewer of these services (home visits every five to six weeks), and still others would not receive certain services, such as home visits. Assignment to level of services was on a strictly random basis, and families had to agree to participate regardless of their assignment before being accepted into the program. Random assignment was a point of controversy among BEEP staff. Some staff objected strenuously when a needy family was assigned to a minimal (C) level of service. Moreover, some parents expressed interest in one or another level of service because of personal wishes or a friend's involvement or because they were concerned about not being able to participate in a service they thought might be helpful. Despite these occasional difficulties, however, the plan was carried out, and all assignments to service level (A, B, or C) were made randomly. No family declined to participate because of the level they were assigned, and no changes in assignment were made.

Following is a timeline showing the events and dates, from the first planning of BEEP to the final evaluation:

1969–1970	Informal planning, Brookline Schools and community
1971–1972	Planning grant, Bureau of Education for the Handicapped and Carnegie Corporation of New York
Nov. 1972	Implementation grants awarded by Carnegie Corporation of New York and The Robert Wood Johnson Foundation
Mar. 1973–Oct. 1974	Family recruitment and enrollment
Mar. 1973–Aug. 1979	Parent and early childhood programs
Sept. 1978, 1979	Children enter kindergarten
May 1981, 1982	Children complete second-grade evaluation

Participants in the Program

Parents joined BEEP for many different reasons. Some thought it sounded enjoyable, some felt isolated and wanted contact with other parents, some wanted information about child rearing, some viewed BEEP as a safety net in case a health or developmental problem emerged with their child, and some wanted to get to know a range of families from different backgrounds. A few had practically no idea why they made their initial visit to BEEP — perhaps to accompany a friend or because someone suggested they find out about it or because a social worker said it was necessary to retain custody of their child. The variety of reasons for joining BEEP reflected the diversity of the participants themselves. Indeed, one goal of the program was to enroll a group of families whose background represented a variety of economic and educational levels, ethnic origins, and family structures. Thus, BEEP was unlike most other early education programs, which tended to target specific types of families or children. BEEP's commitment to serving the entire population of the community prevented BEEP from becoming a program that had a stigma attached to it; BEEP was regarded as a program that served all types of children and families, not only children with problems or families living in poverty. In this way, BEEP operated from a public health and public school model, rather than from a social work model.

Serving a wide range of families was also important in helping to demonstrate how BEEP might work in other settings as part of a regular program available to all types of families. One of the goals BEEP set was to establish a program that could be replicated in other communities. At the time BEEP was established, no other comprehensive early childhood program included such heterogeneous participants. It was important to us to know if heterogeneity in and of itself created benefits for children and families as well as if certain groups of children or families derived more benefits from the program.

Recruitment Process. The original recruiting goal was to enroll close to 300 families. This figure was determined by estimating the number of children who would need to remain in the project through the second grade for us to draw valid conclusions about the effects of the program. We assumed an attrition rate of about 10 percent a year, based on the experiences of other programs, the annual transiency rate in the Brookline Public Schools, and the turnover rate of patients reported by pediatricians in the area.

To be eligible to join BEEP, families had to be expecting a child to be born within a specified enrollment period (during

1973 or 1974). In addition, families had to reside in either Brookline or Boston and have no plans to move from the area in the next few years.

Recruiting families for a new program of free education and health services sounds like a remarkably easy task. Yet the process was frustratingly slow and difficult for several reasons. First, the birthrate in Brookline had dropped more than 50 percent over the prior three years. Although we intended to enroll all participants in one year, the decline in birthrate made us change our expectations. Rather than reduce the number of participants, we extended the enrollment to families with children born during a twenty-month period. This resulted in two cohorts of children, each of which would enter the public school kindergarten program during succeeding years, depending on the year of birth. Therefore, we lengthened the period of enrollment from one year to two, creating two groups of children.

We were seriously concerned that the enrollment quota would quickly be filled by educationally oriented families who actively seek educational opportunities. Children from these families could be expected to do quite well academically in elementary school, without any intervention, and, therefore, the impact of BEEP on them might be hard to determine. We developed an extensive outreach program to recruit families who ordinarily would not hear of or seek out an innovative educational program. Some recruitment plans involved contacting families directly, others included contacting staff members of community agencies and organizations for help. The latter strategies were especially important in reaching low-income families. We were also committed to hiring staff members with backgrounds that would be roughly comparable to the range of people that we were trying to attract to BEEP.

We anticipated many concerns that prospective participants might have: Is my child just going to be a guinea pig in a research project? Are they going to tell me that I've done a poor job of raising my other children? Will my older child feel left out? How will I have time to go to BEEP when I can't find the time to do anything else now? Are these just a bunch of so-called experts who don't really know what it's like to raise a kid?

Are they going to blame me for being a single parent and having to work? I don't speak much English; how can I talk to all those other parents? As the project's services were described to prospective participants, it became apparent that what constitutes early education was much more obvious to us than to parents. It was clear that all the parents wanted the best possible opportunities for their children, but it was not so clear that BEEP could always meet the parents' perceptions of what was needed. Many parents held the misconception that the program would try to accelerate children's development, perhaps, as some parents hoped, by teaching number or letter recognition at an early age. We had to make it very clear that BEEP would not be able to provide unlimited day care or social services. In addition, even though participating children would occasionally receive health examinations at BEEP, we had to explain very clearly that BEEP could not provide any primary health care but that staff members would refer parents to appropriate sources of medical care. Similarly, although social workers were on the BEEP staff, their role was to link parents with the appropriate agency, not to provide direct service.

Although we stressed to parents the importance of enrolling several months before the birth of their baby (66 percent of participating families enrolled before the child was born), enrollment was permitted during the child's early infancy. Many parents were sufficiently anxious and superstitious about having a healthy baby to preclude them from making commitments and specific plans before the baby was born. However, during the first few weeks and months of the child's life, some parents became very receptive to the idea of joining BEEP. The baby's cries in the middle of the night, finicky eating behavior, and diaper rashes were real. Parents began having questions about their baby's behavior or development that led them to consider joining BEEP. As parents realized they could use information and support, and particularly as they heard that their friends enjoyed the program, they became receptive to the opportunity. Consistent with the research design, no child was enrolled after six months of age, although we did receive requests for later enrollment from families who had just moved to town or who had not heard about the program earlier.

Recruitment Strategies. We employed multiple recruitment strategies to reach a wide range of prospective participants (Nicol, 1978). Health providers were one important group that we contacted. Believing that many pregnant women would not join an early education project without the approval of their physicians, we worked to acquaint the medical community with the project's objectives. The task was made difficult by the extraordinarily large number of doctors who deliver and care for babies in the greater Boston area. School records showed that about 150 pediatricians cared for Brookline's approximately 400 kindergarten children.

BEEP staff members made personal calls and follow-up visits with the doctors who delivered or cared for the most Brookline babies. Staff members contacted dozens of obstetricians and pediatricians. For the most part, the response of these doctors was encouraging and supportive; they displayed BEEP brochures in their offices and mentioned the program to pregnant patients. Often the receptionist or nurse was the one who remembered to refer patients to BEEP.

BEEP staff members also explained BEEP to members of the Visiting Nurses Association and asked that they mention it to the pregnant women they encountered in their work. BEEP's nurse and nursing student also enlisted the aid of clinic nurses who serve pregnant women and infants. They visited the major hospitals and clinics in the Boston area, leaving brochures and posters. Several groups of nurses from these institutions visited the BEEP Center.

The directors of both the Brookline Health Department and the Brookline Mental Health Clinic were valuable allies in the recruiting campaign. Their staffs provided leads to groups engaged in childbirth education, to other community resources, and to expecting families. The medical director of the Martha Eliot Health Center, located in the densely populated Mission Hill district of Boston and affiliated with Children's Hospital, helped us to establish a recruiting room within the center. A part-time community worker at the center coordinated the enrollment of black and Hispanic families for BEEP.

Two strategies were designed to allow us to meet parents of kindergarten children. Staff members attended spring preregistration of children for the fall kindergarten term. They spoke individually with parents about the project and asked them to mention it to friends who were expecting babies in the near future. Staff members also visited the school areas or school bus stops where mothers congregated at noon to wait for their returning kindergarten children. It was easy for staff to talk informally with mothers about BEEP at these settings.

Guidance counselors of the Brookline schools held two meetings to learn about BEEP and to suggest ways in which they might help recruit families. BEEP staff members visited each elementary school to explain BEEP to those nurses and teachers who were most in contact with young mothers of the district. They left brochures and posters at each location.

Since many high school students are baby-sitters and therefore might know of families who were expecting a child, we contacted them through their guidance counselor. Students were asked to help inform any pregnant mothers they knew about the BEEP program. BEEP staff members met with all psychology classes at the high school on several occasions to present films and lead discussions about infant development. BEEP's objectives were covered as well.

Two BEEP staff members attended a weekly luncheon meeting of the Brookline Clergymen's Association, explained the programs, and furnished brochures for the ministers and rabbis to give to expectant parents. Several clergymen asked for statements they could insert in their weekly bulletins.

The director and social workers of the Brookline Welfare Department gave valuable assistance by recruiting among families and single mothers in their caseloads. Nursery schools, day-care centers, playgroups, and other early childhood referral services were contacted by BEEP staff members and encouraged to inform their participants about BEEP.

Posters and brochures were distributed by staff members to public libraries, supermarkets, toy stores, and maternity shops. Brochures with Spanish inserts were left where appropriate. Staff members placed several articles and announcements in the local newspapers. In addition, staff members described the project on a number of local television and radio programs and invited involvement.

Recruiting of minority families in Boston was largely accomplished through established organizations in minority neighborhoods. In each case, the key people in these groups visited BEEP several times and explored all sorts of ramifications of the project for minority families. Since the minority communities have frequently been exploited by well-intentioned projects, these leaders wanted to check out the project and evaluate the trustworthiness of the administration before giving their approval.

All of the minority advisers and staff were leery of university researchers. They had heard some psychologists criticizing women for working rather than staying home with their children and were concerned that such experts had little understanding of the daily economic concerns of many minority families. Moreover, minority parents were sensitive to the deficit theory implied by various training programs for parents — that is, they feared the experts would maintain that minority parents were somehow inadequate in their methods of child rearing. The minority families who chose to join BEEP did so only when they realized that minority members of BEEP's staff would act as strong advocates for minority concerns. In particular, we assured parents that data would not be reported by ethnicity; this agreement was made to eliminate the possibility of misinterpretation of any findings.

Fundacion Puente, an organization serving the needs of Boston's Hispanic communities, assisted the project not only in understanding the problems of various Hispanic groups but also in recruiting BEEP staff members and families. In addition, a social worker employed part time by BEEP, who is Chinese and is thoroughly acquainted with the Chinese communities in Brookline and Boston, informed Chinese families about BEEP. She also provided Chinese translations of some of the project's materials. A number of BEEP's initial staff members were actively involved in social service or advocacy organizations (such as the Urban League), and through their work with those organizations, they made others aware of the services offered at BEEP and the program's commitment to ethnic diversity.

Not surprisingly, we found that particular approaches

were more productive in recruiting different types of participants. Once a core group of participants had been recruited,
they served as the most productive source for recruiting new
families simply through word of mouth. Personal contact with
other parents enrolled in BEEP was thus the most effective
recruitment strategy for all types of families. For college educated families, newspaper articles about BEEP were the next
most effective source of recruitments. In contrast, for less educated families, the staff at public health clinics proved to be a
productive recruitment source. For all families, the next most
effective recruiting strategy was personal contact from BEEP's
staff members, which occurred at various sites throughout both
Boston and Brookline. Mass mailings of letters to parents of public school students were unproductive — only four families joined
the project as a result of these letters.

Although precise cost figures for the many methods used
in the enrollment campaign are not available, records of planning sessions and meetings support some conclusions about cost
in relation to yield. First, newspapers articles not only brought
in the largest number of families but also entailed the least ex-
penditure of staff time — usually only two or three hours of preparation for each article. By contrast, staff contacts with the medical community required literally dozens of hours from the nurse,
several educators, and the program director. Only thirty-four
families enrolled as a result of all this effort, which cost, on a
per-family basis, much more than any other form of recruitment. Brochures and posters were useful in that they put the
information directly into the hands of those recruiting for the
project, but by themselves, they brought in only sixteen families. Some families did mention that there was a cumulative
effect for them of seeing the posters and reading of the project
in the paper, so that when a clinic nurse or a neighbor mentioned the project to them, they were already partially convinced
they should look into it.

Characteristics of Enrolled Children. Enrollment for the
project took place over twenty months. A total of 282 children
were enrolled by the end of the enrollment period. We achieved

our goal of recruiting a wide range of families, and the demographic characteristics for families enrolled in the three levels of service were remarkably similar. A total of 37 percent of the families were of minority background, and 17 percent did not speak English at home. Roughly equal numbers of girls and boys were enrolled, and about 50 percent of the children were first-borns. The majority of the mothers were in their twenties, and only 9 percent were adolescents. About 50 percent of the sample of mothers were college graduates, while 11 percent of the mothers did not have a high school degree. The majority of children lived with both parents, although 11 percent lived only with their mother.

Although over the course of nine years between the time the last child was enrolled and the time the last children entered second grade, attrition occurred at a slightly higher rate (about 15 percent per year) than we had anticipated (primarily due to family transiency), the basic demographic profile of the participants remained about the same (see Appendix D, Table D-1). Differential attrition was not a major factor affecting this group of children and families as they advanced from the BEEP program into elementary school.

Chapter 6

Parent Education and Support

I needed BEEP. I knew nothing. I really thought being a
mother would be so easy. But then someone from BEEP
came to my house. She asked about getting my baby's room
ready. I hadn't. I really had trouble coping with the crisis of
being just another womb. I thought an intelligent woman
would be at law school. But BEEP changed my whole attitude. After Barbara was born, Sarah (my home visitor from
BEEP) would ask, "Why do you think she did that?" instead
of just saying, "Isn't she cute?" I suddenly realized that
mothering wasn't just sitting around the house. Nothing at
college prepared me for this.

My little one, Juanita, I take to BEEP. And I see that she
gets community, children, you know. She learn how to play
with the children. And when my other boy—he live in Mexico without me—came to live with me, I see how different my
little one was. She was—I don't know how to say it—like
confidence with her. She learn so many things and she has
confidence.

The prevailing wisdom in early
childhood circles in the early 1970s was that parents are the first
and most influential teachers of their children; that most parents desire to improve their knowledge and skills as their children's educators; that parents want their children to be healthy,

happy, and successful; and that children's performance in school can be improved through an effective parent education program. BEEP's challenge was to involve parents and build a successful parent education program based on these assumptions.

The dramatic changes in family composition that began to take place in the early 1970s in the United States (Bloom and Steen, 1988) were also seen in the Brookline and Boston school populations. Fewer and fewer "traditional" families, with a working father and at-home mother, were found in Brookline and Boston when the BEEP children were born in 1973–1974. In Brookline, types of parents included single-parent mothers (constituting the parents of over 40 percent of the school-age population in two of the eight elementary schools), single-parent fathers, working mothers and at-home fathers, dual-career parents, grandparents raising children instead of parents, parents plus grandparents or aunts and uncles, family and friends filling parenting functions in communal households, homosexual couples as parents, and two sets of parents—through divorce and remarriage with joint custody.

We did not want to exclude any children because of family life-style and certainly did not want to limit participation only to the declining numbers of traditional two-parent middle-class families. Yet it was increasingly clear that different families, even those that shared a particular life-style, required different kinds of assistance in order to be more effective primary educators of their children. Furthermore, the needs of families change over time, with maturity, birth of another child, job opportunities, marital stress, and so on.

The parent education and support program of BEEP had to serve families with different needs and families at different points in their parenting experience. In general, the parent education program was designed to serve three basic functions: (1) to offer valid information about child development, (2) to provide support for and understanding of the demanding and changing role of the parent, and (3) to facilitate a sense of community among participating parents.

The education and support program, designed to respect each family's culture, background, current situation, and parenting style, used a number of strategies to support the parents' role as the primary educators of their child. Two of the major components of the program for parents — home visits and parent groups — are described in this chapter.

Home Visits

Home visits were an integral part of BEEP for many families during their child's infant, toddler, and, to a lesser extent, preschool years. In general, families assigned to the most intensive level of services (A level) received an average of fourteen to eighteen home visits during their child's first two years of life. Those parents assigned to the middle intensity level of service averaged ten to twelve home visits during that time period. The home visitor was often a parent's major link to BEEP and served a critical function for many families during their child's first two years of life. Home visiting of families whose children are not ill or disabled was an unusual concept in this country at the time BEEP initiated these visits. It is still quite unusual for families with children developing normally to participate in a home-visiting program, so we describe this aspect of BEEP in some detail, beginning with the theory guiding the approach taken at BEEP.

Theory and Goals. The importance of the home environment, family resources, and parental involvement in the educational process of children had been documented prior to the development of BEEP (Coleman and others, 1966). Therefore, many programs operating in the 1970s that attempted to affect the behavior of very young children involved parents, usually the mother, and often were didactic or tutorial in manner (such as Gordon, 1969; Levenstein, 1970). Programs using this type of approach seemed far more promising than programs that attempted to substitute professional teaching for mother-child interaction (Gray and Klaus, 1970). In an influential review of the effects of early education programs, Bronfenbrenner (1974) speculated that the effectiveness of the tutorial mode is due to the interplay of three factors: maternal interest and involvement in the teaching process, motivation of the young child to attend to and learn from the mother, and the sustained momentum and continuity of learning resulting from constant physical proximity of the mother and child.

BEEP extended the involvement of parents far beyond the concept of parent training. The program operated in a more global sense, functioning as one element in a system of school and community resources available to meet the needs of parents, so that they in turn could provide optimal support for their children. We recognized the fallacies of a narrow model of parent education. We knew that to be effective in enlisting and maintaining the interest of parents, the program had to anticipate a wide variety of parental expectations, goals, abilities, and life-styles. The program also had to establish an alliance with each family that allowed parents and educators to serve as resources for one another so that each could take an active role in the child's education. This interactive model of learning so often espoused for children (Kamii and DeVries, 1977), had seldom been applied to adults in prior early education programs, most of which focused more on training parents than on helping parents gain insight into their child's behavior. From this rationale and underlying theory, we adopted a series of commitments to parent education:

- Parents are the most significant educational force in the life of the child; therefore, parents and staff need to become partners during all stages and in all components of an early education program. Both parents and staff members need to be involved in planning for the child's educational program.
- Respect for individual family styles and cultural preferences is a critical part of providing support to families. Rather than prescribing specific ways for parents to interact with their children, staff members need to help parents find effective ways of interacting that are compatible with parents' abilities and values.
- The strengths, needs, and resources of families differ; therefore, the services available to parents need to be tailored to individual needs, not prepackaged and imposed on families.

Similar themes (such as a child's reluctance to be away from his mother) need to be approached in different ways for different families.

Characteristics of Home Visitors. Believing that the success of BEEP would depend greatly upon the success of each home visitor, we devoted considerable thought to identifying the qualities that characterize an effective home visitor and the procedures for evaluating these qualities. We reviewed the experiences of other programs that had used home visitors (Gordon, 1969; Levenstein, 1970) and solicited the opinions of a range of families. Five characteristics were the key considerations in assessing a candidate for the role of home visitor: gender, parental status, professional training and experience, background, and personal qualities.

Most of the contacts between the family and the home visitor during the first two years of the child's life took place in the home, often with only the home visitor, the mother, and the child present. All of the home visitors were women to optimize communication and minimize complexity for mothers, many of whom expressed discomfort about the possibility of having a male home visitor. Male teachers, who were valued for their ability to offer advice to fathers on child-rearing issues, were placed in the BEEP center and school-based activities but were not used as home visitors.

At the specific request of parents involved in planning for BEEP, we tried to avoid the posture of child-rearing experts. Parents did not want home visitors armed with theory but lacking experience. As one parent said, "At nine o'clock in the morning, after I've been up all night with a screaming kid, I don't want to hear some graduate student talk about Piaget." Since all home visitors serving families during the first year of a child's life were required to be parents, rapport and mutual respect between parents and home visitors developed quickly. Over time, the empathy for parenthood fostered by home visitors who were also parents was very important.

Home visitors were required to have training or experiences in early childhood education or a related field, which included nursing, social work, and special education. Although most of the home visitors held at least a bachelor's degree, neither academic degrees nor certain certifications were prerequisites for the position. Since we were concerned about maintaining a mix of socioeconomic backgrounds in the staff and encouraging empathy with parents, we placed a higher priority on inservice than on preservice training. Home visitors were discouraged of the notion that opinions on child rearing are merely a matter of personal preference by the requirement of initial expertise and continual updating of expertise.

In addition to the commitment that the teaching staff be diverse in terms of race, ethnicity, language, age, marital status, family size, and area of residence, we sought home visitors who brought a special knowledge or training to complement the expertise already assembled in the existing staff. For example, one home visitor had a background in nursing, another had been an elementary school teacher, one had been a learning disabilities specialist, and others had worked in day-care or nursery school settings. Staff discussions of goals, predispositions, and biases were broadened in a manner that could not have been possible without this staff diversity.

When families enrolled in the program, they were asked whether they had any preference in the characteristics of the home visitor who would be assigned to them. Although it was not always possible to meet all requests, some families did express a preference for home visitors of certain demographic characteristics. For instance, some black families requested a black home visitor, and the majority of parents with large families preferred a home visitor with experience in raising more than one child. Single-parent families often requested a home visitor who was a single parent and the youngest mothers usually preferred the youngest home visitor. Non-English-speaking families were always assigned to a home visitor fluent in their language (either Spanish or Chinese).

We solicited verbal and written references from the supervisors, colleagues, and clients of candidates for position of home visitor. In search of idealistic individuals who were willing to work thirty-five hours per week for salaries equivalent to that of a kindergarten teacher, we looked for individuals with the following personal attributes:

- Sensitivity to the expressed and unexpressed needs of families from a wide variety of backgrounds and with a wide range of experiences
- Versatility in adapting goals and teaching strategies to meet families' needs
- Availability to meet the needs of families by making some home visits during evenings or weekends
- Openness to suggestions and supervision from supervisory personnel, team leaders, and peers
- Organized and systematic approach to the work situation so that services would be provided on schedule and necessary records kept
- Maturity to handle a variety of situations in a nonjudgmental way
- Discretion to know when to disclose and when to withhold information
- Perseverance to establish and maintain contact with families, often under difficult circumstances
- Willingness to try new ideas and to admit the need for help

Finding people who met these high standards was not easy, but we were impressed with the large number of capable and committed individuals who were interested in this demanding level of work. The extensive time and care that we devoted to the hiring process resulted in the appointment of home visitors who were well qualified, enthusiastic about the position, and compatible with the other staff members. This selection and hiring process set the tone for a team-oriented operation in which each member of the group had a stake in his or her colleagues' success.

Functions of Home Visitors. Although any effective teacher fills a variety of functions, a teacher of parents is probably expected to fill more roles than most teachers are. Among the many functions that the teachers who were home visitors for BEEP were expected to perform were those of observer, model, source of information, listener, social service resource, and consultant on the results of developmental and health assessments.

Each home visitor had to be sufficiently aware of the normal course of child development to be able to assess informally the child's developmental progress. In a casual, playful way, the home visitor had to elicit relevant behaviors from the child (such as having the child grasp a toy) or ask specific questions that encouraged the parent to describe the child's progress (such as, What are the child's favorite activities?). Frequently, the home visitor brought along one or more toys or books, either produced commercially or made by the visitor. The toys and books were often chosen because they would allow the home visitor to observe the child in a new way, such as to see how the child might solve a simple problem like getting an object out of a box.

For some families, the home visitor might model a particular behavior or way of interacting with the child. For example, the home visitor might suggest different ways to encourage a three-month-old to reach for a toy. Or the home visitor might model ways of helping a toddler anticipate what would occur next in the daily routine by saying, "First we play, then you eat lunch." The home visitor might then comment on how well the child is beginning to understand simple sequences (if the child appears to be doing so) and how helpful that understanding will be for the child in the future. In some cases, modeling was not made explicit; it was done without comment. In other cases, the parent's attention was drawn to what was being done or to the results. When the parent articulated a problem, asked for help in managing a situation, or requested specific suggestions for activities or learning experiences for the child, the home visitor responded more directly.

In almost every family, the home visitor was regarded as one source of information on issues related to child development and child rearing. The home visitor's opinion may not have been the only or even the final opinion the family sought, but most families valued her input.

The home visitor would always plan for each home visit and was prepared to talk with the family about a particular topic that she thought would be relevant. For example, in planning a home visit to a family with a six-month-old, the home visitor might focus the visit on a discussion about stranger anxiety and the range of reactions children exhibit. On the other hand, if the home visitor knew a critical issue for a parent was the relationship between a sibling and the new baby, she would continue to focus on that issue, and only briefly address the topic of stranger anxiety. The way the home visitor approached the topic at hand varied considerably from one family to the next. Some parents enjoyed reading information and then discussing it with the home visitor. Most preferred a less formal, more experiential approach, in which theoretical constructs were couched in terms of the child's behavior at a particular time. The home visitor tried, in effect, to put the child's moment-to-moment behavior into a broader context of understanding for the parents.

The home visitor always individualized her approach to match the families' style and needs. Many families asked questions that served as starting points for discussion and information. (Appendix A lists the questions, categorized under twenty-three headings, that parents frequently asked home visitors during their child's first two years of life.) For example, a mother who was distressed by the difficulty she had leaving her child with baby-sitters often had many questions about what she could do to make the situation less stressful for her child and herself and what might be the possible consequences of her actions. The home visitor had to be prepared to answer these questions, make suggestions about how to get through the difficult time, reassure the mother, and follow up the concern on subsequent visits.

One of the most sensitive roles the home visitor played was that of a listener. Many families found it helpful to have a sympathetic and knowledgeable person allow them to discuss their uncertainties. As an outsider, the home visitor was removed from the immediacy and the responsibility of the situation and could offer a different perspective. The home visitor's professional status gave her the necessary distance from the situation, and her demonstrated concern for the family allowed her access to issues that needed to be discussed.

Home visitors tried hard to avoid the role of therapist and to determine when they should refer parents to other community resources better able to offer therapy. Almost every family encountered ups and downs in child rearing. Often parents needed to discuss their concern about the way their child was developing, their questions or reservations about their own adequacy as parents, their feeling of isolation from the rest of the world, or many other issues.

If the home visitor believed that the concern raised by a parent was either short term or fairly typical in scope, her role was to listen and, if appropriate, validate the parent's view. For example, one father was concerned that because his child walked at a late age, she would be delayed in other areas of development. In this case, the child had an excellent ability to understand language and to use people in her environment to meet her needs. The home visitor was able to point out the child's strengths and also discuss the child's emerging abilities that indicated a high level of cognitive competence. This discussion enabled the father to see a positive pattern in his child's abilities and to create reasonable expectations for her.

If the home visitor was concerned that the parent was seriously disturbed or unable to cope or that the child's development was not progressing as it should, she presented the situation immediately at an education or diagnostic team meeting (which included staff members such as a social worker, a nurse, an educator, and a psychologist in addition to the home visitor), and a plan of action was determined. This plan sometimes involved referring the family to other agencies. For example, one mother, who was a single parent, expressed grave concern over the development of her two sons, both of whom were older than the child she had enrolled in BEEP and one of whom she believed had been sexually abused by her former husband. This situation was well beyond the domain of the home visitor and required immediate and specific psychiatric intervention.

Sometimes a parent expressed a concern for which there was no immediate solution. For example, for a long time one mother felt overwhelmed with the responsiblity and the physical demands of raising four small children all under six years old. Her husband's work involved a large amount of travel for long periods of time. Although the home visitor made practical suggestions (neighborhood baby-sitters, extra child care at BEEP, involvement with BEEP's parent groups, or talks with BEEP's social worker), she had to acknowledge the mother's anger and frustration before the mother was able to implement any of the ideas. The home visitor listened for a large part of each home visit over several months until the situation had eased.

Home visitors were encouraged not to allow the listening role to dominate the home visit, but whenever possible to turn the focus of the visit toward the child and the child's educational development. It was insufficient, however, for BEEP to be concerned with the child in isolation, as the relationship of the primary caretaker (usually the mother) to the child is critical to the child's development. Moreover, the parent-child dyad could not be separated from the rest of the child-rearing support system. Because the mother or caretaker was the real deliverer of BEEP's services to the child, the home visitor often had to be able to adjust the planned lesson and address the more immediate concerns of the mother or caretaker. In order to make an alliance with the home visitor—and ultimately with BEEP— the mother at first had to satisfy herself that her home visitor was responsive to her needs as well as knowledgeable about her child's development. This often meant that the home visitor needed to allocate a time for listening. For many families, a small portion of every visit was spent this way. In others, the first few visits were devoted almost exclusively to listening.

The most acute need of many families was for social services: housing, food, medical care, evaluation of other children, jobs, and educational opportunities. Although the program's original intention was to refer these families to existing agencies within the community for help, a great deal of the home visitor's time during the visits was spent helping families to procure services that took unduly long periods to obtain after referrals were made. Creating alliances with families who had many needs and who had had poor experiences with social service agencies often meant providing tangible demonstrations that some small part of these families' lives could be made better.

We hired two social workers to whom these needs could

be directed. Their role was considered essential in working with a population as diverse and heterogeneous as that of the participants in BEEP. Often the combined efforts of the home visitor and the social worker were necessary to locate services and facilitate the family's use of them.

Before each health and developmental assessment (described in Chapter Nine), the home visitor participated with the members of the diagnostic team in a brief preexam conference. At this time, the home visitor described her perception of the child and the family at home. During the first year of a child's life, some home visitors administered the developmental portion of the assessment, while others did not. Home visitors were not objective evaluators of children they had visited for a long time, so they did not function as the developmental evaluator after the child's first year of life.

The home visitor sometimes was present during assessments of the child, depending upon the baby's awareness of the presence of others and the parents' need for the support of a familiar person. In every case, the home visitor participated with other evaluators in the feedback session at the end of the assessment. At this time, information about the results of the assessment and its implication were discussed with the parents. If necessary, the home visitor addressed parents' concerns or worries during subsequent meetings.

Themes of Parent Education. The home visits and other parent activities were centered around a series of themes the home visitors were expected to discuss with parents. Team meetings and instructional videotapes on each theme were used to train the staff. Specific questions, relating to the various themes, were developed to ensure consistency among the home visitors and to help home visitors steer a drifting conversation back to the education agenda. (See Resource B for an expanded list of the themes and specific questions developed to assist home visitors.) Some examples of the themes and questions home visitors asked at different stages of the child's development follow:

1. What are the baby's new and emerging skills? For example, is she beginning to try to pull herself up while holding on to furniture?

2. What are the baby's interests? For example, are there toys or activities he especially enjoys or shuns?
3. What activities are immediately available to the baby in the home? For example, can she reach the toys that are intended for her use?
4. Have all aspects of safety in the home been considered, given the baby's present and emerging skills? For example, do all outlets have covers?
5. How do members of the family relate to the baby? For example, do siblings play roughly with the baby?
6. How does the mother regard the baby's temperament? For example, does she see him as very demanding or unusually passive?
7. What does the mother enjoy doing with the baby? For example, does she have a repertoire of appropriate social interaction games, like peekaboo, to play with the baby?
8. What are the baby's sleeping, eating, and toileting routines? For example, does she manage finger foods?

Home visitors also used a curriculum guide, developed by staff at BEEP (Yurchak with others, 1975), to aid them in anticipating the next stage of the child's development in the following areas: postural development, growth and coordination of the visual field, visually directed reaching, social development, audition and language, and cognition. Since no similar set of curriculum sequences for this age group was available, home visitors found the curriculum guide an invaluable resource. The curriculum sequences were designed so that home visitors could offer practical suggestions for ways parents could expand their enjoyment with their child. And the curriculum suggested the normal sequence of development, allowing for individual differences. Through staff training and use of the curriculum guide, home visitors became aware of the need for multiple observations of the child—especially if the home visitor suspected that a child was lagging in development—and the tendency for old skills to reappear when new ones are emerging. The sequences suggested in the curriculum guide, therefore, were not considered to be fixed, but were to be understood within the context of the normal ebb and flow of human development.

Problems Encountered. Although the home-visit component of BEEP was generally quite well received by parents and rated highly by them (this rating by parents is described in more detail in Chapter Ten), several problems were encountered in this aspect of the program. First, upon occasion, respect for a family's sense of values and personal approach to child rearing ran counter to current knowledge about ways to support children's optimal development. A fairly common example of this involved the child's need for exploration. Some families believed that infants, and particularly toddlers, should spend a large portion of their day in playpens. In contrast, BEEP's home visitors encouraged parents to make certain areas of their home or apartment childproof and to allow the toddler to explore and even to have certain cupboards or drawers of his or her own. Parents sometimes could not see the need for such freedom and did not wish to change such an essential part of their living arrangement. In each case, these differences were resolved individually, but conflicts between two essential values of BEEP — imparting information about children's development and respecting each family's sense of values — were not easy on the staff.

A second type of conflict emerged during home visits. We viewed the program's primary function as providing information and support, rather than intervening in the lives of families in a therapeutic sense. Sometimes, however, a family needed more intensive and more direct intervention. Home visitors had to be skilled enough to recognize the signs of the need for intervention. The line between the need for support and the need for therapeutic intervention was not always clear. For example, a mother described herself as not being able to sleep and as having difficulty performing everyday activities. That description is typical of many parents who are experiencing some sleep deprivation but also may be a sign of more serious depression. Whenever a home visitor felt a sense of discomfort with her ability to sort out a situation, she was able to discuss it with the social worker, nurse, or other relevant professionals at BEEP. Group meetings served an important function for all staff members and often prevented minor concerns from developing into major ones.

A third type of problem was encountered by both staff

members and participating families: how to form a relationship that did not result in the families becoming overly dependent on BEEP. In interviews about BEEP, families described their sense of reciprocity with the program. BEEP provided them with information and support, and they provided BEEP with data to be used for research purposes (Weiss, 1979). Moreover, the families described BEEP as one source — but seldom the only source — of information they used in making parenting decisions. Staff members also had some concerns about families becoming overly reliant on them, especially families who were involved with other agencies, such as social service agencies, but had encountered difficulty with those relationships. BEEP's staff members could serve as liaisons for those families with other agencies, but their intervention would undermine the family's sense of independence. As a result, we worked with parents to develop strategies for the parents to use in resolving the dispute with or asking for assistance from other agencies. Nevertheless, in rare instances, a staff member did contact other agencies directly on behalf of a family, but only if the family had exhausted its own resources.

Another problem emerged because of the research nature of BEEP. The needs and strengths of families assigned to the more intensive levels of service (A and B) became well known to the staff through the home visits. In contrast, the families assigned to the minimal level of service (C) did not receive home visits and tended to establish their relationships with staff members more slowly, usually through the diagnostic assessments or possibly the use of the BEEP libraries and other facilities. When staff members became aware of some of the multiple and pressing needs of a few of the families assigned to the C level of service, they were frustrated by their inability to offer the families more of the services of BEEP. In particular, staff members believed home visits to be especially valuable for families with multiple needs and were concerned that those families who might benefit were not able to receive home visits. The conflict between the requirements of the research design and the needs of individual families did not resolve itself during the first two years of the program. As the children from those multineed families entered the children's programs at two years of age, and, therefore, the families were receiving some outreach from BEEP's staff members, this conflict diminished. Although other programs will not be as constrained by research design as BEEP was, they will be constrained by resources, and conflicts are bound to emerge about which families are most in need of (or will benefit most from) a given set of resources.

Parent Groups

Discussion groups for parents were initiated to allow parents to discuss common issues, to help reduce parents' isolation, and to provide parents with information and an opportunity for reflection about parenting in a less costly manner than through home visits. Parents who participated in the most intensive service level attended an average of eight parent group sessions over the first two years of the program and those in the middle-intensity group attended an average of five parent groups over the first two years. Although parents in the least intensive service level did not have group sessions organized for them, they could use BEEP's facilities if they wished to organize such a group themselves; some parents took advantage of this. Parent groups were generally restricted to a maximum of ten participants and met for a series of six sessions.

Theory and Goals. Parent groups were developed at BEEP for three purposes: (1) to offer information about child rearing to parents, (2) to create an increased sense of community among parents, and (3) to provide a means of social support to parents. Parent groups complemented the home-visiting program, which by definition was home based and individualized. Through groups, parents could meet other families in BEEP and extend their community of families in BEEP beyond those they occasionally met in the toy- or book-lending libraries or in the child-care room. Parent groups also functioned as a means of social support to families, a way of establishing an interconnected network of helpful relationships.

Although not widely acknowledged by the research community at the time BEEP was developed, the value of social support networks for parents is currently received increasing attention in the research literature. Informal social support systems (usually comprised of friends, neighbors, and relatives) can act as powerful buffers of some of the stress of parenting (Crnic, Greenberg, Robinson, and Ragozin, 1984). Parent groups can help isolated parents by providing increased social support, and the value of such groups for some parents, although not all, is beginning to emerge. For example, parent discussion groups have been effective in increasing participants' knowledge about parenting and in improving mother-child interaction in some adolescent mothers (Wandersman, 1987). Participation in parent groups has been found to be associated with decreased levels of stress (Shapiro, 1989) and with increased use of informal social supports by new parents (McGuire and Gottlieb, 1979). In general, the literature on the effectiveness of parent groups has reported that these groups appear to be most effective for individuals who are somewhat skilled in parenting and have sufficient personal resources to interact effectively in a group setting (Wandersman, 1987).

Functions of Group Leaders. Various staff members at BEEP served as leaders for parent groups. These leaders included social workers, home visitors, preschool teachers, psychologists, nurses, and the program's director. The group leader served as a guide to initiate discussion, refocus discussion, and offer information or a means of obtaining information.

Themes for Group Discussion. Two types of parent groups were offered. The first concentrated on general issues related to raising a child of a particular age (such as a two-year-old). The other type discussed specialized topics, including parenting alone, raising a child with siblings, preparing for another baby, coping with the unexpected, managing a job and a family, being a father, dealing with issues related to ethnicity, and living in Boston but sending children to school in Brookline.

Some topics were initiated by parents. For example, several fathers became interested in developing a group to concentrate on issues related to being a father. Other topics were initiated by staff members in response to issues they observed to be common across families.

Problems Encountered. Although parent groups were popular with some parents, others were reluctant to attend. During interviews conducted about BEEP, parents pointed out two specific problems related to parent groups. First, some parents felt that at least one of their groups had been dominated by one or two individuals. Some parents were intimidated by such domineering individuals, others simply lost interest in attending the group because of the lack of opportunity for input, and others were reluctant to discuss issues in a group that they had not participated in convening. To some extent, this problem could have been alleviated through additional training of group leaders, but the individual personality "mix" of each group could not always be anticipated, yet it appeared to make a difference in participants' satisfaction with the group.

A second problem was one found in other programs that incorporated parent groups. Certain families, usually those with less education or those who lived in poorer neighborhoods than the majority of families in the project, felt uncomfortable with the group process. They described being intimidated by other parents or having an entirely different set of concerns about their parenting role (Weiss, 1979). Although all parents might want information about the typical behavior of a two-year-old, many of the daily concerns for parents differed according to their personal and economic resources. Thus, although it might appear that single parents would have much to share with each other, being a single parent in a public housing project requires a different set of coping skills than being a single parent in a middle-class neighborhood. We struggled with a resolution to this problem but achieved no entirely satisfactory solution.

Finally, despite their name, parent discussion groups were designed for mothers. The topics, style, and time of group meetings were developed around the needs and schedules of mothers, not fathers. Some of the fathers at BEEP became increasingly vocal about the absence of their views in a program that was supposedly focusing on parenting, not just mothering. In response, we established a father's discussion group that met on Saturday mornings. Unfortunately, the enthusiasm for the group diminished quickly, and few fathers attended more than two or three sessions. We were not able to develop an alternative that was more suitable for fathers. The need to involve fathers is certainly an important lesson.

The BEEP Style

While the two program components of BEEP described in this chapter — home visits and parent groups — differed substantially in structure, they shared a similar philosophy about the way professionals should interact with parents. The approach assumed by BEEP's staff members came to be considered a characteristic style and was described by parents as possessing six critical facets (Weiss, 1979):

1. Openness and accessibility
2. A positive sense of child rearing
3. A nonjudgmental approach to parenting
4. A tendency to provide alternatives rather than directives
5. A willingness to offer direct and honest feedback
6. An unpressured approach

The "BEEP style" became evident during the early days of the program when home visits and parent groups comprised the bulk of services provided to parents. This characteristic approach continued, however, throughout the toddler and prekindergarten phases of the program, in which programs for children and parents became increasingly school based, as described in the following chapters.

Chapter 7

Educational Philosophy
and Approach

Tasha's personality was really established young. I wouldn't
have picked up on that except Lana (Tasha's preschool
teacher at BEEP) brought it to my attention. I certainly
wouldn't have picked up on her staying on task or anything
like that. But her personality was developed, and it's gonna
be with her.

I watched Ernesto in his classroom at BEEP, and I realized
my outlook on school: you never finish. Knowledge just
keeps coming, and so when you feel you can't take in any
more knowledge, you're finished with the universe! I do have
great hopes for Ernesto. And I feel whatever he does in life,
that he will be great at it.

As children approach toddler-
hood and preschool age, they and their families have different
needs than during the children's infancy. Children become increasingly interested in other children, in investigating the world
beyond their home, and in communicating their interests, needs,
and desires. In addition to responding to the changes in their
children, parents often also become consumed with daily survival issues such as balancing work and family time, preparing
for another child, or finding suitable child care. The thrill of
caring for a baby is replaced by the reality of negotiating life
with a toddler.

As the needs of children and families change, service systems must respond to those changes. The BEEP program responded to the needs expressed by parents by adding school-based children's groups as children approached the age of two years. A playgroup for children met weekly for two-year-olds, and a prekindergarten program met five times a week (or, at parents' option, three times a week) for three- and four-year-olds. We introduced children's groups as children approached the age of two years for five key reasons.

First, children can develop a critical set of social and task competence skills in a group setting that complement those developed at home. One of the major goals of BEEP was to reduce the number of children entering school with low levels of competence, so we tried to develop ways of helping children become more proficient in a classroom setting. The important tasks of early childhood — making friends, selecting and completing activities, establishing trusting relationships with adults outside of the family — were all aspects of BEEP's preschool curriculum. We reasoned that the way children negotiated these tasks during their preschool years would have important implications for their future success in school.

Second, parents can learn a great deal about their child's development by observing the child in a group setting. Children reveal different aspects of their development in a group setting than they do at home, such as their way of relating to other children, their choice of activities, and their way of responding to teachers. We believed that by observing their child in a group, parents could view the child's behavior and learning style from a different perspective. Moreover, parents could see how other adults played with, talked to, and comforted their child, and thus could determine some new approaches or strategies that might apply to them.

Third, an education program for young children in the public schools can assist parents in forging alliances with teachers. The partnership developed between parents and teachers during a child's schooling can be an importance force in the child's life, yet some parents, especially those who had not fared well in school themselves, are so threatened by schools and teachers that they do not attempt to create such partnerships. The parent-teacher relationships developed through BEEP during the child's toddler and preschool years provided both a natural extension to the relationships developed between parents and home visitors and a bridge to future relationships parents might forge with public school teachers during their child's elementary school years and beyond.

Fourth, high-quality preschool programs provide important models for kindergarten and primary-grade teachers. Theories of how children learn in the preschool years are also applicable to the early grades of elementary school, so programs for young children offer important in-service training opportunities for elementary schools teachers. The preschool programs at BEEP served as important demonstrations for elementary school principals and curriculum supervisors, most of whom had little training or teaching experience with children under ten years old. The program's role modeling of teaching from a developmental perspective was also important for kindergarten and primary-grade teachers, who, because of declining enrollment and few new hires, were older and who tended to have a skill-based, rather than a developmental, approach to the education of young children.

Fifth, continuity is an important aspect of an early education program. The group programs for children offered parents continuity of support and services from their child's infancy through the child's preschool years. Although only some of the staff of these programs had been home visitors at BEEP, the BEEP style, with its low-key and supportive approach to parents, continued to be an integral part of the programs. Moreover, the support staff, such as social workers and medical personnel, continued to be available to consult with parents. The transition to a school-based program was gradual for children and families; the home-visiting program continued for two-year-olds and was supplemented by the weekly playgroup. During the prekindergarten program (when children were three years old), a less frequent home-visiting program supplemented the school-based program.

The gradual introduction of a theoretically sound center-based program that builds upon the foundation of an earlier home-based program was supported by research reviews of early education programs. Bronfenbrenner (1974) and Clarke-Stewart (1977) both concluded that the effectiveness of early education programs could be enhanced by first providing a home-visiting program and then adding a center-based classroom program as the child approaches the age of school entry. They emphasized, however, that the shift from the home to the center should be gradual and that the role of the parents should not be diminished when center-based programs predominate.

We attempted to ensure that parents and staff did not view the playgroup and prekindergarten components as the points at which "experts" took over work with children. The teacher-parent alliance continued as a major focus of the program even when the preschool teaching staff met with the children five days a week. For example, we continued parent education that encouraged parents to adopt an advocacy role for their child both within BEEP and with other institutions.

Theory and Goals

The theory behind the playgroup (for two-year-olds) and the prekindergarten programs (for three- and four-year-olds) was eclectic in that it drew from developmental theory, educational philosophy, and specific curriculum models. In this section, we discuss the various influences from which BEEP's programs for children were derived.

Developmental Theory. As in many early childhood programs, the work of Jean Piaget (1954) served as a foundation for an understanding of the child's cognitive perspective of the world. Indeed, Piaget, the Swiss philosopher and biologist whose writings span several decades in the twentieth century, has probably had the greatest impact of any individual on psychologists' understanding of how the child's mind works. Although Piaget's work is essentially a theoretical description of children's cognitive development, several aspects of the theory have important implications for education.

First, Piaget emphasized that the child's intellectual development progresses through a series of hierarchical and qualitatively different stages. Thus, the young child thinks and views the world quite differently from the adult. Second, the child gains knowledge through action and through discovering relationships between objects rather than by being told facts by adults. Third, play is the medium through which the child learns to assimilate new information or accommodate his or her actions to activities. Thus, play is essentially the "work" of the young child.

Other developmental theorists have stressed the importance of the young child's development of language (for example, de Villiers and de Villiers, 1979). Language is the symbolic representation of experience. It serves humans as the means for organizing and structuring perceptions, experiences, and ideas, and thus becomes the cornerstone for both cognitive and social development. The growth of receptive language enables children to understand the world depicted by others. Expressive language allows children to share their experiences with others and to make their feelings and desires known.

Like other areas of the child's development, language develops as a result of both the child's maturation and interaction with the environment. Language development and other aspects of symbolic functioning appear to be more susceptible to intervention than certain domains of development such as motor skills that may be more linked to maturation. For example, parents and teachers can encourage a child to learn language through expanding and recasting the child's comments (Nelson, Carskaddon, and Bonvillian, 1973).

Socioemotional aspects of children's growth have also been emphasized by some developmental theorists. For example, Erik Erikson (1964) stressed the importance of autonomy for the young child. According to Erikson, toddlers are best able to develop a sense of independence if during infancy they developed a trusting relationship with their parents. The toddlers' sense of independence and autonomy is critical to their future understanding of self and relationships with others.

The importance of relationships with peers during the preschool years has been studied by Hartup (1983), among others. Close relationships with peers provide children with a sense of mutuality, sharing of emotions, and some experience in conflict resolution. Moreover, the child who has no friends is at risk for difficulties in socioemotional development (Hartup and Moore, 1990). Therefore, negotiating friendships is an important part of participating in a group for the young child.

Although no one theorist has provided an overarching theory of child development that considers in sufficient detail all aspects of development, taken together the various theories we have described yield several critical implications for developing programs for young children. We derived four principles from developmental theory and applied them to our education programs for children.

First, children learn through play. Children are inherently curious. They learn by being active participants in a variety of problem-posing situations and social relationships. Through play, children are almost continually involved in forming concepts and thus clarifying and extending their understanding of the physical and social world.

Second, children need to develop a sense of autonomy. Learning to be independent often means for the young child acquiring self-help skills related to dressing, eating, and toileting. But an integral part of learning such skills is the child's acquisition of a sense of self that is independent of others but has an effect on others. As children grow in competence, they develop conceptions of themselves as independent agents. If they are provided with a stable, consistent, and secure environment, children are more capable of influencing both the physical and the social aspects of that environment and of recognizing their influence. They achieve a greater sense of self-worth and become more sure of their abilities to cause things to happen.

Sometimes children must assert themselves to show independence, and they may be assertive at inopportune times for others. Recognizing a child's assertiveness in the context of the development of autonomy is an important challenge for teachers and parents. An adult's interpretation of a given behavior as independence instead of defiance can have important consequences for the adult's feelings and behaviors toward the child and ultimately for the child's feelings and future actions.

To develop a sense of autonomy, children must also understand that they have some control over their own behavior. As toddlers, children learn to make choices, follow routines, and, increasingly, control the behavior of themselves and others through language. As three-year-olds, they learn to select tasks, ask for help when needed, and complete activities. As four-year-olds, they learn to make plans and to complete them. At all ages, children can describe what has happened and anticipate what will happen next, although with varying degrees of sophistication. Eventually, children can learn that they have control over initiating and inhibiting action. Adults can model these skills, establish their worth, and reinforce their acquisition.

Third, language is an important tool for the young child to develop fully. The use of language by children can be successfully encouraged in a classroom setting. Children need to talk about what is interesting to them and to describe what they see and what their feelings are. They also need to learn to use language to assist in solving problems in social or task-related situations. An environment in which adults both encourage the child to take the lead in conversation and respond by expanding, demonstrating, and recasting the child's comments will facilitate the child's language acquisition and use (Schaffer, 1977).

Fourth, making friends and getting along with others is an important part of a school experience. Families vary greatly in the opportunities they provide children to develop friendships. Moreover, some children readily make friends and become leaders in a classroom setting, but others need adult assistance to understand how to successfully negotiate relationships with peers. A school setting provides opportunities for children to meet other children, begin to develop critical skills such as how to take the perspective of another, and have the safety and security of adults ensuring that relationships developed among the children are egalitarian.

Educational Philosophy. In contrast to Piaget, who seldom mentioned the role of education in development, Maria Montessori (1964) constructed a philosophy of education for children's development. Montessori, a physician and founder of the

Montessori method of preschool teaching in the early 1900s, believed that children have "sensitive periods" when they are especially ready to learn a particular skill. Although the curriculum she developed relies heavily on a specific set of materials developed to encourage children to discover the physical properties of objects, her view of the child and of the teacher is an important part of her philosophy. She emphasized the importance of children's self-initiated learning and their natural cycle of activity, concepts that involve the selection of a task as well as its completion. She also stressed the inherent importance of independence and a sense of personal accomplishment for the young child; the child's satisfaction with learning is self-initiated, not teacher directed.

The role of the teacher is a critical part of Montessori's philosophy. She viewed the teacher as a keen observer of the child and as a key provider of a nurturing and consistent classroom environment that optimizes learning. According to her approach, if a child appears unmotivated or behaves inappropriately, the environment—not the child—is ill prepared.

The child's natural tendency to be interested in learning and to desire independence and the teacher's role as observer and planner of the environment were aspects of BEEP that we derived from Montessori's philosophy. Teachers at BEEP interacted more with children (especially through language) and provided a wider range of activities than teachers in a traditional Montessori setting, but like Montessori teachers, BEEP teachers approached children and learning with respect.

Curriculum Models. Two curriculum models, both of which had roots in the developmental theory of Jean Piaget, were influential in the development of BEEP's education program for children. First, in an application of Piaget's theory to preschool education, Constance Kamii and Rheta DeVries (1977) emphasized the value of children constructing their own knowledge through active exploration in the classroom. In their approach, classrooms are designed for children to select their own tasks and, with encouragement by teachers, achieve two cognitive objectives: (1) to develop interesting ideas, solve problems, and generate questions, and (2) to understand the relationships among the physical properties of objects. Kamii and DeVries also recognized the value of social interaction, an area of development sometimes overlooked in more cognitive approaches to applying Piaget. They stressed that play with peers advances children's development in a way that interaction with adults cannot. Nevertheless, teachers have a role in enhancing socioemotional development by guiding children in their ability to take the perspective of another.

The curriculum developed at the High/Scope Educational Research Foundation (Hohmann, Banet, and Weikart, 1979) also influenced several aspects of the BEEP curriculum. In particular, the curriculum's notion of assisting children with their skills related to planning and selecting activities became an important part of the BEEP curriculum. In BEEP, children were encouraged to articulate their choice of activity, consider the materials they might need, and think of the first few steps involved. For example, if a child wanted to make a marble ramp, she would be encouraged to think of the materials needed (such as wood, glue, nails, hammer, marbles), discuss the various ways the ramp could be constructed (such as a double or single incline), and think of the first few steps in the process (such as to select a base and place another piece at a right angle to it). Some activities naturally lend themselves to planning more than others do, and when children in BEEP selected more open-ended activities such as dramatic play, planning may have involved the selection of props, but teachers realized that props could change as the theme of the play evolved.

We also emulated the High/Scope curriculum's use of teacher-directed activities for small groups of children. These activities, added to the BEEP curriculum as children approached four years old, allowed teachers to observe and assess children's skills with activities that the children might not select on their own. For example, a teacher could observe children's ability to use scissors, to construct a tower out of small blocks, or to grasp a pencil. Teachers' assessments of the strengths and weaknesses of individual children's skills were used to develop curriculum activities that appealed to both the interests and needs of individual children. For example, a teacher might encourage a child who enjoyed playing with cars but resisted fine motor tasks to build a maze or roadway of small blocks for small cars.

Rather than merely implementing a set of curriculum activities, teachers at BEEP used the objectives proposed by Kamii and DeVries and the ideas developed by High/Scope and other developmental programs (such as Forman and Kuschner, 1977) to guide them in developing activities themselves. Thus, curriculum development was an ongoing and critical task for teachers at BEEP. It required teachers to continually observe, reflect, analyze, and try new tasks that would appeal to the specific needs and interests of the children they were teaching. Although some activities were adapted from curriculum guides of other developmental programs, teachers were encouraged and supported in developing their own ideas. These ideas were discussed during weekly staff meetings and documented in an in-house newsletter.

Drop-In Center

BEEP's programs for children were geared to the age of the child, beginning with the relatively informal drop-in center and respite child care offered during the first two years of the child's life. The drop-in center was designed to be a cheerful, comfortable place that children and families would enjoy. Open on weekdays, Saturday mornings, and occasional evenings and Sunday afternoons, the center functioned as a gathering place for families enrolled in BEEP. Toy- and book-lending libraries were available to supplement the collections that stayed in the center. Many of the toys in the center, as well as those made in toy-making workshops held for parents, illustrated the point that toys did not have to be expensive to be enjoyed by children. The kitchen area in the center was organized to give parents ideas on how to arrange a safe area for toddlers. For example, plastic utensils were placed in the lower cabinets, the place where toddlers inevitably love to play. The program had a van and could provide free transportation to the center, upon request, for families who lived beyond walking distance.

Playgroups

Weekly playgroups for two-year-olds marked the transition of the program from primarily home based to primarily school based. When a child reached his or her second birthday, the child entered the toddler phase of the program and became eligible to participate in a playgroup, which met once a week for two hours. (Children who manifested developmental delays or whose families experienced unusually stressful circumstances attended two playgroup sessions a week.) At this point, the locus of activities shifted from the home to the center, with home visits being curtailed as activities increasingly focused on the child. Parents were still considered to be the major educational force in the child's life, but BEEP's staff members began to develop independent relationships with the children through weekly playgroups.

The playgroups were staffed by professional preschool teachers. The teachers, in conjunction with other staff members, developed a curriculum meeting the interests, abilities, and needs of two-year-olds and using the principles described in the previous section on theory. The playgroups each enrolled between six and eight children, although sometimes the size and composition of the group changed throughout the year because children entered the playgroup when they turned two years old. A staff ratio of one teacher to five children was maintained throughout the year.

The playgroup classroom included manipulative materials, art activities, sand and water play tables, a block area, activities for gross motor play, and props for dramatic play. Children chose among the activities available in the classroom, although teachers assisted children by encouraging them to verbalize their choice, follow through, and return the activity or material to its original location when they were finished with it. Thus, one emphasis of teachers in the playgroup was on helping children understand an appropriate sequence of activities in a classroom setting. Teachers also emphasized social interaction, and although parallel play was the norm for children when they first entered the program, the older children often interacted with each other. When conflicts occurred, teachers provided children with verbal strategies for their resolution. In addition, children were encouraged to function independently in the classroom and to learn basic self-help skills related to toileting and dressing, such as putting on a snowsuit. The playgroups also included a brief meeting time when children could participate in group songs or stories and were introduced to the concept of being part of a group.

Many of the children's initial playgroup sessions were spent helping the children feel secure and comfortable in a group setting without their parents. Often parents would attend parent discussion groups that were designed to meet at the same time as the playgroups.

Prekindergarten Classroom Program

From around three years of age until their entrance into kindergarten, children attended a daily classroom program five days a week. Each class was made up of eighteen to twenty children and was staffed by two classroom teachers and an assistant teacher. The classes were three hours long and met five times a week, although parents could choose a three-day option or an extended day program (which met until the end of the elementary school day). A diagnostic teacher, trained in early childhood special education, met with all teachers on a regular basis and sometimes worked with individual children in the classroom. The classes were held in the elementary schools, although one class met at the BEEP center. Teachers occasionally conducted home visits, but for the most part, activities during this phase of the program were school based.

Individual Goals for Children. Although the broad objectives of BEEP's education program were similar to those of other developmentally oriented programs (such as that of Forman and Kuschner, 1977), BEEP differed from other programs in its emphasis on individualization. The individual approach adopted by the staff is analogous to a diagnostic/prescriptive paradigm used in programs designed for special needs children (Deno,

1973; Lovitt and Haring, 1979). Staff, with some input from parents, selected a hierarchy of both long-term and short-term goals for each child enrolled in the education programs. The child's progress toward the goals was evaluated annually during an educational review attended by an interdisciplinary team consisting of classroom teachers, the program supervisor, a nurse, social workers, and psychologists. Teachers selected goals through discussions, review of the child's developmental history as recorded in periodic health and development exams, and classroom observations of the child's daily functioning. The goals formed a framework for specific programs designed to meet the needs and strengths of each child.

The goals for children were stated in the form of behavioral objectives. Each objective focused on one or more of the following developmental areas:

1. Organization of behavior: practice in planning and initiating tasks, in maintaining attention on relevant aspects of a task, in self-correcting one's efforts through successive trial and error strategies, and in completing tasks
2. Cognition: opportunities to classify and seriate objects, to understand temporal and spatial relationships, to understand cause-effect relationships, and to generalize from one task or situation to another
3. Language: opportunities to enhance receptive language (understanding and following directions) and to practice expressive language (using language to get needs met, to converse with peers and adults, and to label or describe events and objects in the environment)
4. Gross motor: opportunities to practice running, jumping, and climbing and to try increasingly complex large-muscle tasks with confidence
5. Fine motor: practice in increasing small-muscle dexterity through using objects such as puzzle pieces, blocks, paintbrushes, beads, and pencils
6. Visual-motor: practice in coordinating eyes and hands while performing activities such as catching a ball or tossing a beanbag at a target

7. Perceptual: opportunities to become more aware of the body in space and to perceive elements of the environment correctly

8. Perceptual-motor: practice with activities that involve selecting part-whole relations, such as puzzles or formboards

9. Socioemotional: practice in developing cooperative peer relationships and in having constructive relationships with adults; having opportunities to develop positive feelings about oneself; practice in expressing emotions appropriately

10. Symbolism: opportunities to construct and make use of visual representations of events and objects

In determining program goals for children, we discovered that it is critical to make goals both global enough so that they have a general focus and specific enough so that they could reasonably be achieved. Staff members and families both need feedback and need to see progress. Goals that are too global often disregard the small but important steps children make along the way, but goals that are too specific can appear trivial. Therefore, we first determined which of the ten developmental areas were the appropriate focus for the child (each child could have multiple areas of focus), and then we listed specific objectives and steps to obtain those objectives. The diagnostic teacher assisted the classroom teachers in developing curriculum activities that matched behavioral objectives.

Teaching Strategies. A child's goals were addressed primarily in the classroom by the classroom teachers and by the diagnostic teacher. Each teacher was responsible for documentation and implementation of educational goals and for parent-teacher conferences for eight to ten families. The two teachers in each classroom worked together as a team in planning strategies for all children in their class and in organizing and managing the classroom. During one part of each school day, the teacher and his or her assigned children met in a group, although the exact composition of this group was flexible in order to accommodate the children's friendship groups, especially prevalent among the four-year-olds. The two teachers in each classroom met daily with each other to document their observations about each child's activities. In addition, each teaching team met weekly to evaluate and revise teaching plans and strategies documented on the individual planning forms. The teachers used the following teaching strategies most frequently:

- Observe for further evaluation
- Provide specifically sequenced activities
- Provide more teacher direction
- Provide supplementary activities
- Provide substitute activities
- Modify time expectations
- Use multisensory approaches
- Alter social environment
- Emphasize consistency in environment and expectations
- Provide teacher outreach for social contact
- Provide teacher support
- Provide clear and immediate feedback
- Provide teacher contact with other school or social service personnel
- Provide indirect teacher support — avoid intrusion

     In addition to recording specific strategies and teaching plans weekly, teachers also rated a profile of goals for each child three times a year. The profile consisted of a list of specific behavioral objectives in each of the developmental areas listed previously. By rating each child in each developmental area, a teacher was able to gain an overall picture of the child, including the child's relative strengths and weaknesses. Teachers used these ratings for assessment and evaluation and to determine if other goals in addition to those developed at the educational case review needed to be addressed throughout the school year.
     Although it was tedious for teachers to complete, the profile served an important purpose. In classrooms in which children are given a great deal of discretion about the activities they

can select, some children tend to choose certain activities frequently and neglect others. By completing the profile, teachers recognized patterns of interest in children and could build on those interests in helping each child acquire or practice neglected skills. For example, one teacher observed that a particular child enjoyed dramatic play a great deal but seldom attempted tasks that had a fine motor component, such as cutting paper. The teacher integrated fine motor activities into the dramatic play enjoyed by this child by suggesting that the child make some signs for the dramatic play area—a task that involved both cutting and drawing.

Staff members revised and extended program goals for each child during the diagnostic case review. These reviews were held on a bimonthly basis for each classroom and were attended by the classroom teachers, the diagnostic teacher, and the education supervisor. Social workers, the consulting psychiatrist, the psychologist, and the nurse also attended sessions when the discussion included families with whom they had extensive contact. These sessions were used as forums for discussing concerns that any staff member had about a child or family and for staff members to gain insight, support, and suggestions from one another.

To summarize, the process of goal development began during the interdisciplinary educational case review. Classroom teachers next constructed weekly plans for addressing these goals in the classroom, documenting specific strategies they intended to use. When necessary, teachers modified goals and strategies based on information they gained during diagnostic case reviews, parent-teacher conferences, and from their own observations. Finally, the child's functioning in the classroom was routinely assessed three times a year by teachers using a rating profile of goals for each child in all areas of development and at the end of the school year by an interdisciplinary team that assessed the child's progress relevant to the goals developed during the educational case review.

Classroom Organization. All prekindergarten classrooms contained the same interest areas, although the specific arrangement of these areas within the room was determined by the individual teaching teams. These interest areas included the following:

- A cozy area for reading books
- Shelves holding small items for children to manipulate and puzzles
- Areas for building with large and small blocks
- An area for art and writing
- A sand and water table
- An area with dramatic play props
- An area for science and discoveries

One area of the classroom was designed so that all children could meet together in a group. Each interest area was color coded to enhance demarcation of that section. For example, in one classroom, the shelving, tables, and easels located in the art area had a yellow color scheme, and the shelves and tables in the area where the puzzles were kept were blue. Materials within each area were kept on low shelves designed to be accessible to children. Similar materials were grouped together, and symbols or signs on the shelves helped children identify where the materials belonged. For example, a picture of paintbrushes was placed on the shelf where the brushes were stored. Teachers ensured that materials were in good condition, that puzzles and construction toys had no missing pieces, and that markers were not dried out.

Daily Routine. All classrooms had similar routines, although minor variations occurred due to bus schedules, public school schedules for the gymnasium and playground, and individual preferences of teaching teams. The seven major elements of the school day were arrival and greeting, planning, work period, snack and recall time, group meeting, gross motor activities, and small-group time.

Children arrived by school bus, in a car pool, or with a parent. Teachers met the children when they arrived and received messages from bus drivers and parents for approximately ten minutes. Generally only one or two areas of the classroom were designated as "open" at this time, usually areas housing puzzles or books. Children were encouraged to choose an activity in the open area while their friends arrived.

After they arrived, children planned their activities for the day. The planning time (approximately fifteen minutes) encouraged the children's task competence. The purposes of the planning session were: (1) to help children understand and articulate the choices available to them, (2) to help children anticipate the materials they would need to complete a project or to participate in an activity, (3) to help children understand and follow the sequence of steps involved in completing an activity, and (4) to help children anticipate the sequence of events in the school day.

Although the teaching staff drew largely on the ideas of others (especially Hohmann, Banet, and Weikart, 1979) in devising methods of planning with young children, each teaching team established its own particular approach. However, the methods they developed were similar, and staff members frequently drew on each other's ideas. Some teachers preferred to plan with children on an individual basis and met with each child as he or she arrived in the morning to establish a plan for the day. Other teachers preferred planning in a group meeting and used the meeting time to discuss the activities available on that day. Some teachers integrated group and individual planning. In all classrooms, however, there was a planning board on which children hung signs to visually represent the activities they had chosen to do that day. Some children required a great deal of teacher guidance to complete this process; others needed only occasional direction.

During the work period (approximately sixty minutes), children carried out the plans they had made. Teachers acted as resources to the children, facilitating children's activities, helping children during moments of frustration, expanding the challenges available to each child, and nurturing or talking with a child as needed. Teachers spent some time observing each child during the work period in order to complete daily records on what each child chose to do and how he or she approached each activity. Teachers also used this time to interact one-to-one with children who learned best with more direct teacher contact.

During the snack and recall time (approximately twenty minutes) that occurred after the work period, each child gathered the signs he or she had placed on the planning board and met in a small group with a teacher. The children were encouraged to discuss their plans, using the signs as reminders. Teachers encouraged children to verbally elaborate on their activities by asking open-ended questions. For example, if a child had planned to make a boat out of wood and nails, the teacher might ask the child to discuss the steps she used in making the boat, what other materials she could have used, what other kinds of boats she could make, and what kinds of cargo a boat might carry.

Next, the children and teachers in each classroom gathered together as a group for about twenty minutes. This time was used for singing, group games, group discussions, stories, or movement activities. Group meetings provided enjoyable and varied activities, encouraged children to follow directions, and gave them the opportunity to participate in a large group.

After the group meeting, children participated in gross motor activities for approximately thirty-five minutes. The weather largely determined the location of these activities. Whenever possible, children and teachers went outside, where children could climb, throw balls, or ride tricycles. Teachers planned some small group games that children could partici-pate in if they wished. During inclement weather, gross motor activities took place in a school gymnasium or a large area of the classroom. Teachers used indoor games to encourage cer-tain children to practice balancing or eye-hand coordination and to help other children decrease their fear of climbing or active play. Children also learned how to dress and undress themselves for outdoor activities.

At the end of the day, children worked in small groups for approximately twenty minutes. In each classroom, children were assigned to one of two or three small groups, led by the teacher who was primarily responsible for the implementation and documentation of their educational plan. Between five and eight children generally were in each group. Small-group time was used principally as hands-on time when children were actively involved in materials and activities designed by teachers. Children worked in pairs or were provided with their own set of materials. Teachers used this time to introduce new materials that were to be available in the classroom, to expose children to activities that some children in that group generally failed to select independently, or to assess the performance of children in some skill area.

Guided Observation

Guided observations were one of the critical components of the playgroup and prekindergarten program. At least twice a year, parents observed their child in the classroom. Parents watched from special booths constructed in the classrooms for this purpose, but they told their child beforehand that they would be observing so that the child would not be surprised or feel the parents were spying. The diagnostic teacher observed with the parents and pointed out the child's strengths and the teacher's strategies both during and immediately after the observation. Rather than focusing only on the activities selected by the child or the child's choice of friends, the diagnostic teacher pointed out characteristics of the child's style of learning or interacting with others. For example, the teacher might point out that a particular child often watched the dynamics of a group engaged in dramatic play before entering the group and why that might be a very positive strategy. Or the teacher might comment on how persistent a child is when engaged in a problem-solving task and how the teacher plans to build on that strength in helping the child learn strategies to overcome frustration.

We considered the guided observations to be an integral part of the children's group program, and we emphasized their importance to parents. Although some parents were reluctant to attend the first observation, once they had attended, they seldom were hesitant to attend again. Helping parents learn how to observe their child in a classroom became an important focus of the education program for parents and an important tool for some parents in learning to advocate for their child's needs in a school setting. The diagnostic teacher would often help parents direct questions to the classroom teacher based on the observations so that parents would become accustomed to initiating discussions with teachers about their child's progress in school. In this way, the parents' role as advocate was nurtured and encouraged.

Staffing Considerations

Regardless of how clearly stated a program's philosophy is, how interesting the curriculum materials are, or how safe and attractive the facilities are, the nature and quality of the teaching is paramount in determining the style and quality of the program. Many of the same qualifications required of the home visitors were required of teachers for the playgroup and prekindergarten program. The teachers were selected from ethnically diverse backgrounds so that they could communicate well with the range of families in BEEP and could learn from each other. At least one teacher in each classroom was required to have several years of experience in a developmental classroom as well as relevant teaching certificates and degrees. Certain characteristics such as an ability to relate well to parents from various backgrounds; solid knowledge of child development; and a tendency to be thoughtful, reflective, analytical, and creative in developing curriculum were critical requirements for teachers.

Problems Encountered

Four problems occurred in implementing BEEP's programs for children. Two involved the development of individual goals for children, and two involved aspects of the curriculum.

First, teachers often found the development of individual goals and the rating of the entire profile of goals (for all areas of development) exceedingly cumbersome. The amount of documentation required of teachers using this method of planning, implementing, and evaluating goals could be overwhelming. We investigated various means of decreasing paperwork while maintaining aspects of the documentation that were considered integral to the development of a high-quality individualized program. For example, during the first year of prekindergarten, teachers rated all items on the profile of goals. This cumbersome method of assessment was changed to global rating for each child in each developmental area. Teachers rated specific items only in areas in which the child needed support and encouragement (that is, had program goals). Critical to the success of this or any method of documentation, however, is the flexibility to allow the staff to use what they consider the most appropriate method within the general framework established by the program's developers.

Second, we did not have a satisfactory way of getting input from parents about the child's goals. We explored various methods of having parents and staff determine together the type of input that parents wished to have in developing educational goals for the children. In one method, parents filled out a form indicating the amount of input they wanted in each defined goal area. However, parents tended to request average or maximum input in all areas. Some parents may have regarded the form as an insurance policy and wished to guarantee maximum input in case they needed it during the coming year. Others might have feared that some services would be withdrawn if they did not specify needs in all areas, and still others might have been confused by what, admittedly, was a complicated form. The staff instead preferred a less formal, one-on-one discussion with parents about what the parents perceived as their own and their child's needs and how staff members could meet those needs. The content of these discussions helped staff develop specific goals during the educational case reviews.

Third, the emphasis on having children learn to plan their activities was novel for most teachers, even those with extensive experience in developmental classrooms. At first, some teachers were concerned that the imposition of planning activities would dampen children's enthusiasm and spontaneity. In fact, it took some time for each teaching team to establish methods of encouraging children to plan activities while still taking advantage of children's need to change activities and to integrate new ideas and materials into their plans. Some activities (such as constructing a structure) clearly lend themselves more to planning than do others (such as dramatic play). Moreover, some children are more able to integrate plans into their activities than are others, a skill we found to be based somewhat on the child's level of development. As teachers became aware of the various ways they could individualize the planning process, the problems initially experienced by the teachers diminished.

Fourth, the child-directed approach in the classroom was valuable for all children, but some children benefitted from occasional didactic intervention from the teacher. Since this type of intervention by teachers was designed to expand but not interrupt children's productive activity, teachers needed to be sensitive to the best time to intervene. Some children required a great deal of direct teacher input because they became easily frustrated, had difficulty initiating or completing new tasks, made little outreach to peers, or seldom presented themselves with new problems to solve. Other children needed little direct teacher intervention, and required only occasional teacher acknowledgement, support, or suggestions.

Teachers wrestled in particular with when to intervene in cognitive tasks. Some children demonstrated their well-developed social skills in the classroom but seldom attempted cognitive tasks voluntarily. Didactic approaches to this problem might help children learn certain concepts but would not necessarily encourage them to select tasks that would challenge them cognitively. Teachers found that one solution was to ensure that cognitive challenges—that is, opportunities for thinking and problem solving—existed in all areas of the classroom. A combination of some individual time with the child with cognitive tasks and "planting" of cognitive tasks in activities the child was attracted to appeared to be a fruitful approach.

Every program encounters unanticipated problems when it moves from a theoretical mode to actual implementation. For BEEP, the solution to such problems involved providing ample opportunity for discussion of concerns at staff meetings, developing a consensus about different approaches that could help resolve such concerns, and, ultimately, maintaining some flexibility in implementing the program.

Chapter 8

The Bilingual Component

Juan asks me, "Mommy when are we gonna talk English?"
And I say, "Not now, because when you go to Puerto Rico,
you can talk to your grandfather."

I keep telling Margarita and Alberto that if I don't have a
career, that I work, is because I want them to have something one day, and they gonna say, "Oh, my mother work
and want me to have something." My son say, "Oh, I'm gonna be a mechanic like my father." And I say, "It's okay. You
can be a mechanic like your father, but you can be *more* than
that, you have to, because that's why we work, and we want
to give you some education." I am a housekeeper; I go to
different houses and clean. And Margarita say, "Mommy, after I finish school, I am gonna help you. I'm gonna be like
you." I say, "No, I don't want to be like that. That's okay.
Any kind of work is good. But, I don't want you to be that.
I want you to be in an office or something like that. To be
something else." So, I hope they, if they can, get some more
education.

W hen we considered how to de-
velop optimum programs for the diverse families participating
in BEEP, some staff members were inclined to treat all children and families alike. Cross-cultural studies of child development suggest that all children progress through the same general

stages of development at roughly the same time periods (Cole and Scribner, 1974; Nyiti, 1976). Perhaps the program could, therefore, just deliver a common body of information to all parents and provide uniform experiences for the children.

Our bilingual/bicultural staff members, however, advocated strongly for flexibility and adjustments in the program to take into account cultural differences. Although BEEP's participants included several different bilingual and non-English-speaking groups (including Chinese and Israeli families), the largest of these groups was Hispanic. Over 10 percent of the families in BEEP were Hispanic. The Hispanic group was very diverse, however, and included immigrants from Cuba, El Salvador, Colombia, Mexico, and Spain as well as many from rural areas of Puerto Rico. All had come to Boston seeking economic opportunity and to be with friends and relatives. As most of these immigrants lacked a secondary education, many were unsuccessful in finding adequate employment. They were unprepared for the cold New England climate and often fearful of the neighborhood in which they lived.

With some exceptions, the idea of early education was an unfamiliar one for the Spanish-speaking families. Many had been taught to respect, fear, and never question institutions. Moreover, the notion of becoming informed advocates in their children's education and health care seemed much less pressing to them than coping with the stresses of finding financial assistance, living in crowded apartments, and keeping warm. Advocating for their children in a strange educational and health care system and in a language that they were not yet comfortable with seemed a remote aspiration. A few Hispanic parents, however, led the way in working with BEEP's bilingual staff by voicing the needs of Hispanic parents to learn advocacy skills and of Hispanic children to learn competence in English at an early age.

During the first phase of BEEP, from a child's birth to his or her second birthday, parents and home visitors were matched for language, and home visits were conducted in the language most comfortable for parents. Staff members advised parents to use the language in the home with which they were most comfortable. Our review of the research on monolingual and bilingual language development indicated that it was more important for the young child to participate in a rich, spontaneous language environment than to hear the culturally dominant language (for example, English) at home (Rogers, 1975).

However, beginning with the playgroup phase, when children were two to three years old, the program emphasized not only responsiveness to each child's individual development and home culture but also the child's competence in the public school setting. As previously mentioned, all children in BEEP, including those who resided in Boston, were eligible to enroll in the Brookline Public Schools at kindergarten. Although the Brookline schools had some provisions for non-English-speaking children, the elementary school classes were conducted in English. Children needed to be fluent in English to gain the maximum benefit from the Brookline kindergarten and elementary school curricula.

Therefore, one of the major goals of BEEP's bilingual program was for Hispanic children to be competent in English as well as in Spanish before entering kindergarten. To reach that goal, we formulated and implemented a Spanish-English bilingual program for children that began when the first Spanish-speaking children entered the playgroup at two years of age. A bilingual Chinese-English group was also planned but not fully implemented because of low enrollment and lack of parental interest. However, a bilingual Chinese-English teacher was part of the program staff during playgroup and prekindergarten.

We developed the Spanish bilingual program based on parents' requests and opinions as well as reviews of research on monolingual and bilingual language development and bilingual programs. We considered parents' views on all aspects on the program. Parents and staff members met a few times for group discussion, but most input from parents occurred on an individual basis. The bilingual staff at BEEP included home visitors, a secretary/receptionist, a psychologist, and a social worker. In general, the alliances formed between parents and those staff members facilitated an interactive process of program development.

Theory and Goals

Bilingual education in the United States is not a new phenomenon. In general, it has reflected the changing views of the role of cultural diversity in American society. In the early nineteenth century, several different immigrant groups established bilingual schools in an effort to maintain their language and culture. At the time of World War I, however, bilingualism fell into disfavor. By the end of World War II, monolingualism was regarded as a national resource that encouraged national unity (Crawford, 1989). Support for bilingualism was rekindled, however, in the 1960s by at least three major forces. First, and possibly most influential, ethnic groups were increasingly determined to retain their identity and to incorporate ancestral life-styles and traditions into their present-day life. Second, public schools were not adequately educating non-English-speaking children, as was evident in the high percentage of these children who dropped out, repeated grades, and needed special services (Epstein, 1977). Third, new outlooks, methods, and procedures for teaching such as team teaching and individualized instruction helped pave the way for new approaches to bilingual education.

The federal government responded to the public's changing view of bilingual education and in 1968 passed Title VII of the Elementary and Secondary Education Act, the Bilingual Education Act (Public Law 90-24). This law determined policy and provided federal monies for bilingual/bicultural projects in public schools and in general gave impetus to the bilingual education movement. By 1981, the government had allocated Title VII $157 million, and Title VII supported over 200 bilingual education programs (Baker, 1988). In 1971, Massachusetts became the first state to enact a law promoting bilingual education (Chapter 1005), and by 1989, thirty states had statutes permitting (although not necessarily promoting) native-language instruction (Crawford, 1989).

Another landmark for bilingual education occurred in 1974 in the Supreme Court decision on the *Lau* v. *Nichols* case. In this case, which was brought by Chinese students against the San Francisco School District, the plaintiffs argued that non-English-speaking students do not receive equal educational opportunity when instructed in a language they cannot understand. The Supreme Court outlawed English submersion programs and recommended a set of guidelines, which became known as the Lau remedies. Although not precise, the Lau remedies allowed a broader view of bilingual education that can include the maintenance of minority language and culture.

Controversy continues to exist about the goals of bilingual education (Spener, 1988) and the efficacy of various bilingual program models (Baker and deKanter, 1983; Willig, 1985). As a result of a reanalysis of federal policy in 1985, the U.S. Department of Education issued a new set of rules governing bilingual education programs that receive Title VII funds. The new rules emphasize the importance of students' acquisition of competence in English and allow local districts to have "maximum flexibility" in the way in which they provide bilingual education, which some districts have interpreted as allowing the native language component to be eliminated (Spener, 1988).

At the time children enrolled in BEEP were approaching preschool age (1975–1976), few visible models of early childhood bilingual programs existed. We examined the bilingual education models developed in response to federal and state mandates, although we recognized that such models were developed for school-age, rather than preschool, children. In general, four models had been developed: the transitional, the bilingual maintenance, the bilingual/bicultural maintenance, and the culturally pluralistic programs.

The orientation of the transitional program (also called English as a second language—ESL) is toward compensatory or remedial education. The use of the home language is usually limited to increasingly smaller segments of the day, and teacher aides rather than teachers are often the only bilingual adults in the classroom. Transitional programs make few efforts to involve parents or to acknowledge cultural traditions. The goal is for children to learn English as rapidly as possible so they can be placed in a monolingual English classroom.

The goal of bilingual maintenance programs is to facilitate children's English language development while encouraging the children to maintain their home language. Classroom teachers are usually bilingual, and they teach most subject matter in the home language. English is taught as a foreign language through prescribed methods of instruction. In general, English is not used to teach other subjects in the curriculum.

Bilingual/bicultural maintenance programs have the same orientation as bilingual maintenance programs except that they place additional emphasis on incorporating into the curriculum various aspects of the history and culture of the non-English-speaking group. If possible, teachers are from the same cultural background as the children. Parents and community groups often play a large role in determining aspects of the curriculum.

Culturally pluralistic approaches (sometimes called balanced bilingual approaches) differ from the previous ones in that they are not restricted to children from a particular linguistic group. All children in the school are involved in the program, and cultural diversity is explicitly regarded as an asset to the learning that occurs within the classroom. The curriculum includes an emphasis on understanding the various histories, manners, cultural characteristics, and values of the cultural groups represented in the classroom.

Within each program model, one of two types of language instruction is generally used: direct instruction or the interactionist approach. With direct instruction, the teacher provides a regularly scheduled language class on a daily basis. In addition, in some programs, teachers repeat their instructions in both languages, often requiring children to do the same.

In the interactionist approach, the two languages are either used during different parts of the day (for example, Spanish in the morning and English in the afternoon) or different languages are used by different teachers in a team teaching setting. The interactionist approach reflects the shift that has occurred in research and theory of language acquisition. In general, the view that language develops as a result of reinforcement or shaping from the environment (for example, Bijou and Baer, 1961) has been replaced by the view that language develops through a creative, constructive process, facilitated by direct interaction with others (for example, Brown, 1973). Some research (Garcia, 1983) has suggested that second-language development occurs through the same self-constructive process as does the development of a first language. The implications of this view are that successful teaching of a second language, at least for young children, should replicate those conditions under which a first language is normally acquired (Hamayan and Pfleger, 1987).

If one subscribes to the interactionist position, then the role that peers play in a bilingual classroom setting becomes vital. Yet the majority of bilingual and bilingual/bicultural classrooms consist exclusively of monolingual non-English-speaking children (Epstein, 1977). Children talk to their peers in their home language, and they have little or no incentive to develop cross-cultural friendships. Since children learn language readily from their peers, informal opportunities to converse with friends in the second language may be an important and perhaps critical ingredient in second-language acquisition (Dulay and Burt, 1978).

A culturally pluralistic classroom, on the other hand, contains an equal number of English-speaking and non-English-speaking peers. Children from both ethnolinguistic groups have the opportunity to benefit from the bilingual/bicultural curriculum. Some proponents of this two-way bilingual program have suggested that in addition to the obvious social benefits, acquiring bilingual language skills may impart cognitive advantages. Research reviews conclude that, although the literature is far from definitive, bilingual children have more "mental flexibility" and are superior in tasks involving concept formation and divergent thinking (Baker, 1988).

The research evidence is mixed on the optimal age for introducing a second language. Children learn a second language more slowly than adults but often surpass adults in their ultimate level of achievement of second-language skills (Snow, 1983). Generally, learners at different age levels appear to excel in different aspects of the language acquisition process (Fathman and Precup, 1983). Even though young children may acquire a second language slowly, the earlier they are exposed to an environment rich in that language, the better they will speak it (Seliger, Krashen, and Ladefoged, 1975).

In designing the bilingual program at BEEP, we determined that we needed to give several elements careful consideration: the program model that best suited both the needs of the children and the philosophy of the parents, the type of instruction that teachers assessed to be most appropriate for the group of students, and the age at which instruction should be introduced. Along with the parents in the program, we chose to implement the culturally pluralistic model because its aim, to engender a respect for and value of ethnolinguistic diversity, reflected the general philosophy underlying BEEP's efforts. We decided not to provide explicit language instruction but rather to establish a rich language environment using two languages. The view that children acquire a second language, like a primary language, through interaction with the environment is consistent with the view of children as constructive learners, an approach that guided all aspects of BEEP's development. We decided to introduce two languages when children entered playgroup at two years old, even though the literature was not definitive about the optimal age for learning a second language. However, with the input of parents, we chose this age because a goal of the program was for all children to be competent in English as well as in their home language before they entered kindergarten. We intended to provide program continuity for the children enrolled in bilingual classrooms by keeping them together as a group for the three years comprising playgroup and prekindergarten.

Program Organization

All children in the BEEP bilingual program received the same services as other children in BEEP. We made modifications, however, in some activities and services to accommodate the child's bilingualism.

Infant-Toddler Phase. During the first two years of the child's life, the program was the same for the non-English-speaking children as for all other participants — home visits, drop-in center, respite child care, and periodic assessments — with a few exceptions. First, more outreach to the child's family was often required to make families comfortable with the program and staff at BEEP and to help families understand the goals of the program. Thus, families whose primary language was not English tended to receive more home visits (within the allotted range) than other families assigned to the same program level. In addition, the children from bilingual homes participated more often in the optional diagnostic assessment at eleven and one-half months. And although staff members encouraged all families to use the BEEP center, the bilingual families used the center less on a spontaneous basis and more often for parties and other functions once they felt comfortable with BEEP.

Playgroup. At two years of age, children from Hispanic families were assigned to a playgroup led by one English-speaking teacher and one Spanish-speaking teacher. Parents of monolingual English-speaking children could request that their child be assigned to a bilingual group, although only those English-speaking children with well-developed language skills were selected for this group. The groups were arranged so that each had an equal number of Spanish-speaking and English-speaking children.

Although each teacher spoke his or her home language in the classroom almost exclusively, teachers worked together as a team. The teacher who shared the child's home language usually dealt with separation issues and other issues of emotional concern to the child. Otherwise, teachers generally interacted with all children using the teacher's home language. Parent-teacher conferences and guided observations were conducted in the parent's most comfortable language.

In addition to the characteristics considered in the hiring process that we have described previously, teachers in the bilingual classroom were chosen because of their understanding of Hispanic culture and their desire to include culturally relevant activities in the daily curriculum. Children learned Spanish and English songs and listened to stories in both languages. Teachers chose snacks and cooking activities based on their appeal to children in both cultural groups. The groups celebrated birthdays and other nonreligious holidays according to the cultural traditions of the child's family. Also, we held a piñata party annually for all families whose children were enrolled in the bilingual program.

During playgroup, children tended to ignore the teacher speaking a language different from their own. When they needed assistance, most children approached the teacher with whom they shared a common language. In general, children engaged in parallel play, infrequently communicating with each other, but language groups mixed freely.

Prekindergarten. Children entered their first year of prekindergarten around three years old and attended the program three or five days a week. The classroom model in the prekindergarten program was the same as that used in the playgroup. Two teachers, one English speaking and one Spanish speaking, worked together as a team, and an equal number of English-speaking and Spanish-speaking children were enrolled in the class. However, because classes enrolled a total of eighteen children, a bilingual assistant teacher was also hired as part of the teaching team. Respect for cultural traditions, values, and mores was an integral part of the curriculum.

During the second year of prekindergarten, as children approached four years of age, some changes were made in the bilingual program. Although the classes still contained an equal number of Spanish-speaking and English-speaking children, continued to observe cultural customs, and had a teacher representing each cultural group, the Spanish-speaking teacher no longer exclusively spoke Spanish. This change helped to prepare the children for the emphasis on English they would encounter the following year in kindergarten. By midyear, the Spanish-speaking teacher spoke mostly English but maintained some Spanish.

The assignment of equal numbers of English-speaking and Spanish-speaking children to the bilingual classroom facilitated a balanced emphasis on both cultures. No one ethnolinguistic group made up a majority of children in the classroom. The benefits of this approach were especially apparent during the second year of prekindergarten, when many cross-cultural friendships were formed.

Just as no single ethnocultural group was dominant in

the classroom, no single language was dominant, at least until the end of the second year. Most important, neither language was relegated only to disciplinary status. That is, teachers did not use English for daily conversation with children and use Spanish only for discipline, but rather they used both languages for both purposes. Even when more emphasis was placed on English during the end of prekindergarten, teachers used Spanish to communicate ideas and not solely to transmit instructions.

Benefits of the Bilingual Program

At the end of the prekindergarten program, all Spanish-speaking children were readily conversant in both Spanish and English, and the staff recommended that all the children attend regular kindergarten classrooms. Almost all of the Spanish-speaking children were significantly above age norms for language use. The only two children below age norms were less than six months below in English and were similarly delayed in Spanish.

An interesting benefit of the bilingual program was that Spanish-speaking parents also became more comfortable communicating in English, a skill they would need in order to advocate successfully for their child in schools and other similar institutions. At the parents' request, an adult education course in English as a second language was held at BEEP. Six families reported at entry to BEEP that they were monolingual in Spanish, but all twenty-seven Hispanic families reported having English as a second language when they finished the program. By the last year of the prekindergarten program, all Hispanic families had made outreach to English-speaking as well as Spanish-speaking staff and had attended several meetings conducted only in English.

The effects of this program on English-speaking children were not as apparent. The goals of the bilingual program for English-speaking children, however, were not explicit; the intent was for these children to learn some Spanish and, more important, to acquire a respect and appreciation for the Hispanic culture. No formal assessment was made of the English-speaking children's understanding of the Spanish culture, but, in general, these children learned a small vocabulary in Spanish.

Although parents were never asked formally about their assessment of the bilingual program per se, they were asked to assess the quality of the "mixed language/cultural groups" during both the playgroup and the prekindergarten phases. At the end of the playgroup phase, over 90 percent of the 123 respondents indicated that they were satisfied with this element of the BEEP program. Only 57 percent of the respondents, however, considered this program element to be crucial or important for a successful program for two-year-olds (Ferb, 1977; Weiss, 1979). In the survey about the prekindergarten phase, 58 percent of the 76 respondents considered the "mixed language and culture groups" to be either an outstanding or very good aspect of the program, and 6 percent considered this to be the program's most important feature (Fort, 1981). However, 10 percent of the parents reported having no opinion about this question, presumably because they had little experience with mixed language groups in BEEP.

The program's staff also positively rated different aspects of the bilingual prekindergarten program. Teachers indicated that they gained personal and professional insight from working with families possessing a variety of opinions and cultural values related to child rearing. Several staff members indicated that the key to the success of a bilingual program is a well-prepared and culturally diverse staff, dedicated to team effort.

Problems Encountered

Four types of problems emerged during the implementation of the bilingual programs for children. The first relates to peer relationships; the second, to the lack of effects on the English-speaking children; the third, to parents' reactions to staffing; and the fourth, to informal visits to the classroom by Hispanic parents.

First, as we mentioned previously, English-speaking and Spanish-speaking children interacted during the playgroup phase for two-year-olds, but most interaction was a fleeting diversion from parallel play, such as showing each other clay snakes, or occurred during gross motor activities, such as climbing with each other. We attributed this minimal amount of interaction to the developmental stage of this age group, as much play was parallel and most conversation was directed to adults. Also, the children only attended this group once a week, and they might have interacted more if they had had more frequent contact with each other.

In the prekindergarten program, the children had more opportunity for interaction and the development of peer relationships than in the playgroup. Also, at the age of three years, children generally make a transition from parallel to associative play. However, unlike in the playgroups, children tended to play only with peers who spoke their language, despite frequent attempts by teachers and parents to change this pattern.

In general, the three-year-olds' pattern of associating mainly with peers who spoke their language reversed itself during the second year of prekindergarten. The four-year-olds were quite familiar with the daily routine and classroom expectations, and they became increasingly involved in developing peer relationships. These friendships began to cross over language barriers and appeared to be based on personality characteristics and common interests, rather than shared home language.

These expanded peer relationships may have more to do with developmental changes in the children than with any changes in the program per se. Two-year-olds are interested in manipulating objects, and such manipulation can be done as easily with peers who speak a different language as with those who speak the same language. Three-year-olds, on the other hand, are beginning to use language to facilitate communication with peers, often over issues of property rights. The exclusivity seen at this age may be merely a matter of concentration by the children on the development of only one skill at a time. By the time children reach four years of age, however, they are better able to adjust their language to the listener and often use language to engage in projects with others rather than only to negotiate the use of materials.

The second problem—lack of apparent effects on the

English-speaking children — may have been due to several aspects of the implementation of the program. The original intent was for the same group of English-speaking and Spanish-speaking children to remain together for a total of three years. Unfortunately, this did not occur. The composition of the English-speaking group in the bilingual classes changed yearly. Some of the changes were due to the wavering commitment of some of the parents of English-speaking children. They were concerned that adjustment to school routine was difficult enough for their child and was further complicated by the introduction of a second language. (A similar complaint was not voiced by Spanish-speaking families, whose children also had to undergo the dual adjustment.) A few of the English-speaking parents were very committed to the program and introduced some Spanish at home. The extent of the parents' commitment may be a critical variable in the program's success. Moreover, if Spanish language instruction would have been available to the children during elementary school, more parents of English-speaking children may have opted for the bilingual classroom.

The third problem involved decisions we made in hiring Spanish-speaking teachers. We hired a Spanish-speaking teacher for the prekindergarten program at midyear who possessed excellent Spanish skills but was not culturally Spanish. Even though the Hispanic parents readily acknowledged the teacher's expertise, they expressed some resentment about this hiring decision. The following year, this teacher was the English-speaking teacher in the bilingual classroom, and a Hispanic teacher was also hired, an arrangement that fit more closely with BEEP's philosophy and with parents' wishes. The importance of hiring a Spanish-speaking teacher whose background is similar to that of the Hispanic children and, if possible, who speaks the same dialect as the children needs to be underscored.

Also, it was critical for the two teachers within each of the bilingual classrooms to work together as equal team members, rather than to function within a hierarchical framework. Hierarchical arrangements can encourage children and parents to respect one teacher more than another, a situation that ran counter to BEEP's goals for this program.

The fourth problem was that, with some exceptions, the Hispanic parents seldom made informal visits to the classroom, as did many of the English-speaking parents. Some staff members thought that certain families were uncomfortable commuting to a community that was appreciably different from their own. Parents were more willing to initiate and make visits if they had formed personal alliances with the staff. Furthermore, the location of the center made its access by public transportation tedious and time consuming, especially for those traveling from the Boston community. Even though BEEP's van was available at parents' request, it often had to be reserved a day or more in advance, which made spontaneous, drop-in visits less possible. In fact, the issue of transportation and accessibility to the center was a consistent theme and a particular problem for participating families from Boston throughout BEEP's history (Ferb, 1977; Weiss, 1979).

Many of the problems we encountered could be remedied by other programs replicating BEEP's bilingual early education component. For example, English-speaking parents might be more committed to a bilingual program if they had a better understanding of the advantages of the acquisition of a second language and of a multicultural classroom experience. Furthermore, preschool classrooms in which children's ages are mixed would offer the younger children models of friendships without cultural boundaries. In addition, a program's designers could try to select a site that would allow both English-speaking and Spanish-speaking parents easy access. And staffing decisions should be based on closely matching the cultural background (not just the language) of teachers and children. In the end, a bicultural program needs to determine whether its goals are for all children to speak English fluently, with the degree of bilingual proficiency chosen by parents, or for all children to be truly bilingual, which requires a commitment by families and continuity from the preschool to the elementary school.

Chapter 9

Health and Development Monitoring

I should have, but I didn't interview my first pediatrician. He didn't have time for well child care questions. So I left him and interviewed six others. BEEP taught me to ask developmental questions. I was interested in far more than illness.

Educators and health care providers have always been concerned about early identification and treatment of children's health and developmental problems. In the past, the child's physician had the major responsibility for early identification and detection of these problems. In theory this arrangement made sense since all children need a regular source of health care and not all children participate in an educational or early childhood setting. Each child and family should have a regular health care provider who knows the child and provides well-child primary care in a continuous manner as the child grows.

Unfortunately, not all children have an ongoing relationship with a physician or nurse practitioner because some families lack health insurance or transportation to health facilities and because other problems currently plague the health care system (Schlesinger and Eisenberg, 1989). Problems in access to health care are more acute for low-income and high-risk urban and rural populations (Select Panel for Promotion of Child Health, 1981).

123

During the past two decades, new state and federal laws about special education have given the educational system the responsibility for early identification of problems that lead children to underachieve or fail in school. The Education for All Handicapped Children Act Amendments of Public Law 99-457 (discussed in Chapter One) requires states to set up systems to identify and assess any child at risk of developmental delay from birth on (Garwood and Sheehan, 1989). To successfully implement these mandates, health, education, and social service systems must collaborate, now more than ever, to provide all children and their families with an ongoing screening and assessment system from a child's birth to the child's entry into kindergarten.

A key component of this screening system is the availability to each family of a well-trained physician or nurse practitioner who can provide primary care. Comprehensive primary care as defined by the American Academy of Pediatrics and other child health groups includes a wide range of components. Components of primary care are a health history; physical examinations; immunizations; screening and assessment for vision and hearing problems, developmental delay, psychosocial problems, nutritional deficits, dental problems, and other conditions (such as anemia); and parental guidance about safety, nutrition, discipline, sibling relationships, and other developmental issues (Green and Haggerty, 1984).

From the inception of BEEP, we integrated a strong health and development component into the educational and family support aspects of the program. The logic for including this component and a link to the child's physician was simple. A child will have a reasonable chance of being successful in school if he or she has adequate hearing, vision, and attentional abilities; nutrition; and socioemotional control. Simply stated, a child's health and developmental status affect the child's competence in school. Therefore, children must be monitored periodically throughout their early childhood years, and health care providers must deal promptly with any concerns identified to alleviate health or developmental impediments to learning. A child's entering kindergarten with a previously undetected or detected but untreated handicap to learning should be regarded as a failure—of the health care and school communities.

Although BEEP did not provide primary care to children, the program did provide ongoing comprehensive health and development assessments, health screenings, information and referral concerning health conditions, communication with the child's physician, and health education and advocacy. This "early school health model" was possible in Brookline because an adequate number of primary care physicians served the community already, making it unnecessary for BEEP's staff to provide direct medical services. Instead, BEEP's staff enriched the primary care provided to the children by giving families extensive feedback from ongoing health and developmental assessments (Hanson and Levine, 1980).

BEEP's early school health model differed from traditional health programs in schools for older children in that it provided for many more contacts with parents, it had a stronger emphasis on behavioral and developmental issues, and it integrated educators more with health care professionals in planning a child's educational experiences. On the other hand, it was similar to traditional programs in that it relied on nurses, provided back-up and consultative care rather than primary care, and offered no medical treatment (Walker, Butler, and Bender, 1989).

Diagnostic Assessments

We elected to conduct early and periodic assessments of children to monitor their development, to establish whether problems in school could be predicted at any one particular age, and to determine whether pediatricians can be effective in helping to diagnose and prevent children's school related problems. All children in BEEP were monitored according to the same developmental monitoring system (Kronstadt, Palfrey, Wolman, and Hanson, 1977). Eight regularly scheduled diagnostic examinations were administered to all children in BEEP from shortly after their birth until their entry into kindergarten. The only optional examination was at eleven and one-half months. This was given to children for whom a concern had arisen in the first three examinations. The target ages and major foci of each assessment were as follows:

1. Two weeks — nervous system
2. Three and one-half months — early visual-directed reaching, responsiveness to social stimulation
3. Six and one-half months — early understanding of language, development of perceptual and gross motor skills
4. Eleven and one-half months (optional) — fine and gross motor functioning, receptive language skills
5. Fourteen and one-half months — comprehensive survey of areas assessed during infancy plus early observation of learning style and activity level
6. Twenty-four months — expressive language, activity level and learning style, problem solving strategies
7. Thirty months — language development, problem solving and abstract abilities, gross motor functioning
8. Forty-two months — areas of functioning most associated with abilities needed in prekindergarten classes
9. Entry into kindergarten — educational readiness skills

Because of the research and development criteria embedded in this component of BEEP, absence of children from two consecutive exams constituted withdrawal from the project.

The developmental stages of children guided our choices for both the age of administration of the assessments and the diagnostic batteries selected. We selected particular ages at which children grow rapidly and experience developmental changes. We wanted to assess children at ages when the children would be cooperative to ensure a valid assessment and to observe optimal development. In the assessments, we monitored the child's health as well as his or her early precursors of language; cognition; and social, perceptual, and motor development, all of which are ultimately related to learning proficiencies in school. The aim was to detect and address the first signs of delays in these important developmental areas so that an educational intervention could be developed in the home-visit, playgroup, or classroom setting.

The first year of a child's life is one of rapid and complex change in the child's mental and physical organization. Many reflexes within the neurological system emerge during this period. The child's physical growth is very rapid, as is his or her development of skills and abilities to deal with the world. Thus, in order to monitor a child adequately during this period, frequent evaluations are necessary. Because we felt that it was impractical to examine children in the hospital, the initial two-week examination was the earliest observation of the child. The first assessment was followed by assessments at periodic intervals only a few months apart during the child's first year of life. We decided not to include an assessment of children at eight months of age because children at that age tend to be anxious around strangers and uncomfortable in unfamiliar settings or situations.

Around the middle of the second year of life, the child's expression of autonomy and separateness increases. Although this is a normal developmental trend, it is very difficult to obtain a reliable and valid assessment of the child's development at this time. Therefore, we scheduled the next examination for twenty-four months. This gap of ten months since the prior examination was not of serious consequence because the rate of development in the second year of a child's life declines somewhat, especially in comparison with development in the first year. The last few exams were scheduled at periodic intervals (thirty months, forty-two months, entry into kindergarten) so that the child's educational readiness skills could be assessed regularly and thoroughly.

We designed a series of diagnostic batteries to identify potential barriers to learning in major areas of functioning: physical and neurological status, sensory (vision and auditory) screening, cognition, receptive and expressive language, perceptual-motor development, gross motor development, and socioemotional adjustment. The procedures and instruments were developed into a comprehensive assessment battery that reflected the state of the art in each of the primary disciplines represented at BEEP (pediatrics, nursing, child development, psychology, and education) (see Appendix C).

Whenever possible, we selected standardized instruments in widespread use. In some instances, however, we had to rely on instruments without an established history because the instruments filled a gap in areas that we judged relevant to learning and school performance. If no adequate measure existed, we developed new instruments or procedures.

The developmental instruments we used included the Bayley Scales of Infant Development (Bayley, 1969), the Harvard Test of Receptive Language (White, Kaban, and Attanucci, 1979), the Harvard Test of Abstract Abilities (White and Watts, 1973), the Denver Developmental Screening Test (Frankenburg and Dodds, 1967), the Stanford-Binet Intelligence Test (Terman and Merrill, 1972), and the McCarthy Scales of Children's Abilities (McCarthy, 1972). In the physical exams, we used the hearing assessment procedures developed by Ewing and Ewing (1944), the Allen Card vision screening, and the neurological examination developed by Prechtl and Beintema (1964). The behavioral ratings were adapted from those used at the Harvard Preschool Project (Ogilvie and Shapiro, 1969), and the parent questionnaire on feeding and sleeping (Kronstadt, Oberklaid, Ferb, and Swartz, 1979) was based on the temperament model of Thomas, Chess, and Birch (1968). The neurological examination we used for preschool children was developed by BEEP's team of physicians and psychologists (Blackman, Levine, Markowitz, and Aufseeser, 1983; Levine and Oberklaid, 1977; Meltzer and others, 1981). (See Resource C for more information on when each assessment instrument was used.)

Steps in Diagnostic Assessment

We designed the ongoing health and development monitoring system to assure maximum cooperation and coordination with the parents and all professionals involved. We followed the same steps before, during, and after each diagnostic assessment. These nine steps are outlined in Table 2.

Three pediatricians from Children's Hospital Medical Center of Boston who were enrolled in a postgraduate fellowship in ambulatory pediatrics participated on a rotating basis as members of BEEP's diagnostic team. As part of their fellowship training in developmental pediatrics, these pediatricians had part-time one-year appointments to BEEP. The pediatric chief of the medical outpatient department supervised from the hospital the fellows' training program at BEEP. The administration of physical and neurological examinations was a major responsibility of these pediatricians. The pediatricians were able to collaborate with BEEP's staff in defining the developmental, social, and educational profiles of the children and families participating in BEEP.

BEEP's nurse, a specialist in community, maternal, and child health, participated in all examinations, provided parent and staff education about outside referrals and health advocacy, participated as a member of the medical resource team, and provided information on health counseling and education for parents and staff. As the only full-time member of the diagnostic team, the nurse served as a liaison between the diagnostic and education components of BEEP (Hanson, 1977).

A psychologist who was experienced in evaluating infants and young children conducted the developmental assessment portion of the monitoring. Along with the doctor, the nurse, and the teacher, the psychologist was responsible for coordinated feedback of information to parents and the education and diagnostic staff.

Whenever possible, the home visitor who was assigned to each family was available in the BEEP center during the exams. She played with the child, helped the parents feel comfortable, listened to the staff discussion of examination findings, and participated in the feedback session with the parents.

A social worker also participated in the feedback session if referrals to other community agencies were under consideration. The social worker made plans to work with the family on noneducational issues that might be interfering with the child's development, including inadequate housing, unemployment, and marital stress.

We maintained a diagnostic file for each child, documenting the results of all evaluations, the conferences, referrals, intrastaff collaboration, and parent contacts with diagnostic and education staff members. Since clinicians are not always ac-

Table 2. Diagnostic Assessment Components.

Part	Contents	Administered by	Time	Other Adults Present
Before exam				
•Postcard (2 weeks before exam)	Schedule exam	Administrative assistant	Less than 5 minutes	—
•Telephone reminder (2–3 days before exam)	Confirm appointment	Administrative assistant	5 minutes	—
During exam				
•Health history	Review of primary health care, sleep and feeding patterns, illness events since previous exam	Nurse	10–15 minutes	Parent(s)
•Development assessment	Standardized test of cognitive, language, perceptual-motor development	Psychologist	30–40 minutes	Parent(s), nurse, home visitor
•Health assessment	Physical, neurological exams, sensory screen, pediatric development assessment	Pediatrician	30–40 minutes	Parent(s), nurse

• Staff conference	Analyze findings	Psychologist	10–15 minutes	Home visitor, pediatrician nurse, social worker[a]
• Parent conference	Feedback of findings	Psychologist	15–20 minutes	Parent(s), home visitor, social worker
After exam				
• Telephone follow-up (2–3 days after exam)	Review of health and education plans	Nurse, home visitor	5–20 minutes	—
• Diagnostic review (biweekly)	Discussion of concerns and coordination of plans	Psychologist	5–15 minutes	Nurse, pediatrician, home visitor, social worker,[a] program supervisors, consultants[a]

[a]Optional, based on child's or family's needs.

customed to keeping systematic records, we devised simple forms, and a research assistant checked each form for completeness prior to filing it. Staff members assured parents in writing that all files were confidential. With the parents' permission, a copy of exam results was sent to the family's pediatrician. Later reference to this copy often led to productive discussions between the parents and the family doctor. Files were shared with other professionals outside of BEEP only when parents gave permission. Parents were able to arrange an appointment with a member of the diagnostic staff to review their child's file and to obtain a copy of any of the contents at any time. Many parents took advantage of this opportunity and viewed it as useful in learning to ask for their rightful access to school or medical records outside of BEEP.

Problems Encountered

Implementation of an ongoing health and development monitoring system presented many challenges to the staff members. First, staff struggled with ethical issues concerning what to tell parents about a particular finding from an assessment. What to tell parents was not a problem when the exam finding was confirmed and all the staff members felt confident that the finding was clearly related to behavior, health, or other development outcomes. But what to tell parents was a problem when the staff was not sure what the finding (such as a slight delay in language or a discrepancy with a prior assessment) meant in terms of the child's future development. Staff members often felt in a difficult position, having to decide between telling parents everything they observed in the exam and withholding some findings. We frequently discussed the trade-offs between telling the parents something that might not be a lasting finding of any consequence but might alarm the parents, and not telling parents, thereby withholding information.

Another set of problems centered on the struggles between professionals from different disciplines who were involved in health and development monitoring. Although we worked as a multidisciplinary team, tensions developed over who should ultimately be responsible for the developmental assessments and interpretations. All of the professionals on the team — the nurse, pediatrician, psychologist, and educator — felt that their training and expertise focused on developmental issues. Especially at the beginning of BEEP, the pediatricians and psychologists disagreed about which group had more expertise in developmental issues, disagreements that were heightened by the pediatricians' development of an exam for educational readiness that their colleagues could use. Disputes may be typical of the initial stages of collaboration across disciplines, but after the initial struggles at BEEP, we worked in a team fashion in which all staff members learned from each other and integrated their skills to help the families and the children.

Tensions also existed, to some extent, between BEEP's staff and the children's primary care physicians, who received reports of all the assessment findings (with parental consent). The BEEP health monitoring model was extensive, and the staff explained the findings in detail to parents immediately after the assessments. In addition, we taught parents to become keen observers of their children at home and at school. Thus, parents involved in BEEP had greater expectations of their primary care physicians than most parents have. They expected the physician to take time to answer questions and interpret exam findings. Sometimes their primary care physician did not do this because he or she had limited training in developmental or educational issues. In other cases, physicians did not spend time discussing development issues because they were under tight time constraints in their busy practices anad were not reimbursed for the extra time by health insurance. In the first year of BEEP, many parents sought a new primary care physician who would be more responsive to their questions than their previous doctor.

Recommendations

The health and development monitoring system at BEEP was designed from its inception to be a research and demonstration effort. Thus, it provided a scope and frequency of services that future school-based programs could not be expected to match. But much that we learned from these frequent assessments by a multidisciplinary team can be incorporated into future school-based early childhood programs.

Parents valued the assessment procedures and felt they were important in helping them to become good observers and teachers of their children. (We discuss this in more detail in Chapter Ten.) An analysis of participation by parents in the assessments during the first two years of BEEP revealed that: (1) the diagnostic services of BEEP were uniformly used by parents assigned to all levels of service intensity, (2) single-parent families tended to use the services of the social worker at BEEP more than dual-parent families (23 percent and 9 percent, respectively), (3) mothers with at least a high school education used the BEEP pediatric staff more than those without a high school education, and (4) the birth order of the child did not correlate significantly with the family's utilization of the various diagnostic support services.

Feedback to parents regarding the results of the evaluations of their child should be candid, direct, and given in a setting that allows ample time for interaction with the examiners. Telling parents the truth conveys a confidence in them that increases their ability to act as effective consumers and advocates for their child. Nevertheless, hearing all the results of examinations can sometimes increase parents' anxiety. It is essential that professionals involved in this type of service be confident and comfortable in communicating with parents.

We learned some important information from the various analyses using all the health and development findings over time from the child's birth through the child's entry into second grade. As others have found (Chamberlin, 1987), we determined that there is no one particular age at which developmental screening and assessment will predict later school competence or problems. Instead, the most effective and meaningful approach to understanding and describing the development of young children is the continual monitoring of their development rather than a one-time screening. Because many thirty-month-old children are apt to act like younger children and be uncooperative during an evaluation session, we found that the most suitable age for the first school-based examination is thirty-six months.

Although there was a high incidence and low prevalence of health findings in the participating children during their early years (Levine, Wolman, Oberklaid, and Pierson, 1982), both health and developmental findings during the children's first two years of life demonstrated a tendency toward instability over time with two important exceptions (Kronstadt, Oberklaid, Ferb, and Swartz, 1979; Levine and others, 1977; Palfrey, Levine, and Pierson, 1984; Wolman, Yurchak, and Levine, 1980). First, concerns identified on hearing screening exams were reliably predictive, even at an early age, of later hearing loss or language delay. We found that effective screening of children's hearing can begin as early as six months of age. In addition, obtaining a family history of hearing loss and a history of ear infections in the child and documenting parental concerns about hearing are useful at all ages in identifying children at risk for hearing loss, a loss that is predictive of later learning problems if undetected and untreated (Palfrey and others, 1980).

Second, children with persistent attentional problems over two or more assessments demonstrated poorer outcomes in second grade reading than children without these problems (Palfrey and others, 1981; Palfrey, Levine, Walker, and Sullivan, 1985; Palfrey, Walker, Sullivan, and Levine, 1987). Children with persistent concerns (14 percent of children in BEEP) also had other risk factors associated with the attentional problems; for example, they tended to be from single-parent homes in which mothers had low levels of education, and they also exhibited other developmental delays and signs of social and emotional problems.

We found that formal visual acuity screening is not cost effective prior to twenty-four months of age, but it increases in usefulness thereafter with the age of the child. Prior to twenty-four months, a structural examination of the child's eyes, a vision history of the family, and documentation of parental concern about vision are more productive than an acuity screening. Effective dental screening can begin when the child is twenty-four months old. We also found that the frequently used Denver Developmental Screening Test does not provide by itself adequate results for making specific educational plans or decisions about infants and preschoolers.

We learned a great deal about the timing and staffing of diagnostic and monitoring programs. Diagnostic evaluation results must be linked to an educational program that provides appropriate services and interventions for children and families. Identification of problems without follow-up intervention is unethical and unwarranted. In addition, educators furnish a different and important perspective regarding the functioning of children and of the context or family in which they live. The program's staff must solicit and document concerns from teachers and parents in any comprehensive assessment of a child's health and development.

Procedures used to evaluate children must reflect a sensitivity to the children's cultural background. When adequate measures are not available, staff must interpret results with the greatest caution to avoid labeling and stigmatizing the children. Bilingual children should be evaluated in the language that is spoken in their home. Standardized measures are often unavailable in languages other than English, so experienced clinical observations in home and educational settings must be substituted for these measures.

A multidisciplinary team approach to evaluating young children provides the most effective means of understanding a child's functioning and developing appropriate interventions based on this understanding. Nurses and teachers, if experienced in work with infants and preschoolers and if carefully trained, can perform valid and reliable developmental evaluations of young children. A nurse with a specialty in maternal and child health can perform several very important functions as a member of the diagnostic team: health advocacy, counseling, and screening with parents; health education of staff; and general health supervision. Pediatricians can play an effective role in the prevention, diagnosis, and treatment of social, behavioral, and learning disorders. Since parents and schools often ask pediatricians for advice on children's learning or behavioral problems, it is important that pediatricians be as informed and effective as possible and willing to collaborate with educators. A social worker is a valuable member of the diagnostic team, not only to provide families with a source of referral to outside agencies but also to offer consultation services to staff members who are in regular contact with all families. Also, a collaborative relationship between the project's medical staff and the community's primary pediatric providers is an essential component of an effective diagnostic program and requires sensitivity to the needs and resources of the local pediatric community.

At BEEP, we found that an early school health program can be successfully integrated with an early education program. Although a period of initial adjustment may be required, educators, physicians, psychologists, and social workers can work together with the goal of promoting optimal health and development in children. Instead of one-time screening measures, we recommend assessments that are thorough (and include measures of attention) and that occur periodically throughout the child's early life. For children without disabilities, slight deviations in development at any one age may right themselves and, therefore, do not necessarily predict later problems. Early and periodic assessments with appropriate follow-up and participation by parents are a key to ensuring that each child realizes his or her fullest potential during early childhood and the first school years.

Chapter 10

What Parents Gain

What BEEP did is it included parents. You know, suggesting
like I should physically go to meetings. So, I'm going to
BEEP and I'm seeing other kids. So now, I'm in it. From the
time Imani was born, then she grew, now she's in school, I
got involved. Right from the start. So, it's like when the next
one was born, I automatically did the same thing. That's
what BEEP did. It kind of turned on a little motor.

The central role of parents in the
education of their children was an integral part of the philosophy
of BEEP. The project was built on the premise that children
whose parents understand and support their development enter
school as competent learners. BEEP offered parents various ways
to gain a more thorough understanding of their child's skills and
approaches to learning and making friends. However, the parents valued some ways of gaining information more than others.

Parents' views of different program components are critical to those who wish to improve a program, replicate a program, or understand the dynamics by which a program operated. No matter how well designed a program component may
be or how extensively it may be based on prior research or theory, if it does not appeal to parents, its effectiveness is limited.
We solicited views of parents at several points during the program to gain an understanding of those components that parents found most appealing and why. Additionally, we were

138

interested in understanding parents' feelings about their experience with BEEP after the program had ended. We also investigated whether parents showed any lasting effects from BEEP, especially in regard to their involvement with their child's school. Parental participation has been cited as a critical factor in children's success in school (Ashton and Webb, 1986), yet the ability of programs like BEEP to affect parents' advocacy for their child in school was uncertain.

In this chapter, we summarize a series of studies (both interviews and questionnaires) conducted with parents who participated in BEEP about the aspects of BEEP they found to be most and least valuable (Ferb, 1977; Fort, 1981; Nicol, 1977; Weiss, Yurchak, and O'Leary, 1977; Weiss, 1979). The studies were conducted at different times during BEEP and on different samples of participants, although each sample was selected to represent the entire population involved in BEEP. Additionally, at the time participating children were in second grade, we asked parents to reflect on BEEP in terms of their relationship with their child's elementary school, and we collected and analyzed independent records of parent-teacher contacts (Hauser-Cram and Pierson, 1984).

The Infancy Phase

After one year of participation in BEEP, 110 parents were interviewed about their experience with the program (Nicol, 1977). Individuals not involved with BEEP conducted the interviews, which focused on home visits and diagnostic exams. In general, the majority of parents (58 percent) believed that they had changed because of BEEP, and they believed that the most persistent change was in their way of relating to their child. For example, one mother said that before being in BEEP she had no idea of what a baby could see or the importance of playing with her baby. Another parent said that her home visitor helped her realize how important it was to talk to her baby before the baby developed language. Other parents described more subtle ways they had learned to extend their baby's interest in objects or other people.

Parents rated the home visits as the most uniformly positive aspect of BEEP during the infancy phase of the program. Nearly all parents who received home visits found these visits helpful (92 percent). Parents were very resistent to changing this aspect of the program, and when asked if parent groups to discuss child development topics would be preferable, 88 percent of parents responded negatively (Nicol, 1977).

Parents said that the following topics were those most often discussed during the home visits:

1. Child management concerns, such as sleeping, feeding, and separation — 30 percent of families
2. Child development information, such as developmental milestones — 24 percent of families
3. Their child's development, such as behaviors to anticipate — 22 percent of families
4. Health and safety — 17 percent of families
5. The parents' role — 7 percent of families

Parents' perceptions of the topics discussed during home visits indicated the extent to which the visits centered on the child and involved the transmission of information. Parents rarely viewed support for themselves as isolated from support for their child's development.

Mothers, who had substantially more contact with home visitors than fathers, were asked to reflect on characteristics of the home visitor. They described the home visitor more as a friend (53 percent) than a teacher (33 percent) or an expert (5 percent). Mothers resisted changing home visitors, and the majority of those who had experienced such a change reported that the change was difficult. The alliance formed with one home visitor could not easily be replicated with another, even when each home visitor possessed outstanding personal characteristics. Mothers felt that having the same home visitor throughout the infancy period was critical.

Although the home visits were clearly parents' favorite aspect of the program during the infancy phase, the diagnostic exams were a close second. The majority of parents judged

BEEP's exams to be more thorough than those provided by their child's physician, and they thought that the exams provided more information about their child's developmental status than those conducted by the physician. Parents received a written summary of the exams and met individually with the diagnostic staff to discuss findings. Parents often mentioned during the interviews about BEEP that the written report and discussion were the most valuable parts of the exam.

A large percentage of parents (72 percent) believed their perceptions of their child had been influenced by the exams (including the reports and discussions). They said that they had gained a greater awareness, sensitivity, and understanding of their child's strengths and limitations by observing the exams and discussing the findings with BEEP's staff. For example, one mother commented that she had no idea that her child had such a great attention span until she observed her in the exam setting. A father remarked that he was surprised at how well his son could follow complex directions, a characteristic he had not noticed before. The exams provided parents with a perspective that is hard to gain when interacting with a child and also gave parents an opportunity to see their child's reaction to individuals who, although skilled in examining children, did not know their child well.

The Toddler Phase

When children completed the playgroup component of BEEP (that is, when they were approaching three years of age), a questionnaire was completed by 123 participating families (Ferb, 1977) and in-depth interviews were conducted with 35 mothers whose families had participated in BEEP for three years (Weiss, Yurchak, and O'Leary, 1977; Weiss, 1979). Over 80 percent of parents who completed the questionnaire indicated that they were very satisfied with the playgroups. Parents rated the three most critical elements of the playgroup as (in order of importance) the personal characteristics of the teachers, the size of the playgroups, and the child-staff ratio. Concerns about playgroups were voiced mainly by families in which both parents were employed; they found the playgroup sessions too infrequent to meet their needs (Ferb, 1977).

Although the questionnaire data indicated generally high rates of satisfaction with BEEP, certain components appeared to present problems for some parents. Transportation to BEEP was often difficult for families without cars. Even though a van was available to transport families to BEEP, families who relied on the van found BEEP to be less accessible than other families. For example, because they had to plan for transportation by the van in advance, spontaneous visits to BEEP were seldom a possibility for these families. This finding underscores the importance of providing neighborhood programs to which parents have easy access, especially for families who do not have their own transportation.

A second component of the toddler phase of the program brought mixed reviews from parents (Ferb, 1977). Parents rated parent groups lower than other aspects of the program. During interviews, some parents indicated that they found parent groups unrewarding because certain parents often dominated the conversation. Particularly troubling to some parents was the contrast in the concerns of parents of different socioeconomic groups. For example, in one group, parents who had constant economic concerns for their family's well-being were distressed by the desire of other parents to use the group to discuss how they could travel to some exotic resort with their child. Even skillful group leaders were not always able to bring the group to a common focus.

The interviews also revealed several other issues that were important for parents in BEEP (Weiss, 1979). First, some parents were aware of the risk of dependency on BEEP, and they described ways in which they maintained their capacity for self-initiation and autonomy. They viewed BEEP as one of several information sources they would go to for suggestions about raising their child. Structuring a relationship that is not dependent required that both parents and program staff value parental autonomy.

Second, some parents were distressed about the way in which a staff member had communicated concern about their child's development. In some cases, the communication occurred in the discussion of the diagnostic exam; in others, it occurred in conferences with the child's playgroup teacher. Parents wanted complete information about their child, yet they often were discouraged because staff members did not have sufficient information about the prognosis or gravity of a concern. In general, parents expected pediatricians, psychologists, and teachers to know more about the course of child development than, in fact, is known by anyone. For example, one parent explained that her child's speech articulation errors were mentioned during one diagnostic exam, and the psychologist was uncertain whether her child would outgrow those errors or whether they would continue to be a problem. Another mother remarked about the playgroup teacher's concern about her child's social skills. She finally decided to ask the teacher if she thought the child should see a psychiatrist. When the teacher quickly responded that the concerns were not that serious, the mother wondered why they had been raised. Thus, parents believed that they should have complete information about their child but also that such information should be supplemented by information about the meaning and gravity of concerns and recommendations for intervention. In reality, even with all the expert advice that a program like BEEP could solicit, our ability to predict the course of an individual child's development was much poorer, in some cases, than parents wanted it to be.

Third, parents reported that BEEP had given them a different set of standards by which they would judge other programs for their children. Their increased awareness of child development fostered a high level of expectations in parents, and few programs could meet such expectations. Parents were concerned about finding quality programs for their other children and about the ability of the elementary school to offer what they believed their child would need.

The Prekindergarten Phase

At the end of the prekindergarten phase of the program, seventy-six families completed a questionnaire about specific features of prekindergarten (Fort, 1981). Over 75 percent of these families rated their reaction to the prekindergarten program as being "very enthusiastic." Parents indicated that several aspects of the program had had a large influence on their child. The majority of parents selected three particular ways in which their child had developed as a result of the prekindergarten program: social skills (such as the ability to get along with other children), mastery skills (such as the ability to select and complete activities independently), and preacademic skills (such as interest in cognitive tasks).

Parents were asked to reflect on characteristics of the prekindergarten program that they considered to be most valuable. They reported the following to be most important (in rank order): the personal qualities of the teachers, the organization of the classroom, and the variety of materials and activities available.

A few parents expressed some concerns about the prekindergarten program. Although one parent commented that the curriculum was too cognitive, others believed that the program did not prepare children to deal with the social interaction they would find in their neighborhoods. One mother remarked that her child had begun to believe that children in his neighborhood would behave like children in BEEP (such as using language rather than physical force to resolve disputes) and did not know how to deal with more physically aggressive children. Another said that although her child would probably have good social skills in the elementary school classroom as a result of BEEP, she would not be able to relate well to her peers at home where the ground rules were different. Thus, some parents believed that neighborhood and classroom social mores were so distinct that BEEP's influence on a child's behavior in the classroom may have been detrimental to the child's social acceptance in the neighborhood. Others, however, believed that the strategies children learned in relating to their peers at BEEP would benefit them in both settings.

More than 50 percent of the parents had had experience with other nursery school programs attended by older children in the family. When asked to compare BEEP's prekindergarten program to others they had experienced, parents indicated that

BEEP's program was more personal, more stable, better organized, better staffed, and more comprehensive. Although some
of these qualities were specific to the prekindergarten component itself, such as the number of staff members, others were
probably related to the fact that the prekindergarten component
was part of a program that was comprehensive in scope.

Entry into Kindergarten

When their child entered kindergarten, parents in BEEP
were asked to consider all of the features of the program and
to indicate which were most important to their family. A total
of 125 parents responded to a questionnaire that asked for ratings of various components of BEEP (Fort, 1981).

As Figure 1 indicates, the diagnostic exams received the
highest overall ratings, followed by home visits, prekindergarten,

Figure 1. Parent Ratings of Program Components.

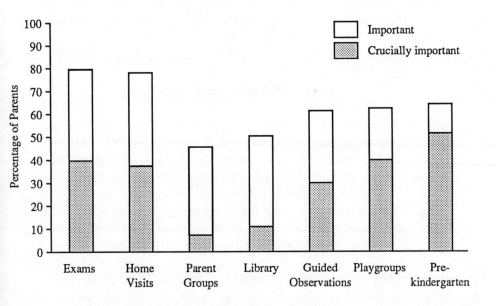

Source: Based on figures in Fort, 1981.

and playgroups. The parent group meetings were the least valued aspect of the program. Fifty-five percent of the respondents considered the prekindergarten component to be "crucially important." Prekindergarten was the only aspect of BEEP that the majority of parents considered to be crucial.

Parents were also asked to judge BEEP's effects on themselves and their child. The majority responded that BEEP helped them achieve a better understanding of child development, in general, and of their own child's development in particular (Fort, 1981). In addition, they felt that they had gained skills to manage their child more adeptly and had increased their enjoyment of parenting. And about 50 percent of the parents responded that they were more confident in relating to school personnel.

In response to questions about BEEP's effects on their child, about 79 percent of parents indicated that BEEP had a positive influence on preparing their child for elementary school, and 48 percent believed that influence to have been large. Parents were asked what they believed would be the lasting effect of BEEP on their child. The majority indicated that they thought their child would be a better learner and have a more positive reaction to school in general. Parents also felt their child would be more secure and self-confident in the classroom and have better classroom social skills because of participating in BEEP.

Effects of BEEP on Parents

When the children who had participated in BEEP were in the second grade, we undertook a study in which contacts between parents and second grade teachers were compared for families who had participated in BEEP and others who had not (Hauser-Cram and Pierson, 1984). We wanted to know how participating parents viewed the program in the context of their experience with their child's elementary school and whether or not they demonstrated sustained interest in their child's school experiences.

Parent advocacy in schools has several different interpretations. Many regard parent participation on school policy-making committees or parent volunteers in classroom events as parent advocacy (Davies, 1981; Salisbury, 1980). However, our view was that parent advocacy consisted of parental interest in sustaining a relationship with the child's teacher about the child's progress in school. We reasoned that one effect of an early education program such as BEEP could be that parents demonstrate a continued interest in their child's academic and social progress in school. Such interest would reflect parents' desire to understand their children's school experience and therefore would enable parents to be better advocates for their children's needs.

This study involved sixty-six families who had been enrolled in BEEP and a randomly selected comparison set of sixty-six families who had children in the same second grade classrooms. Teachers of all the Brookline second grade classrooms agreed to keep records of their contacts with all parents for a twelve-week period. For the most part, teachers were unaware of whether or not a family had participated in BEEP.

In order to ensure that the records would be as accurate and reliable as possible, a project supervisor met with each teacher individually at the beginning of the study, one week after data collection began, and every two to three weeks thereafter. Teachers recorded personal conversations and personal notes between themselves and parents on a form developed with the assistance of several teachers. The form included spaces for the following information:

- Family member contacted (mother, father, other)
- Date of contact
- Initiator of contact
- Form of contact (phone call, note, school visit)
- Length of contact (estimated in minutes)
- Description of content or topic

We found that many interchanges between parents and teachers involved more than one type of information. For example, a teacher may have called parents to ask them to sign a field trip form, yet the parents also wished to discuss their child's math homework. All information was recorded for each contact so that the data would reveal how many times each family discussed a topic as well as how many contacts each parent had with teachers.

We organized the content of the contacts that the teachers recorded into four categories. The first category covered interactions about a child's progress, including all discussions about a child's academic skills, classroom behavior, health status, and general progress; family concerns; and routine conferences. The second category covered interactions that involved an exchange of administrative information, including discussions about general school policies, dates at which homework was due, and particular classroom issues such as the class size or ethnic makeup. The third category covered friendly discussions between parents and teachers about topics unrelated to school. The fourth category covered interactions about class participation, including discussions about classroom visits, field trip supervision, school events, and attendance at class workshops.

Overall, more than 80 percent of the families in the study had at least one contact with a teacher to discuss their child's progress during the time the study was underway. About 75 percent of the families had a discussion with a teacher about administrative issues; about 33 percent of the families had at least one contact with a teacher that was regarded as simply friendly or social; and about 33 percent had at least one discussion about class participation. In general, the rate of contact was reasonably high for all families.

Although we found no difference between parents who had been in BEEP and other parents in the total number of contacts they made with teachers, the pattern of contacts did differ. A higher proportion of contacts made by families who had been in BEEP involved discussions about their child's progress — 47.4 percent as compared to 34.1 percent of contacts made by families who had not participated in BEEP.

When only those contacts initiated by parents were considered, the effects of BEEP on parents became more apparent. Those parents who had participated in the program differed significantly from other parents in their tendency to initiate more discussions concerning their children's progress in school. The parents who had been in BEEP initiated contacts 48.9 percent of the time to discuss their child's progress. Only 27.4 percent of the contacts initiated by comparison parents involved their child's progress.

In order to understand more fully the thoughts and assumptions underlying the actions of parents who had participated in BEEP, staff members interviewed twenty of these parents when their child was in second grade (Hauser-Cram and Pierson, 1984). The interviews revealed several strategies motivating parents' high rate of contact with teachers. Families varied widely in their descriptions of why they had been so active. Some described their behavior as simply a friendly reminder to the teacher of their interest in their child's school work. Others used more aggressive terms, such as the need for "muscling in" or the importance of "staying on the teacher's case."

Parents gave three general reasons for their frequent communications with teachers. First, some referred to their vigilance as a type of preventive measure—a way of ensuring that if a problem arose it would receive prompt attention. These parents described the importance of altering teachers' tendencies to contact parents only when major problems occur. The parents reasoned that if they made frequent contact and were easily accessible, the teacher would be more likely to mention even minor concerns, which could then be prevented from developing into major problems. The majority of parents who applied this reasoning attributed it to their experience at BEEP, where the staff had been readily available to them.

Other parents described the reasons for their vigilance less in terms of preventive measures and more in terms of the possible benefits for their child of daily interactions with the teacher. They observed that teachers cannot dole out equal amounts of time and attention to all students. From their perspective, students get extra attention if they exhibit learning or behavioral problems or, more relevant to these families, if they have parents who maintain a high level of interest.

A third reason parents gave for their close monitoring of the classroom was to make sure that their child was properly challenged academically. Most of the minority parents interviewed feared that their child would not be challenged academically or expected to be a high achiever. Although few parents reported confronting teachers directly about their impressions that teachers demanded less of their child because of race or ethnic status, many described strategies they had developed to make sure that the teacher assessed their child's abilities appropriately. Some pointed out that their experience with BEEP had taught them to expect high standards for their child in any program. They felt they had an important role in ensuring that those standards were met.

Almost all parents interviewed pointed out that they regarded the first parent-teacher conference of the year as a time to determine whether the teacher understood and appreciated their child. Parents emphasized that the continuity in BEEP had ensured that playgroup and prekindergarten teachers understood the individual characteristics of their child. They felt that their role as parents was to help teachers continue to view their child as an individual with unique traits. Thus, rather than advocating for more services, these parents viewed their advocate role as that of helping teachers appreciate the personal characteristics of their child.

Chapter 11

Children's Future Success in School

As the children who had partici-
pated in BEEP entered kindergarten and proceeded through the
elementary grades, they encountered many new experiences.
Teachers and parents expected them to function as part of a
large class, often led by only one teacher; develop new friendships; and master academic skills, such as reading and compu-
tation. Had BEEP prepared them well for these experiences?
The goal of BEEP was to minimize the number of children who
would fail to function competently in school rather than to increase children's IQ scores. Did BEEP succeed in this goal? In
this chapter, we discuss the problems encountered in evaluating BEEP, describe the evaluation process, and present the
results of the evaluation of child outcomes in kindergarten and
second grade.

The Challenges of Evaluation

The early childhood literature is replete with testimony
about the difficulty of adequately evaluating early childhood programs (Cronbach, 1982; Gordon, 1979; Hauser-Cram, 1990;
Travers and Light, 1982). Most programs that provide services
to young children are not "pure experiments" conducted in lab-
oratory settings but rather are programs trying to assist families with a wide variety of needs by providing a wide variety

of services. The diversity and flexibility of service-oriented programs pose many challenges for evaluators. How do we compare the effects of different programs when the programs often
serve different types of families in different ways? Some of the
challenges in designing evaluations occur across programs, but
others are unique to a particular setting. In planning the evaluation of BEEP, we considered three major sets of questions:

1. What is the best time (or times) to evaluate effects? What
    are the best age points to use in evaluations?
2. What kind of comparison group (or groups) should we use
    for assessing the impact of BEEP on the children who par-
    ticipated? Should some kind of randomized trial be em-
    ployed? How should groups be identified and recruited?
    What trade-offs should we make between research require-
    ments and service-related considerations? How practical or
    realistic are some of the alternative approaches?
3. On what school competencies should comparisons be made?
    What are the appropriate measures to use to test those com-
    petencies? How adequate are the available measures for
    young children from diverse backgrounds who will even-
    tually be in a variety of classroom settings?

These sets of questions — along with a number of additional issues related to the overall evaluation — received a great
deal of our time and attention throughout the project. In each
instance, we did not develop a single "best" answer or solution,
but often we used two or more alternative approaches to address the evaluation challenges. The major questions, some of
the options that we considered, and some of the answers that
we developed are discussed in more detail here.

Ages for Comparisons

A major issue in the evaluation of BEEP was selecting
the ages at which comparisons would be made. Some researchers had argued that evaluations of early childhood programs
tended to be carried out too soon after the program ended

(Stearns, 1971). By considering the effects of a program several years later, researchers could detect different patterns of findings. As was noted in the early evaluations of Head Start, effects demonstrated immediately after a program ends may fade in time (Datta, 1969). Alternatively, sleeper effects may not become evident for years (Lazar and Darlington, 1982). For example, improvement in children's cognitive or attentional skills might not result in dramatically different performance by these children in kindergarten, but the improvement might begin to emerge as the children face more academic tasks, such as reading or mathematics. Or some of the effects seen at kindergarten might become translated into somewhat different effects later on in school. For example, children's early skills in interacting with adults during kindergarten might lead to improved academic performance during the elementary school years.

We decided to evaluate the children's classroom skills at two time points: when the children were in kindergarten and when they were in the second grade. The decision to assess children during their first year in school was a natural one because the central goal of BEEP was to help children develop competence in a school setting. The decision to assess them again at second grade required more extensive thought. Together with school personnel, we determined that in the second grade academic demands on children begin to accelerate and referrals to special services often increase sharply. Moreover, child development research indicates that by seven years of age — when they generally are in second grade — children have passed through a major developmental period, called the "five-to-seven shift" (White, 1970). At seven years old, most children are more able developmentally to be attuned to the academic demands of school than at earlier ages. The second grade period thus seemed to be a critical time at which to examine children's functioning in school.

By assessing the children's school functioning at these two points, we could determine a great deal about the effects of BEEP. For example, if we found effects of BEEP at kindergarten that were not sustained under the pressure of a more academic environment in second grade, we would have information about the limitations of this type of early education program. On the other hand, if new effects began to emerge when the children were in second grade, these effects would demonstrate the potential strengths of early education programs, such as BEEP, on children's later functioning in an academic environment.

Comparison Groups

Comparing Participants to Nonparticipants. In designing BEEP, one of the major questions we considered was whether to conduct a truly randomized study — that is, a study in which individuals who had volunteered for the project would be randomly assigned to a control group (that would not be offered the program) and a treatment group (that would be offered the program). Since a truly randomized study is considered to be the best research design for determining the true effects of a program (Gilbert, Light, and Mosteller, 1975), why did we not select this approach?

First, when we discussed the plans for BEEP with community representatives from health clinics, public housing projects, the welfare department, day-care centers, and the schools, it became apparent that these individuals were interested in a program that would provide services for the families they would refer to it. They saw the needs of these families as being pressing and immediate, and they were reluctant to recruit participants for a program in which some of the families would be randomly assigned to a control group and would thus receive no services at all.

Even if we could have overcome this problem, however, and used a randomized design, we anticipated that other problems would have compromised the overall plan (Tivnan, 1988). Some of these additional problems later became much more widely recognized and discussed in the evaluation literature as important threats to the validity of evaluation studies — even those studies that appeared to have been well designed when they were begun (Cook and Campbell, 1979). For example, in a communitywide program such as BEEP, participating families would be in contact with control families and would impart some of what they had learned in BEEP to these families through "diffusion." Thus, the control group would not represent a pure control. A second important concern was that families assigned to a control group might become resentful of the public schools or find a way of obtaining compensatory services; both possibilities would compromise our ability to generalize the results of the study.

As a result of a variety of concerns, some of them based on the practical difficulties that we anticipated in actually trying to carry out a truly randomized trial over such a lengthy period of time, we developed some alternative approaches. Instead of a truly randomized design, we selected an approach that combined some aspects of a randomized experiment with some aspects of a quasi-experimental approach (Cook and Campbell, 1979). Quasi experiments allow comparisons to be made among groups that are provided with different aspects of the program or among similar (but not randomized) groups that do and do not participate in the program. We decided not to rely on a single comparison group but instead to take advantage of several different strategies for making appropriate comparisons (Bryk, Wohlleb, Malson, and Mathis, 1975; Dougherty, Bryk, and Pierson, 1975).

First, for the evaluation of children in kindergarten, we compared participants in BEEP to children and families residing in the same communities (Brookline and Boston) who had not participated in the program. The comparison children, however, were born in the years preceding the years for enrollment in BEEP. We believed that this group would provide a better comparison than children born the same year as children in the program, whose families may not have volunteered to participate in BEEP. For example, those families who did not volunteer to participate may have been distinctly different from those who did in critical ways, such as being less interested in or oriented toward education-related issues. Moreover, through examining birth records of families in Brookline, we found that over 50 percent of those families who had not enrolled in BEEP (but were eligible based on the date of their child's birth) had moved or planned to move away from Brookline before the child would enter kindergarten. Therefore, a comparison group of nonparticipants would have had a high attrition rate as well as possibly been biased in other respects.

Instead, we decided that one of our strategies would be to compare BEEP's participants to similar families who might have been interested in BEEP had it been available when their child was born and who intended to stay in Brookline. Thus, families whose children were from the same communities but were born in the years just before BEEP was available were recruited to become the comparison group. We felt that these families and children would be quite similar to the participants in many ways. This sample provided the standard to which we compared children who had participated in BEEP during their kindergarten year. Furthermore, this sample was used for comparative purposes in developing measures for the pediatric community (as described in Chapter Nine), for developing the classroom-based measures that would be used in the evaluation of BEEP, and for comparing general developmental trends of children with the BEEP group's developmental trends.

For the second grade evaluation, we used a different approach in developing a comparison group for two reasons. First, despite the anticipated similarity between BEEP's participants and the comparison group, we found demographic differences between the groups at kindergarten, and we adjusted for those in our analyses. We were concerned, however, that those differences would increase by second grade, especially if families from traditional risk groups (such as families whose mother had a low level of education, which proved to be a critical variable) continued to drop out of the comparison group. BEEP was able to retain certain types of families, such as families in which the mothers had not completed high school, that were not retained in the comparison group. Although some of these demographic differences could be taken into account in our analyses, statistical control of such differences is never entirely adequate. Given the sample size that would ultimately be involved, relying solely on statistical adjustments would be especially risky.

Second, the size of the BEEP sample in the Brookline Public Schools had dwindled to 104 children. When the evaluation of BEEP was originally planned, we assumed that attrition would be about 10 percent per year over the course of the project and that a sample of 100 children by second grade would be sufficient. In fact, such a sample size was indeed adequate to answer general questions about the effects of BEEP. But for questions about the effects of BEEP on subgroups of participants, such as families with lower levels of education, a sample size of 100 children was meager. Fortunately, at the time the children entered second grade, sixty-five families who had participated in BEEP had moved from Brookline to communities in the Boston area and were willing to have their child participate in the evaluation of the program. Therefore, we decided that each child who had participated in BEEP would be compared to another child of the same gender selected randomly from the same classroom. This resulted in a matched pairs design. The matched pairs design provided a large sample size while controlling for classroom or school effects that could not be sufficiently controlled by using the comparison group of children enrolled only in Brookline schools. As described later in this chapter, the matched pairs comparison group was remarkably similar demographically to the BEEP group.

Comparing Program Intensity Levels Within BEEP. Although random assignment of families to participant and nonparticipant status was not a part of the evaluation design of the program, we did randomly assign families to levels of service. As described in Chapters Four and Five, participating families were provided with either an extensive level of service (A level), a moderate level of service (B level), or a minimal level of service (C level). The differences in the levels of service occurred largely during the infant and toddler phases of the program. Families assigned to the C level did not receive home visits or attend parent groups, whereas A and B level families participated in those two program components, although to a different extent.

BEEP's staff members routinely analyzed records of contact with each family to determine if families participated according to their assigned level. Assignment to level of service was truly random and was successfully maintained throughout the program. Demographic characteristics of the families were similar across the three program levels, with approximately 25 percent of each group composed of families with low socioeconomic status. Differences in attrition over the course of the project for the three groups were minimal.

We wanted to know if a minimal level of service would be sufficient to produce effects or if certain types of families would require moderate or intense levels of service. The heterogeneous composition of the participating families (and adequate sample size) allowed us to respond to critical questions about who benefited from each intensity level.

One way to approach the question of who gained the most benefit from a program is to analyze the results for subgroups of participants who have similar characteristics. We could have looked at several subgroups when evaluating BEEP. For example, Brookline and Boston families could have been analyzed separately. We decided against this possibility because, to a large extent, Boston families were either black or Hispanic, whereas Brookline families tended to be Caucasian. The parent advisory group at BEEP strongly voiced their concern over any division of participants into ethnic groups in reporting the results of the program. Some of this concern was in reaction to the still festering wounds inflicted on ethnic groups by social science research (such as Jensen, 1969) that suggested biological or genetic explanations for the apparent differences in the educational performance of various ethnic groups. Therefore, we decided to plan the evaluation around subgroups based on demographic characteristics other than ethnicity or neighborhood.

Appropriate Measures

Concerns about the selection of appropriate constructs and adequate measures of those constructs are integral to any evaluation. Although the central question of the measurement aspect of evaluation appears straightforward—Given the goals of a program, what are the appropriate measures to assess impact?—the answer is often elusive. One of the major concerns with evaluations of early childhood programs is the overreliance on standardized measures of intelligence (Hauser-Cram and Shonkoff, 1988). Often evaluators have attributed importance to constructs that are measurable, such as an intelligence quotient, rather than to constructs that are important but are not easy to measure, such as social skills (Walker, 1973). Many researchers use standardized IQ measures because these measures possess psychometric properties such as high internal consistency (that is, test items tend to be correlated statistically) and high test-retest reliability (that is, individuals tend to receive similar test scores over two shortly spaced intervals) that many other measures lack. IQ tests can also be used to gather data easily because they can be administered during a single session and require only that the examiner be sufficiently trained on the measure, although group-administered IQ tests lack even that requirement.

Despite the ease of administration, IQ tests as the sole measure of the effectiveness of early childhood programs are quite limited (Zigler and Trickett, 1978). Moreover, such tests are often biased against minority groups (Mercer, 1974) and are a poor match with the goals of a program such as BEEP. Indeed, some standardized test scores were collected on children who had participated in BEEP (the McCarthy Scales of Children's Abilities at the children's entry into kindergarten and the California Achievement Tests when they were in second grade). These tests were used to determine if the development of participating children was within the normal range. The purpose of BEEP, however, was not to improve children's scores on standardized tests, such as IQ tests, but rather to enhance children's functioning in classroom settings. As a result of these considerations, we used some alternatives to standardized tests in assessing the impact of BEEP on children's performance in school.

The Construct of School Competence. Although school competence as a construct is very appealing, it does not lend itself to easy definition. We described in Chapter Four the process by which BEEP's staff and school personnel determined a definition

of school competence. School competence includes the following attributes for the child entering kindergarten:

1. Selects activities and tasks that are consistent with his or
   her abilities
2. Focuses and maintains attention
3. Displays organized behavior in the classroom by selecting
   and planning tasks, choosing appropriate materials to accomplish the tasks, and completing the tasks successfully
   with minimal distraction
4. Perceives the many relationships between objects and actions such as size, function, order, position, and time
5. Understands and uses language effectively
6. Performs age-appropriate motor activities and fine motor
   tasks
7. Plays alone and with others
8. Interacts successfully with adults and other children

In general, these eight attributes relate to three aspects
of children's behavior in the classroom: social skills (that is, the
ability to play and interact successfully with others), mastery
skills (that is, the ability to choose, organize, attend to, and complete tasks successfully), and academic skills (that is, the ability
to understand the relationships among various characteristics
of objects and to demonstrate a range of appropriate skills). The
evaluation of BEEP focused on these three aspects of children's
classroom functioning. We selected a combination of instruments
and approaches to measure these areas, including classroom observations, teacher rating scales, and data on referrals to special services.

Classroom Observations. After analyzing the properties of
a wide range of child-related measures (Walker, Weiskopf, and
Weiss, 1975), we decided to select measures that would both
match with the purpose of BEEP and measure the functional
characteristics of children that teachers believe to be important
in the early school years. The best way of measuring such characteristics is through naturalistic observation, that is, observation

of the child's typical behavior in his or her classroom (Walker, 1973). Although costly in terms of time and effort, observational measures offer an unobtrusive snapshot of children's behavior.

Ideally, we wanted an observation instrument that would yield information about children's social behavior (such as interaction with peers) and mastery behavior (such as ability to select and complete tasks). Few such measures existed at the time that we were selecting evaluation measures. After analyzing the properties of several measures, we selected the Bronson Social and Task Skill Profile (Bronson, 1985), an observation measure that had recently been developed for use with preschool-age children and that we modified extensively for use with kindergarten and second grade children. The Social and Task Skill Profile proved to have good interrater reliability (that is, two people would rate the same child's behaviors the same way using this scale) and test-retest reliability (that is, an individual child's behavior over a short period of time appeared fairly stable using this scale).

The Social and Task Skill Profile enables the researcher to record a child's performance in planning and organizing work, interacting with others, and carrying out social interactions and mastery on school-related tasks. Both social and mastery activities can be called "executive skills" because they involve using effective strategies for choosing and reaching goals.

The profile covers eleven different types of classroom behavior. Three of these types of behavior fall under the heading of "mastery skills," and were designed to measure a child's success in planning and carrying out tasks. They include the extent to which the child (1) completed tasks successfully, (2) used appropriate "task attack" strategies, and (3) was able to sustain attention and resist distractions. Four of the behaviors are related to social skills. These behaviors involve the extent to which the child (1) had cooperative interactions with peers, (2) used effective coperative strategies, (3) was successful in influencing others, and (4) used language rather than physical force to persuade and gain the attention of others. Four other behaviors are related to how the child was involved and made use of time in the classroom setting: (1) the rate of the child's social acts or interactions,

(2) the proportion of time the child spent in social activities, (3) the proportion of time the child spent in mastery activities (these two could overlap), and (4) the proportion of time the child spent without any focused activity.

Trained observers who did not know which children had been enrolled in BEEP followed each child individually and recorded his or her behavior in the classroom for six ten-minute periods. The modified time-sampling procedure we used required that three of the observations begin at the start of a social interaction and three at the start of academic work (which we termed *mastery*). When observing the second grade children, the observers made certain that at least one of the academic tasks was a language arts task (that is, reading or writing) and one was a math activity. Each ten-minute observation was scheduled for a different day, spread out over no less than three and no more than six weeks.

The observers recorded both what the child was doing and how long he or she stayed involved. The basic approach was to watch the target child and record the child's behavior every fifteen seconds based on a series of categories. Observers were trained to a criterion of 90 percent interrater agreement with the observation supervisor, and their reliability was periodically checked.

As the system for collecting the observations was being developed and refined, we began to address the question of how to interpret the results. What should the criteria be for defining adequate or competent behavior? This was a critical and difficult decision because of the local or situation-specific nature of the observations. We had no national norms to go by, so we developed criteria through an extensive review of the several years of data we had collected with the Social and Task Skill Profile on children who had not been in BEEP. We established a set of cut-off points for determining whether a child's behavior should be considered adequate or not. For the sake of making a discernible difference from the norm, we identified natural breaks in the distribution of behaviors and set the cut-off points at least one standard deviation below the average level for that behavior. We identified about 10 to 15 percent of these children as showing difficulties or inadequate levels of school performance.

Teacher Rating Scales. Although we selected classroom observations as the major outcome measure in the evaluation of BEEP because data could be collected through observations in an unobtrusive way by unbiased independent observers, we realized that teachers' views of children's competence were also important. Indeed, remedial and other special services are often provided to a child on the recommendation of a teacher. Thus, a comprehensive definition of school competence needs to incorporate the classroom teacher's assessment of a child as a part of the evaluation effort (Swartz and Walker, 1984). Teachers and other Brookline school personnel recognized the importance of teachers' views of children and worked with BEEP's evaluation consultants to develop two rating scales, one to be used in kindergarten and another to be used in second grade.

The Kindergarten Performance Profile includes eighteen items covering performance in five main skill areas: social, work, motor, reading readiness, and numbers. (The Kindergarten and the Second Grade Performance Profiles can be obtained from the Brookline Early Education Project, c/o Superintendent of Schools, Public Schools of Brookline, 333 Washington Street, Brookline, MA 02146.) These skill areas and the specific indicators of them were designated by Brookline teachers as necessary for a child to function successfully in kindergarten. The social area covered leadership, peer interaction, communicative language, and classroom participation. Some of the items teachers rated in the work area included persistence, use of classroom time, following directions, and following classroom routines. The motor area included dressing and tying shoes, catching a ball, skipping, using a pencil, and using scissors. Reading readiness involved knowing sound-symbol relationships, recognizing isolated words, and decoding new words. The number concepts area included knowing numerals, counting objects, and counting and matching sets of objects.

Children were rated individually on each scale. Using a criterion-referenced approach, teachers compared each child to a set of specific descriptions or standards. Teachers were instructed to select the response that best described the child's current level of functioning. The categories for each item were arranged in a progression from least to most competent and represented the range of behaviors typically exhibited in kindergarten and second grade classrooms in Brookline.

In a manner similar to the design of the system of classroom observations, the rating scale was developed and refined over several years, as teachers reported information about more than 1,000 kindergarten and second grade children in Brookline (Walker, Ferb, and Swartz, 1978). We involved teachers as well as educational consultants in determining the levels of functioning necessary for successful performance in school. For example, teachers contended that kindergarten children should be able to engage in simple positive dialogue with their peers. If a teacher indicated that a child "listens but does not engage in conversation," "makes only direct responses to questions," or "uses language only to influence others' behavior," the child was considered to have a low score on that item.

We also developed an instrument to be used by second grade teachers. The Second Grade Performance Profile was similar to the kindergarten measure in that it was a criterion-based rating scale developed for use by teachers. It consists of fifteen items related to classroom skills, including items related to task persistence, behavior, use of time, peer interaction, writing and communication skills, computational skills, attitude toward reading, and reading level. Although all items required an element of judgment on the part of teachers, questions about reading level were more objective in that teachers were required to list the various reading series used in the schools to determine the reading level of a particular child. Like the kindergarten measure, the Second Grade Performance Profile was tested extensively before it was used in the evaluation of BEEP. Frequency distributions on the sample used for instrument development (over 1,000 children) indicated that the instrument flagged fewer than 25 percent of children as demonstrating inadequate performance (Swartz and Walker, 1984).

All kindergarten and second grade teachers were trained

in the use of the rating scales. Children's membership in BEEP or the comparison group was not revealed to the teachers, but some of the teachers knew that certain children had been in BEEP either because the teacher was involved in the planning for BEEP or had contact with the children's parents. (Indeed, in some cases the children themselves were glad to announce that they had been enrolled in BEEP!)

Referrals to Special Services. When the children who had participated in BEEP were in second grade, we collected information from the school records about the referrals to special services made for these children or comparison children. These services included social and psychological counseling for the child and or parents, remedial reading, speech or language therapy, math tutoring, learning disabilities tutoring, assignment to a learning center or resource room program, and any other special education services (such as placement in a special education class for part or all of the day). In addition, we asked teachers to indicate whether they had to make any modifications in the classroom for the target child and whether the child had been retained in any grade level (including kindergarten).

Results at Kindergarten

Characteristics of the BEEP and Comparison Groups. The first evaluation focused on the 132 children who had been in BEEP and entered the Brookline Public Schools for their kindergarten year. As described earlier in this chapter, the children who attended BEEP were compared to a large sample ($N = 366$) of similar children who had been born the two years prior to the initiation of BEEP. The characteristics of these two groups were similar on many, but not all, of the relevant variables. In general, the differences between the two groups appeared to offer advantages for the comparison group on demographic factors that are traditionally associated with success in school. For example, the comparison group had slightly higher percentages of girls, firstborns, families who spoke English as a first language, highly educated fathers, older mothers, mothers who completed high school, and two-parent homes. (See Table D-1 in Appendix D for a fuller comparison of the groups' characteristics.)

Although the two groups were generally comparable, even small differences between them could confound results. Therefore, the analyses were conducted both with and without adjustments for background characteristics (Pierson and others, 1983).

Analysis Strategy. Since the principal aim of BEEP was to reduce the proportion of children who lacked competence in school, we selected a strategy of analysis that would yield interpretations about the proportions of children who scored below designated criteria for specified variables. The proportion of children in the comparison group who exhibited a problem was compared to the proportion of children who had been in BEEP who exhibited the same problem. The technical term for this approach is *analysis of the odds-ratio.* If proportionately fewer participating children displayed a particular problem than children in the comparison group, the odds-ratio would be greater than 1.0. If the proportion of children in the comparison group showing the problem was smaller, the odds-ratio would be less than 1.0. For example, if 5 percent of the children who had been in BEEP fell below criterion on an outcome variable and 10 percent of the comparison children fell below criterion, then the overall rate of difficulty would be twice as high in the comparison group (10 percent versus 5 percent), and thus the odds-ratio would be favorable for BEEP.

The advantage of this approach is that it allowed us to use a statistical technique called logistic regression to adjust for the effects of background characteristics. Because the BEEP and comparison groups differed on some characteristics such as parent education that are often related to school outcomes, the odds-ratios could be adjusted statistically to take such differences into account. Although the computational details are sophisticated (odds-ratios are derived from the beta-weights in a logistic regression analysis), the results are quite easy to interpret.

Results from Classroom Observations. The results from classroom observations of children's behavior during the fall and spring of kindergarten showed significant differences favoring BEEP's participants, particularly in the areas of social skills and in use of time in the classroom. Specifically, we found that in the fall children in the comparison group had more difficulty than children in the BEEP group in using cooperative strategies with peers (comparison children were over five times as likely to have a problem in this regard) and had much higher rates of time in activities uninvolved in the classroom (comparison children were ten times as likely to exhibit a problem in this area). Overall, comparison children were almost six times as likely to have a problem in the areas observed in the classroom than children in the BEEP group.

We also carried out a series of analyses to determine whether these differences could be accounted for or influenced by any of the family background characteristics of the groups. The analyses indicated, however, that no major changes in the pattern of differences were apparent when the background variables were considered. The results were quite consistent, whether or not any background variables were included in the analysis, although adjusting for background characteristics increased the magnitude of the findings in favor of the BEEP group. We found that during the spring of the kindergarten year three times as many comparison children as children in the BEEP group displayed at least one problem in the areas of competence that we observed (as indicated by the odds-ratio of 3.29).

We conducted additional analyses to see if there was evidence of differential impact for different subgroups of children. We found that the advantages for BEEP's participants were consistent regardless of demographic factors and regardless of the level of service (A, B, or C—that is, extensive, moderate, or minimal) to which the participants had been assigned. (See Tables D-2 and D-3 in Appendix D for more information on our findings.)

Results from Teacher Ratings. The results of the teacher ratings of children's classroom performance displayed a somewhat different, but related, pattern compared to the results from the classroom observations. In terms of overall effects, there were only two significant results. The first highly favored the BEEP group in the ratings in the fall (but not in the spring) of reading readiness; comparison children were almost eight times as likely to have difficulty in this area. The second showed slight advantages for the comparison group, which was slightly less likely to demonstrate problems in the area of work skills in the spring. (See Table D-4 in Appendix D for more information on the teacher ratings.)

Although few differences in overall effects for either fall or spring occurred on the teacher ratings, such findings were modified when the background differences of the BEEP and the comparison group were considered. In contrast to the observation data, we found many more significant relationships between teacher ratings and the family background variables. Moreover, we found important interactions between participation in BEEP and demographic factors that were related to the teacher rating outcomes. These interaction effects, while not completely consistent, point to a number of advantages on the teacher ratings for children who had been in BEEP who are from subgroups traditionally associated with being at risk for school problems. These advantages occurred particularly among families in which the father had less than a high shool education (especially in ratings in the fall). In families where the father was more highly educated, the overall rate of problems was much lower, and there were generally no differences between the BEEP and the comparison groups (and occasionally slight differences favoring the comparison group).

In the fall ratings, children in the BEEP group who had fathers with less than a high school education showed lower rates of school problems on the teachers' ratings of performance in social and other skills. The rate of problems for the comparison group on social skills was over two times the rate for the BEEP group, as indicated by the odds-ratio of 2.34. On work skills, the rate for the comparison group was about 1.6 times the BEEP group's rate. On motor skills, the comparison group was almost four times as likely to have a problem, and on number skills, the rates were similar but favored the BEEP group. The rates for reading readiness skills were about the same for the two groups, and there were no statistically significant differences after adjusting for the background variables. The composite rating of kindergarten skills in the fall revealed that for children with fathers who had less than a high school education, over two times as many comparison children had difficulty in at least one area of development. In the spring teacher ratings, advantages for the BEEP group were found for a group of children traditionally seen as vulnerable for school-related problems, children from families with adolescent mothers.

Interpretation of Findings. We interpreted the results from both the observational data and the teacher ratings at kindergarten as encouraging. The observations of children's behavior in the regular classroom settings indicated that the children who had been in BEEP were in fact having many fewer problems than the comparison children. Even though at entry to kindergarten the two groups of children had no significant differences in terms of general development, based on the McCarthy Scales of Children's Abilities (mean score = 107.3 and 110.4 for the BEEP and comparison groups, respectively), the percentage of the BEEP group who were not reaching the standards considered appropriate for success in kindergarten was lower than the corresponding percentage of the comparison group on every one of the areas assessed in the classroom observations. These differences were particularly strong (and statistically significant) in the area of social skills and use of time in the classroom. The overall summary scores indicated that the rate of difficulties or problems for the comparison children (that is, presumably the "normal" rate of problems in the Brookline schools) was about six times higher than the rate for the BEEP group during the fall and about three to four times higher in the spring.

On the ratings obtained from the kindergarten teachers, the overall results were not as striking. Yet here, too, we found evidence of the positive impact of BEEP on reducing the numbers of children who were having difficulties in meeting the basic requirements for successful performance in kindergarten. The robust overall effects of BEEP found by independent observers contrasted with the more subtle indications of differential impact noted by the teachers.

The results of the observations and the teacher ratings both revealed that the advantages for the children who had been in BEEP were somewhat larger during the fall than during the spring. One interpretation of this pattern might be that the impact of BEEP — even though the population served and the links with the public schools were quite different from other early education programs — was similar to that of many preschool programs of the 1960s and early 1970s. The evaluations of those programs indicated that the positive effects demonstrated by children immediately after participating in the program often dwindled by the time the children were in the third grade (Datta, 1969). Alternatively, we hypothesized that new patterns of findings could emerge in second grade, as academic requirements on the children increased.

Results at Second Grade

The second grade evaluation was very similar to the kindergarten evaluation but had two important differences. First, we included a larger BEEP group than we used previously in the analyses and they were compared to a matched sample of peers (Bronson, Pierson, and Tivnan, 1984; Pierson, Walker, and Tivnan, 1984). This affected the type of analyses we conducted. Second, we collected data only in the spring, rather than in the fall and the spring (Bronson, Pierson, and Tivnan, 1984).

Characteristics of the BEEP and Comparison Groups. For the second grade evaluation, we collected information on 169 children who had participated in BEEP through prekindergarten. As discussed earlier in this chapter, we made a decision to gather information from children who had participated in BEEP but who were not attending Brookline Public Schools because their families had moved to nearby towns. These children were compared to other children of the same gender and in the same classroom, selected at random. Thus, the comparison group at second grade was different from that at kindergarten, but even more comparable to the BEEP sample.

The children were spread out over eighty-two classrooms in over fifty different elementary schools. The education levels of the families ranged from those with less than a high school education to those with college and postgraduate degrees. Over 10 percent of the families spoke languages other than English as their primary language. (More information on the demographic characteristics of the two groups can be found in Table D-5 in Appendix D.)

Results from Classroom Observations. The differences between the average scores of the BEEP group and the comparison group on the classroom observation behaviors showed significant advantages for the BEEP group over the comparison group in both mastery and social skills. We found the strongest effects in the mastery skills area. (See Table D-6 in Appendix D.) For example, children who had been in BEEP had higher percentages of tasks completed successfully, a higher rate of task attack strategies, and a higher percentage of time attending to tasks than the comparison children. In the social skills ratings, the BEEP group had a higher percentage of time in cooperative interaction with their peers and were more successful in influencing others.

To be consistent with the way in which we analyzed the data from the kindergarten year, we also analyzed the percentages of children who were having difficulty performing up to the standards expected of them in second grade. Again, the BEEP group showed significant advantages over the comparison group in both mastery and social skills, with the strongest effects in the mastery skills area. The BEEP group had fewer overall problems. Of the BEEP children, 14 percent had overall difficulties in classroom behavior, in contrast to 29 percent of the comparison group. In social skills, only 2 percent of the BEEP children, compared to 8 percent of the comparison children, had difficulties. Few children in either group showed problems in the use of time. The BEEP group had fewer children with problems in more than one area than the comparison group.

For example, although 25 percent of the comparison children had two or more scores below the criterion in the mastery skills area, only 12 percent of the BEEP group exhibited such problems. (See Table D-7 in Appendix D for more information on our findings.)

In further analyses, we found a distinct relationship between children's classroom competence, their mother's education, and the level of services the family had received (A, B, or C — that is, extensive, moderate, or minimal). We found that for children with highly educated mothers (usually families with relatively large resources in other areas as well), the differences between the BEEP and comparison groups were quite consistent regardless of the intensity level to which the family had been assigned (95, 90, 96, and 76 percent were classified as competent for the A, B, and C program levels and comparison group, respectively). For these families, even the minimal level of service resulted in significant advantages. For the children whose mothers were not so well educated, however, the picture is somewhat different. Only the most intensive of BEEP's levels appeared to show a significant advantage for the BEEP group over the comparison group for children whose mothers were not college graduates (78, 70, 70, and 64 percent were classified as competent for the A, B, and C program levels and comparison group, respectively). Thus, clear and important differential effects of BEEP on families began to emerge when the chidren were in second grade. We also analyzed the classroom observations of those children in the BEEP and the comparison groups who were receiving special services in second grade. Twelve percent of the BEEP children and 19 percent of the comparison children received special services during the second grade year. Although this was only a small group, we found significant differences on several critical variables from the classroom observations for those children in the BEEP group receiving special services compared to their peers receiving special services.

BEEP children who received academic remedial services had significantly fewer social difficulties than comparison group children with academic problems. Only 4 percent of BEEP children receiving special services for academic assistance had concomitant social difficulties, whereas 25 percent of the comparison children receiving special services demonstrated social difficulties. This finding suggests that although BEEP did not prevent all children from having academic difficulties, it did prevent the children who had such difficulties from developing concomitant problems in the social realm. Early education programs like BEEP may play a critical role in limiting the damaging and often extensive effects of learning difficulties.

Results from Teacher Ratings. The teachers' ratings at second grade revealed an overall low rate of problems in the areas of children's work and social skills. While differences tended to favor the BEEP group in both social and work skill ratings, the differences were not large enough to be statistically significant. (Similarly, for those children enrolled in the Brookline Public Schools, California Achievement Test Scores, while favoring the BEEP group, did not reach statistical significance. Battery total means were 70 and 68 for the BEEP and comparison groups, respectively.) However, we found one important exception to this pattern of findings. Teachers' reports of children's reading levels (using the basal reader selected for the child's reading group) indicated important differences for the children who had been in BEEP in comparison to their peers. Significantly more comparison children were considered to be reading below grade level or to be having difficulty in keeping up with the normal expectations for children in the spring of second grade. Teachers reported that 32 percent of comparison children — nearly one-third of the group — were unable to decode or comprehend stories in a 2-2 level basal reader. For the BEEP group, on the other hand, the overall rate was only 19 percent.

In further analyzing this finding, we found the results to be consistent with the results from the observations of classroom behaviors in terms of the effects of various intensity levels of BEEP. For children whose mothers were highly educated, there was only a modest relationship between the level of program resources and the achievement of "on grade level" reading performance in second grade. These children displayed relatively low rates of below-level reading performance (3, 10, and 12 percent for, respectively, the A, B, and C program levels). The comparison group baseline for children from relatively less well-educated families showed that 50 percent of the children were reading below the 2-2 level. For comparable children in BEEP who had been assigned to the minimum intensity level (C), the overall rate was quite similar (52 percent). At the moderate and intensive levels (B and A) these rates were substantially and significantly reduced to 32 and 29 percent, respectively. For this outcome, the effects of BEEP were certainly most pronounced for the children from families in which the mothers had not received a college education.

Summary of the Effects on Children

The findings we have outlined in this chapter are important and are especially valuable for those who are considering the introduction of an early education program in the public schools. First, we found that the effects of BEEP were evident in both the social skills and mastery skills areas for children in kindergarten. In the fall of the kindergarten year, the children who had been in BEEP demonstrated significantly greater strengths in social skills in contrast to the comparison group. Those strengths diminished slightly by spring, but certain aspects of mastery skills (notably task attack strategies) began to emerge as an advantage for the BEEP group at that time. By second grade, the BEEP group demonstrated strength in a full set of mastery skills (that is, completing tasks successfully, having appropriate task attack strategies, and spending time attending to tasks). These children also continued to show strength in aspects of social behavior as compared to their peers. The use of cooperative strategies was the strongest consistent social skill of the BEEP group in comparison to their peers, both in kindergarten and second grade. During both kindergarten and second grade, significantly fewer children who had been in BEEP than comparison children had difficulties in either mastery or social skills.

Had we concluded our evaluation of BEEP when the children were in kindergarten, our overall conclusion would have been that the program had its greatest effects on the social skills of children and that these effects occurred regardless of the level of program intensity. The second grade findings, however, extended our understanding of the program's effects. By second grade, the BEEP group demonstrated a more competent set of skills related to academic tasks and still demonstrated some superior skills in social interaction. For both social and mastery tasks, these children demonstrated a wider range and application of strategies than their peers. For example, whether attempting a difficult math problem or solving a dispute with a friend, they called upon a variety of approaches to bring about an adequate solution or resolution. Although the strengths in all areas of social interaction seen in the BEEP group in kindergarten were less dramatic by the time the children were in second grade, strengths in the mastery skills of the children became evident.

Why did we find different patterns of strengths at the different grade levels? We offer two possible explanations. First, the expectations for children in the classroom at kindergarten and second grade may be quite different. In kindergarten, social skills are an important focus, and much of the curriculum emphasizes the value of cooperative social interaction. By second grade, the major focus of the classroom has shifted from the children's attainment of social skills to their acquisition of basic academic skills such as reading and mathematics. In second grade, children have less opportunity for a variety of social interactions that fully test their skills in this area, whereas their academic skills are increasingly challenged. Our data may be reflecting this shift.

Second, the acquisition of adequate social skills may be a prerequisite for children's establishment of a solid set of mastery skills. Children who develop a broad foundation of social strategies and other social skills will later be able to translate these into strategies they can apply to academic tasks. Our data, therefore, may be indicating that a developmental shift in children's skills has occurred by second grade.

Based on our data, we cannot indicate which of the explanations is more accurate, but our second grade findings point to another critical program effect that would have been missed had the evaluation of BEEP stopped at kindergarten. The level of program intensity did make a difference, especially for children whose mothers were not well educated. Although few mothers of children in the BEEP program were poorly educated (that is, had not received a high school diploma), children of mothers who had not received a college education showed the greatest benefits in both classroom behaviors and reading levels *if the program had been of sufficient intensity.* A minimal intensity level was insufficient for these children to demonstrate benefits. For highly educated families, we found few differences based on program intensity.

These findings have important policy implications. The differences of program levels reflected primarily differences in home visits, parent groups, and other parent education components during the first two years of the child's life. The addition of these components appeared to have been crucial for later effects on children in the less well-educated families.

Thus, in general, BEEP was successful in increasing the number of children who demonstrated competence in the classroom. In kindergarten, this competence was demonstrated primarily in social skills; in second grade, it was displayed by mastery and academic skills. All types of families appeared to have benefited from BEEP, with the greatest benefits occurring for those with the lowest levels of education who received the more intensive levels of services. Our findings underscore the value of early education for all children and the importance of program efforts directed at outreach to families with minimal or modest educational backgrounds.

PART THREE

Implications for Policymakers

Chapter 12

A Better Education for All Children

Any time educators plan, implement, and evaluate a program, they learn a great deal more than the objective data reveal. They learn about the barriers to implementation, the way that unanticipated problems and consequences (both positive and negative) shape the actual program, and the extent to which a program requires a series of negotiations between staff and participants. BEEP was no exception. In the course of planning, implementing, and evaluating BEEP, we not only investigated several critical research questions but also grappled with a number of problems and arrived at some conclusions about the productive implementation of an early education program in the public schools. We derive some of our conclusions directly from objective data gathered over the course of BEEP's history. Others are based on more subjective impressions. Our findings about the effect of BEEP on children's competence in school point clearly to the long-term value of early education. As important as our findings are, we believe that the lessons we learned from the implementation of a school-based early education program are also valuable. In this chapter we consolidate the knowledge—both quantitative and qualitative—that we accumulated over the course of many years of implementing and evaluating this program. We also take into account how the context for early education programs has changed over the last two decades and propose a series of standards to guide the development of future programs, in light of the pressing need for early education and the current debate about the role public schools should play in the lives of very young children and their families. Finally, we discuss the adaptations we would make if BEEP were implemented today.

Clear Need for Early Education

When BEEP was begun in the 1970s, the need for early education was not as widely recognized as it is today. Questions were still being raised about the efficacy of programs that served preschool-age children. The percentage of women in the work force was relatively small, and families seldom voiced a need for child care. Moreover, many educators assumed that schools could reduce the numbers of children who failed in school by concentrating on basic skills and enforcing standards for achievement, for example, by holding children back a grade who did not perform at the expected grade level on standardized tests. Early childhood education was regarded as a luxury for those people who could afford it or as a social service for those in dire need of help.

Today, assumptions about early childhood education have changed in several respects. Unprecedented numbers of women, from both single-parent and dual-income families, have entered the work force and are desperate for high-quality and reliable child care. Moreover, it is painfully obvious that the number of children who are living in poverty and entering urban schools with little likelihood of success has reached epidemic proportions. In comparison to their peers living in more economically advantageous circumstances, such children are more likely to achieve at low levels, need special services, become teenage parents, begin using drugs, and drop out of school.

For more than a decade, the federal government, the nation's governors, state legislatures, and various professional and private interest groups have called for school reforms to address low achievement and related social problems. But new curricula, threats of greater accountability, reforms in teacher education, and more teacher participation in school decision making have not addressed the fundamental fact that schools in this country were organized to fit the perceived needs of an earlier time. Minor adjustments will not help schools motivate children who, for the first five years of their lives, have watched as much as 10,000 hours of television programs, many demonstrating antisocial role models, while spending virtually no time listening to and discussing imaginative stories read by caring adults.

Schools ignore fundamental knowledge about the importance of early childhood development by waiting until five years of age to enroll children in high-quality school programs, by failing to form effective alliances with parents, and by trying to isolate education from adequate health care and child care. Research continues to confirm the profound effect of experiences during children's first five years of life on their attitude and strategies for learning (Ramey and Campbell, forthcoming; Weikart, 1989). Research also points out that the child's parents and home environment have a great influence on the child's enthusiasm for the process of learning (Bradley and Caldwell, 1984; Bronfenbrenner, 1986; Radin, 1981; Rutter, 1985), and evidence is accumulating on the value of productive alliances between parents and schools (Henderson, 1987). Furthermore, research has demonstrated that consistent health and medical care ("primary prevention") can be a critical factor in limiting costs and in preventing or alleviating conditions that may permanently restrict the child's ability to learn (Chamberlin, 1987; Upshur, 1990). In an era of demands for zero-based budgeting (that is, each program being funded on its own merits rather than on historical funding levels), the neglect of the early childhood years by the public schools is difficult for anyone to justify.

Preschool and parent education programs are a sound investment for schools to make for all children and families because such programs can have a fundamental impact on the way children approach learning. Our results indicate that, in comparison to their peers, children who had participated in BEEP functioned more competently in the elementary school classroom. They applied more effective strategies to problems; they were more organized in the way they set about completing tasks; they were better able to develop positive relationships with other children; and they demonstrated better skills in one of the most important academic skills of early elementary school — reading. The findings from BEEP, when added to the array of findings about the long-term success of other early education programs like the Perry Preschool Project (Berreuta-Clement and others, 1984), the Yale Project (Seitz, Rosenbaum, and Apfel, 1985), and others (Lazar and Darlington, 1982; Ramey and Campbell, 1984), point directly to the value of early education in helping children become students who value learning and who function well throughout their lives in school.

Rather than simply building on the results of prior studies, the BEEP findings, in fact, suggest the mechanism by which the success noted in other studies occurs. The children who had attended BEEP, although not more intelligent than other children in the classroom, approached tasks in ways that made them more successful learners in second grade. Such success can stimulate a child to define himself or herself as a learner and school as a positive environment. Perhaps that is why the longitudinal studies of early education find few differences between participants and nonparticipants on intelligence tests yet demonstrate such powerful results in preventing school dropout and the need for later remedial services.

The benefits of enhancing competence for the individual child are apparent, but are not limited only to that child. Children learn from their peers, especially in classrooms in which active, cooperative learning occurs (as contrasted with passive listening). All children benefit if the number of children who model independent and cooperative behavior in a school setting increases.

Early education programs are cost effective. Schools can make fairly reasonable estimates of the savings they will incur if fewer children enter school unprepared to learn and thus fewer children need remedial services. Furthermore, if we assume, consistent with our findings, that in a class of twenty-five children the number having difficulty can be reduced from six (that is, approximately 25 percent) to three, the amount of teacher attention and quality of instruction will be enhanced for the other nineteen children in the class.

Parents play a critical role in influencing the course their children's lives will take in school. Involvement in an early education program can help parents become advocates for their children. We found that parents in BEEP anticipated that their children would be successful in school and attributed the success less to BEEP's direct effects on their children and more to the insights they had gained as parents participating in the project. Individual parents gained these insights in different ways — through talking with the home visitor, watching developmental assessments, observing children in the classroom, or talking informally to staff. Perhaps the most convincing evidence of the confidence parents gained as advocates for their children was the frequency with which they initiated contacts with second grade teachers about children's progress in school. Three years after their last contact with BEEP, the parents were still actively invested in their children's lives in the classroom.

Although all parents need support and encouragement in their role as parents, some need more than others. Many parents view schools and teachers either as "the experts" or as unapproachable, perhaps based on their own school experiences. Some parents need support in building the confidence to form an alliance with schools and to expand their children's access to learning. We found that outreach to parents with limited resources and educational backgrounds, especially through home visits during infancy, was necessary to involve them in their children's education. Home visits are relatively expensive when compared to a center-based model, but we believe they are crucial in supporting and involving hard-to-reach families.

Introduction of Programs into Different Communities

Despite the public's increased awareness of the potential benefits of early education, a debate has lingered regarding the principal sponsorship of the program. In general, private childcare providers believe they should serve as lead agents; teacher unions argue for the schools; public health and mental health agencies offer themselves as leaders; and nonprofit groups, such as community action agencies, that operate Head Start sites maintain that they have the most expertise. The participants in the debate seem unwilling or unable, given the vested interests involved, to reach a consensus.

Because the capabilities and resources of institutions vary considerably from one community to the next, each community needs to determine its own lead agency and the best resources for supporting an early education program. We have found the set of guidelines presented in the following list to be useful in introducing an early education program into a community.

1. The mayor (or superintendent of schools) appoints an early education advisory committee. This group, representing a cross section of the community, is charged with conducting a needs assessment to identify gaps, redundancies, and capabilities of early childhood services in the community.

2. An early education advisory committee formulates and presents a statement of philosophy and goals for formal adoption by the school board or other appropriate body. (Resource E is a copy of the statement adopted by the Brookline School Committee as an illustration.)

3. The school board (or other lead agency) hires a fully qualified director to work with the advisory committee and initiate operations, including to plan specific program offerings, develop collaborations among professionals in the community, secure funding, hire staff, recruit families, and plan evaluation for a pilot program.

4. Based on the results of the pilot program, the director and the advisory committee submit recommendations to the sponsoring body to continue, discontinue, modify, or expand the program's scope and focus.

Regardless of what agency takes the lead, representatives from various sectors, such as public schools, public and mental health agencies, community action agencies, and Head Start and private preschools and day-care providers, must participate in the planning to aid coordination and prevent duplication of existing programs.

Public Schools as Sites for Early Education Programs

If the public schools can develop and implement a developmentally appropriate and comprehensive program, they are a particularly suitable agent for communitywide early education. Public schools offer universal access, continuity between programs, links to other resources, and mechanisms for funding.

Universal Access. The open enrollment policies of public schools are intended to ensure that every child has a sufficient opportunity to obtain a free, high-quality education. Today, however, it is obvious to school personnel that, from the outset, many children lack the skills that are prerequisites to effective functioning in a classroom setting. Without intervention, these children are unlikely to experience success in school. A variety of strategies — none particularly successful — have been devised to cope with this problem.

Some children who are eligible for kindergarten, but relatively young compared to their classmates, are held out of school for a year so they can be among the oldest in their grade. Other children, who start school with their peers, are retained a second year in kindergarten or in the primary grades. Still other children are assigned to a "transition class" for a year either before or after kindergarten to gain the necessary skills or behavioral control to move on in the school curriculum. Each of these approaches raises some questions about universal access and cost effectiveness, especially if an early education program could better address the issues of maturation and readiness without the child experiencing the stigma of failure.

In addition to these strategies, a number of federal and state policies are designed to ensure that children who are at present risk of failure in school receive some help before they are five years old. Head Start, for instance, is regarded by many people as one of the most successful social programs in this country for children from low-income families. Chapter I, also designed for children who live in poverty, is aimed at alleviating these children's documented learning deficits. Public Law 99-457 mandates that preschool children with special education needs receive educational and related services. Unfortunately, these well-intentioned categorical programs fall short of providing equal educational opportunity for all children. None of them offers children who are at the greatest risk for failure in school the optimal educational experience of functioning in a group of normally developing peers and of receiving services without being stigmatized as "moderately handicapped" or "low income." If public schools began supporting early childhood programs for all members of a community, children with disabilities and children from homes in which education is not a priority could benefit enormously from being in school with children from their community who demonstrate a variety of skills and interests. Certainly we found this to be true in BEEP.

Continuity Between Early Education Programs and the Primary Grades. Early education can be a sound investment for a community only if connections are forged between the early education program and the primary grades. If the early education program and the elementary school operate in isolation from each other, early gains made by children may go unrecognized.

Public schools are in a unique position to take advantage of many opportunities for continuity between programs. Discussions between a child's preschool teacher and parents and the child's prospective kindergarten or elementary school teacher can help the child's new teacher to appreciate his or her approach to learning and, thus, make the child's transition to the new classroom as positive as possible. Moreover, the alliances forged between the parents and the preschool teacher could begin to be transferred to the new teacher.

Collaboration between the preschool and the elementary school program can serve another function as well. If school principals and teachers attend in-service activities as part of the initiation of preschool programs (as they did at BEEP), the school's expectations of young learners may be transformed. Indeed, we found that the introduction of early education focused the entire school community on more effective applications of research to educational practice. When an early education program is organized around what is known about how young children learn, it follows that other school programs could also be based on what is known about how children of different ages and from different cultures learn. Early education can be the impetus for a reevaluation of many traditional school practices such as tracking, grade retentions, double-session kindergarten, teacher-dominated instruction, and unsupervised homework that are not as effective as once thought.

Links to Community Resources. Because of mandates for special education screening and services, public schools have gained experience in working with health and social service agencies. Many school health programs collaborate with other agencies for sensory screening, nutritional counseling, drug and alcohol abuse education, sex education, child abuse and neglect concerns, and other matters that affect children's ability to learn. Furthermore, schools are increasingly being used as centers for quasi-educational programs such as extended day programs, summer camps, and senior citizen groups. Thus, many schools already have relationships with other community resources and serve as a focus for a range of community activities.

Mechanisms for Funding. Funding early education programs is often difficult. Parents, especially single mothers with young children, are the most impoverished group in our society. They cannot adequately pay for a program by themselves. We charged a sliding-scale fee for the daily prekindergarten and extended child care components of BEEP, but even then, the program was not self-supporting. The communities most in need of public education and human support services, like the families, are least able to afford them.

Since states are empowered by the Constitution to set educational policy, state support for local education offers the most realistic option for financing early education programs. If we accept the premise that all children are entitled to equal educational opportunity and that by starting school at five years old some children are at a significant disadvantage, then support for public education for the years before kindergarten should follow. If education is truly a national priority, then federal incentives should be offered to encourage states to support preschool education. In some states, such as Minnesota and Missouri, funding incentives are already available to school districts that offer certain forms of parent education. State governments must modify their aid formulas by incorporating per-pupil reimbursements for early childhood education at the same rate that reimbursements are calculated for older students. If funds beyond the reimbursements are required, then modest parent fees plus local public and private funds must be sought. We maintain, however, that the state reimbursements and other public support should be subject to compliance with standards of quality, for only through adherence to such standards can the promise of early childhood programs be realized.

Recommended Program Standards

The planners of an early education program must anticipate the inevitable pitfalls in implementing such programs. Prompted by the urgency of the need, the unselfish commitments of professionals who work with families and young children, and the willingness of chief administrators to approve programs if local costs are negligible, some program planners will be tempted to embark on early education programs prematurely before they have clarified their plans or gained sufficient support and resources. We believe, however, that unless it is possible to set and maintain certain high program standards, it may be less harmful to children to delay a program rather than to create unrealistic expectations that cannot be met. Through both self-assessment and more objective evaluations, program planners should determine if their programs consistently have clear goals, a committed leadership, a well-qualified staff, the participation of parents, a developmentally oriented curriculum, and comprehensive and preventive services.

Clear Goals. A clear statement of purpose is necessary to focus the energies that staff and parents invest in the program. Early education means different things to different people. Some might, for example, expect an emphasis on early reading skills, whereas others might desire a program that stresses social skills. In BEEP, we focused on the overall goal of increasing the percentage of children who function competently in school. Frankly, although we started with a general notion of what "school competence" meant, we collaborated at length with elementary school teachers and other staff members of BEEP to develop operational definitions (that is, descriptions that could be measured) of competence. We all worked hard to determine, for example, that a competent child could select, attend, and complete tasks independently as well as make friends and resolve disputes with peers. In determining how to describe competence, we had to choose among competing priorities and reconcile different viewpoints. Eventually, we achieved a strong consensus about the goals we set and support for them, at least partially because we involved teachers. Different early childhood programs might state their goals differently, but if the goals are clear to everyone, the program is more likely to be well coordinated and appropriately evaluated.

Committed Leadership. The superintendent of schools, as chief administrative officer of a program, and the school committee, as the local policy-making body, must understand the goals and provide unequivocal support for a school-based program. The competition for scarce resources is so keen and the pressures for broadening of goals so strong that if the superintendent and the school committee are not committed to the program, interested parents and school staff should collaborate with a capable community agency that can take the lead role in delivering early education.

In addition to the support of the superintendent and the school committee, a successful program needs the participation of a broad-based advisory group. The group must reflect the multicultural diversity of the participating families as well as the professional and nonprofessional interests in the community. The advisory committee, if well chosen, serves an important role in maintaining credibility and support within the community as well as in providing expertise on various aspects of program development and implementation.

The advisory committee should take on the difficult task of anticipating and providing a mechanism for resolving ethical issues. Some of the ethical questions we faced at BEEP are likely to emerge in other communities, such as: How can we distinguish between acceptable and inappropriate (or even harmful) differences in child-rearing practices, given different cultural mores and life-style choices? At what point and in what way should potential (or even slightly unusual) concerns about a child's development be conveyed to parents? Should a parent's educational background make a difference in what we tell the parent? How much information about a child or family should be given to the elementary schools or collaborating community agencies?

Well-Qualified Staff. To the participating families, the staff members personify the program. The most carefully conceived plans will not succeed unless parents feel that the staff empathize with them and appreciate their child as a unique individual. The program's teachers must have experience in early childhood programs and the ability to convey useful information about child development and parenting issues in a non-threatening way that empowers parents rather than makes them dependent or resentful. Staff also need to be sensitive to cultural interpretations of child-rearing practices. Hiring teachers from the variety of backgrounds represented in the community and encouraging them to observe and discuss the intersections between culture, teaching, and parenting ensure their sensitivity to cultural issues.

Professionalism among early childhood teachers must be fostered, recognized, and compensated. Otherwise, as frequently occurs, the program will be weakened by high staff turnover and low morale. We recognize that at least 80 percent of the cost of any education or human service program is made up of staff salaries, and that high staff salaries mean a high overall budget that makes a program less attractive to policymakers. Quality early childhood programs require teachers who are well trained in child development, dedicated (but not to a point of self-sacrifice beyond that demanded of other professions), and capable of providing invigorating, yet consistent and stable, environments for young children. Teachers deserve to be well compensated for their work; early childhood teachers should be paid at the same salary level as their elementary school colleagues.

Participation of Parents. Enrollment and continued participation by families in an early education program depend largely on two factors: trusting relationships between families and staff and accessibility of the facilities to families. Personal recruitment by currently enrolled (and satisfied) families or staff is the most effective recruitment strategy. If families must travel a distance to reach the school, then reliable transportation must be provided for them. Even then, the opportunities for informal communication between teachers and parents may be lost.

Early education is effective only if the parents are engaged in a concurrent parent education program. Parents must be well informed about the nature of children's development and learning, in general, and their child's development, in particular, if they are to complement the school curriculum at home and learn to be effective advocates for their child in subsequent years in school. The empowerment of parents as successful advocates for their children will require more outreach for some parents than for others. Home visits, especially during the infant year, may be necessary to engage the participation and trust of parents who are poorly educated and who have not established a tradition of relating successfully to schools.

The proper approach, we believe, is a partnership in which parents and teachers each bring useful information and insights to discussions of the child and develop appropriate educational strategies. An early education program should provide a combination of information and support to parents while avoiding, at one extreme, a model that fosters dependency and, at the other extreme, a laissez-faire model that implies that all approaches to child rearing and teaching are equally valid.

Developmentally Oriented Curriculum. Although many curriculum models exist, we maintain that the most appropriate models for early childhood programs view the child (as well as the parent and the teacher) as an active, continually developing learner. The best curricula offer extensive opportunities for the child to learn how to plan and execute tasks, solve social and cognitive problems using a range of strategies, extend language development, and engage in experiential learning (for example, by collecting data, developing manageable experiments, and playing roles). Rigid time blocks and artificial subject areas should be avoided in favor of time planned according to the activity and needs of the children. Curricula should be organized according to interdisciplinary themes that integrate learning experiences. As described by the guidelines for developmental education issued by the National Association for the Education of Young Children (presented in Chapter Three), this approach is distinguished from the diluted elementary school or "academic" kindergarten approach, with its emphasis on worksheets and other seatwork.

To develop a curriculum, teachers working in a particular classroom must continually think about and discuss developmentally appropriate activities for the children in that classroom. By maintaining a profile of goals for each child, teachers can analyze the array of each child's strengths and interests and build upon these through the curriculum to expand other areas of the child's development. The profile of goals and curriculum plans should be accessible to parents. Moreover, parents should be expected to visit the classroom to observe and discuss with the teachers their child's activities as well as the teachers' strategies to extend their child's growth in the classroom setting. Teachers and parents also can discuss the possible applications to the home of certain aspects of the curriculum for a particular skill or interest of the child.

Comprehensive and Preventive Services. One attribute of successful programs is that they are comprehensive and do not operate within traditional professional boundaries (Schorr, 1988). The health and education of young children cannot be separated as if they are isolated, independent components of children's development. We found that periodic health and developmental assessments can yield educationally relevant findings, including the early detection of chronic ear infections and hearing loss, prevention of unnecessary delay in language development, referral for orthopedic concerns, early detection of anemia and lead paint poisoning, identification of amblyopia and other vision concerns, and the early recognition of neglect and abuse.

Periodic health and developmental assessment cannot be replaced by a one-time screening, a screening that we found to be unreliable. We found that the group of children identified as showing unusual developmental growth at any one point during the first few years of life was substantially different from the group identified at another point. The main exception to this conclusion proved to be the children with major attentional deficits, who tended to show consistent profiles over several examination periods.

Pediatricians and other health professionals, when properly trained, can contribute to the monitoring and treatment of educationally relevant health concerns. Furthermore, the availability of a health monitoring component tends to increase family participation in early education. The assessments, individual conferences, and referrals for specialized care in BEEP represented tangible benefits to families who were unaccustomed to personalized health care.

Recommended Adaptations to BEEP

If we were starting an early childhood program today, we would try to build on the knowledge we gained from BEEP but would adapt the program to the realities and needs of today's families. We would also address certain concerns that were never adequately resolved in BEEP. In this final section, we reflect on those changes.

Participation of Parents. Because BEEP was designed as a research project, it operated under certain constraints. First, parents were randomly assigned to certain levels of participation. This type of random assignment within a program caused considerable friction. Parents who were assigned to the level of minimal services were frustrated when they learned that their neighbors who were assigned to more extensive levels of participation could enjoy so many more opportunities. At one point during the program, parents assigned to the minimal level initiated their own discussion group. Such competition within the program for resources does not foster positive growth.

Second, BEEP did not involve parents in as many stages of program development and implementation as we would recommend. The research nature of BEEP brought with it many experts, all desiring to have an effect on the program's design. Parents, although clearly the focus of the program, were seldom included in discussions about budgeting, hiring staff (with occasional exceptions, such as the hiring of the bilingual staff), or developing the curriculum. We recommend that future programs offer parents a more collaborative role.

Finally, BEEP was essentially a program designed for mothers and children. Although this was not intentional—for example, home visitors suggested to parents that visits could occur at times when fathers were at home—it was often the case that fathers were simply on the periphery. Even in homes in which both parents were employed, the mothers usually took the primary responsibility for child rearing and education, while the fathers served more of a gatekeeping function, getting involved at major decision points or crises. At the request of some fathers, we did form a fathers' discussion group, but participation in it was often erratic. Although we do not have a successful answer to the question of how to include fathers in early education programs, we hope that future programs will be creative in including fathers and will not assume that mothers alone affect the educational lives of children.

Education of Parents. Parents repeatedly informed us that they found the parts of the program that were quite individualized, such as the home visits and the conferences after diagnostic exams, to be the most valuable. On the other hand, parent groups (that is, discussion groups of particular topics) were less well received and appear to have been the least effective program component. Parents preferred the more informal opportunities for getting to know each other. We would recommend that programs take advantage of informal events for allowing parents to forge their own relationships with each other. Those parents who wish to form an interest or support group should be offered resources such as a place to meet, materials to use, or staff to discuss particular issues.

Role of Minorities. Given the realities of U.S. society today, the majority of policymakers who will decide the merits and focus of early childhood programs will be Anglo men, and the majority of participating parents will be minority women. The risk of paternalistic biases in the programs is great. We hope that the complexion of the policy-making community changes, but we also realize that such changes will take some time. In BEEP, we consciously made a decision to select program and office staff to reflect the ethnic composition of participants, to make available translations for all written communications, and to choose initial staff who were parents themselves. Although the staff members represented the range of ethnic groups served in BEEP, the administrative leadership and pediatricians did not. We would recommend that future programs make extraordinary efforts to recruit minority staff at all levels of the program's organization.

Interdisciplinary Collaboration. The collaboration of staff members of Children's Hospital with BEEP's staff was a strong advantage for the program. The services provided by the physicians, nurses, and social workers were highly valued by parents. In addition, the interdisciplinary staff meetings, which focused on coordinating the education and health needs of specific children, were mutually informative to all the professionals involved. Moreover, the developmental assessment procedures developed by the pediatric team have been widely disseminated and now enhance the diagnostic capabilities of significant numbers of physicians. But, as we mentioned in Chapter Nine, these interdisciplinary alliances were forged slowly and sometimes were fraught with tension. As a result, we did not learn as much from one another as we could have learned. Other programs should anticipate tension between professionals from different disciplines and develop methods of defusing it rapidly. Easing tensions will require the programs to have methods of establishing trust among professionals from different fields and a clear and common focus.

Full-Day Options. Although BEEP was implemented at a time before the current surge of women with young children appeared in the work force, current programs must take the working lives of both parents into account. For example, the one-half day per week of playgroup that toddlers at BEEP enjoyed would clearly not satisfy the needs of many working families with toddlers today. The extended day option that BEEP offered for the prekindergarten program would need to be the norm, not the exception, for most children. Also, the program would need to operate on a year-round basis and not be limited to the school year. Parents participating in a program like BEEP today would probably be interested in the options the program offered for child care. Although parents need options in their choice of early childhood education arrangements, children do not benefit from shifts of group size, composition, staff, and routine from day to day. Therefore, the options made available must be ones that serve both the needs of the child and the needs of the parents.

Periodic Monitoring. In BEEP, the schedule for frequent health and developmental exams was intentionally gauged to learn as much as possible about the children's development, rather than to provide ongoing, cost-effective monitoring. We learned that the monitoring should be neither one-time nor delayed until shortly before the child enters kindergarten. We advise an initial developmental exam when a child is six months old. Observation and discussion of this exam can heighten the parents' awareness of the rapid learning taking place in all areas of the infant's development and of the influential role that parents and other caretakers have in that development. Any concerns can be referred to a specialist and further observation or interventions can be recommended.

Beyond the initial exam and referrals, assuming a child has regular primary health care, developmental exams should be offered at least twice before the child enters kindergarten, to focus on specific educational skills that can be nurtured during the prekindergarten program. The ages of thirty-six months and forty-eight months seem most appropriate for this purpose. Moreover, objective information about the child's functioning in the classroom should be provided as part of the exam process. If parents know about their child's profile of skills and interests and know about approaches to enhance home and school collaboration, the child is more likely to be successful in school.

Coordination with Categorical Programs. Programs serving heterogeneous groups of children must be coordinated with programs providing intensified attention and outreach to children who are most in need of help. In most communities today, some families who can afford excellent early education opportunities for their children are able, with determination, to locate and secure those opportunities. But only a small portion of the families who lack such means are able to participate in analogous publicly supported programs. Resources must be maximized by coordinating opportunities available through provisions such as Chapter I, Public Law 99-457, Even Start, and Head Start with funds allocated by state and local sources. In addition, parents who can afford to pay should be expected to subsidize the more expensive program components, such as full-day options for children.

Teenage Parents. One of our society's most troubling problems today is the explosion in the rate of births to teenage parents. While we had some experience in working with adolescent parents at BEEP, the magnitude of the challenge has far surpassed anticipated levels. If early education programs and secondary schools are coordinated, young mothers and fathers in school can stay in school, improve their own educational status, and reduce the likelihood of repeated pregnancies during their adolescent years. Indeed, operating early education programs from the high school, rather than from the elementary school, is one option that many communities are exploring for school-based early education. Thus, one adaptation that we recommend is a priority in shaping future early education programs to the developmental learning styles and needs of adolescent parents.

Bilingual Education. Due to limited prior experience and a paucity of research on bilingual early education, BEEP designed its own bilingual prekindergarten program. The need for programs that serve families who speak little English is more prevalent now, especially in urban areas, than it was when BEEP began. At the same time, much more is known about the way in which children acquire first and second languages. It is important that future programs collaborate with parents in determining the goals and strategies with respect to bilingual education for young children.

Some Final Thoughts

Communities invest relatively little in the education of children before five years of age. Yet early education clearly produces future benefits for those who participate. BEEP has demonstrated that one of the important effects of early education is that children become better students: they can plan and organize strategies for the cognitive and social problems they encounter in the classroom. We found that as a result of early education, children approached learning in a more productive way. Such differences may have profound effects on the course of their lives in school.

In the final analysis, however, the decision to move forward with early education programs should not be based solely on whether such programs can produce future returns or on gaining a fair share of the education dollar. The decision should be based on the affirmation that the quality of life during the first five years is as important as during any other period of an individual's life. A responsible society takes the necessary and proper steps to care for its children, not only because they will become valuable citizens but because they are valued members of the human community.

Questions and Issues Parents Have Raised

The Brookline Early Education Project

1. Why was the program started?
2. What services are available?
3. Why are there three program levels?
4. How are families assigned to a program level?
5. If I think the services available at my level are not appropriate for my family or for me, what can I do about it?
6. Who are the personnel and what are their qualifications?
7. Can I drop in any time?
8. Will I find other people there like me?
9. What do I do if I need help?
10. What tests and examinations will be done on my child?
11. What records will be kept?
12. Who else has access to them?
13. What happens if you find something wrong with my child?
14. Do you ever communicate with anybody else about my child?

Anger and Aggression

1. My son gets angry and hits me or his sister; how should I respond?

Source: Yurchak with others, 1975.

199

2. What outlets are there for my two-year-old's anger?
3. Sometimes my child gets angry and throws food; what can I do about it?
4. Lately my child "fights" me when I dress, feed, or otherwise restrain him. Why does this happen? Is this hostility?
5. If my child lies on the floor and screams, how should I respond?
6. My child holds his breath when I don't do what he wants me to do. Is it dangerous? What can I do about it? Is this behavior unusual?
7. Sometimes when children visit my child, he becomes very aggressive. He hits and bites the other children. How should I deal with this behavior?

Child Care and Separation

Short-term separations
1. Who should care for the baby?
2. Does father's care matter?
3. How do I select a baby-sitter?
4. Why does my baby cry when someone else holds her or cares for her?
5. Do babies prefer men or women to care for them?
6. Are men or women more frightening to babies?
7. Should strangers care for the baby?
8. How often should the baby be left with a baby-sitter?
9. How long should the baby be left with a baby-sitter?
10. Is it better to have one regular baby-sitter or several different ones?
11. Will my baby prefer her baby-sitter to me?
12. How do I know what's really going on while I'm gone?
13. If I have a choice, is it better to leave the baby in her own home or in someone else's?

Long-term separations
14. Is it all right to leave my baby if I have to go away for several days?
15. How long can I stay away?

16.   How do I prepare him for my absence?
17.   What behavior should I expect when I get back?

Regular short-term separations
18.   What are the effects of day care?
19.   How do I select a day-care program?
20.   If I must be gone often, is it better to leave him with relatives?
21.   How do I let the sitter know what I want him to do?
22.   How do I let the day-care center know what I expect?
23.   How will I ever know what they expect of my child at the day-care center?
24.   Is there a good or bad time to start leaving my baby regularly?

Crying

1.   What should I do when my baby cries?
2.   Should I respond to every cry?
3.   How soon should I respond?
4.   What if I let her cry a little?
5.   At what age does a baby understand that her cries will cause a parental response?
6.   Can you "spoil" a young baby?
7.   Is it harmful for a baby to cry? For a long time?
8.   Why does my baby cry?
9.   Is it good for a baby to cry once in a while?
10.   My baby whines a lot and it bothers me. How should I handle it?
11.   She never cries with her father, only me. Why?
12.   My husband (or parents or parents-in-law) will never let her cry but I do. Does it matter if we do things differently?

Feeding and Nutrition

1.   What are the relative advantages of breast feeding and bottle feeding for baby? For mother?
2.   Should breast fed babies receive bottle supplements? How often?

3. How do you know the baby is getting enough to eat?
4. My baby likes to go to sleep with a bottle. Should I let him?
5. What is bottle mouth?
6. Which is better, demand or scheduled feeding?
7. Who establishes feeding schedules?
8. Can you modify a baby's feeding schedule? How?
9. When should he be weaned?
10. Should he be weaned to a bottle or a cup?
11. How do I wean him?
12. Which are better, homemade or prepared baby foods?
13. What's wrong with prepared baby foods?
14. When should I start my baby on solids? Which ones?
15. Are there any foods to be careful of?
16. Can my baby taste the difference in foods?
17. How can I be sure he's getting a balanced diet?
18. When can he start feeding himself?
19. How do I encourage him to feed himself?
20. He used to be such a good eater but now he's just not interested. Why? What shall I do?
21. Should I make him finish his meat?
22. Should I regulate the amount of sweets he eats? How?
23. Should I give him food as a reward for good behavior?
24. Should I punish him by withholding a treat he likes?
25. Should he have snacks? How many? When?
26. What are some good snacks for children?

Group Experience

1. When will she be ready for playgroup or preschool?
2. How do I know when she is ready?
3. What kinds of group experiences are available?
4. How do I judge which is best for her?
5. How do I know what is expected of me and my child?
6. How do I let the others know what I expect?

Health and Related Issues

1. How often should I consult my pediatrician?
2. When should my child start to have his teeth brushed?

3. When can he brush his teeth by himself?
4. When should I take him to the dentist?

Independence, Autonomy, and Negativism

1. All of a sudden my baby wants to do things by herself. Why?
2. Why does she say "no" so often?
3. I used to be able to take her everywhere, now she's impossible! Why?
4. Why does she suddenly want to do all the things she's not supposed to do?
5. It almost seems as if she's testing me. Could this be true?
6. What shall I do when she refuses to do what I ask her to?
7. What shall I do when she purposely does what she knows she should not?

Language

1. Why is it important that I talk to my child?
2. Does he know I'm talking to him?
3. When will he understand what I say?
4. When should he learn a second language?
5. If I am bilingual, which language should I use with my child?
6. If my child speaks only Spanish at home, how will he do in school? How will he learn English?
7. How can I preserve my mother tongue if he hears only English at school?
8. What kinds of language experiences are necessary for my child?
9. When should I start to read stories to him?
10. How should I talk with my child?
11. Is it important that I
    label objects
    expand his utterances?
    interpret his utterances?
    answer his questions?

Mother's Well-Being

1. Why am I tired all the time? How can this be helped?
2. Why am I so moody? How can this be helped?
3. Is it natural for me to want to get away from my baby?
4. Sometimes I don't even like her. Is there something wrong with me?
5. How can I get some time to myself?
6. It frightens me to have so much responsibility. Do other parents feel this way?
7. Sometimes my husband seems jealous of the baby. Is this natural?

Pacifiers

1. Why does my baby want (need) a pacifier?
2. Should my baby use a pacifier?
3. How much should he use one?
4. When should he be able to give it up?

Parental Concerns

1. Why am I sometimes scared (anxious or angry) about the baby?
2. What will the delivery be like?
3. Will I really be able to take care of my baby?
4. Does it matter what kind of medication I have at the delivery?
5. Who can I talk about this with? When should I talk about it?
6. Will the hospital tell me if the baby is not all right?
7. When will I know that it's time to go to the hospital?
8. Will it hurt?
9. Should my husband be there when I deliver?
10. What about rooming-in? Are there advantages for my baby?

Protection Against Weather and Other Natural Forces

1. How do you dress a baby during very hot weather?
2. How do you dress a baby during very cold weather?

3. Are there special safety measures necessary for hot or cold weather? What are they?
4. Should I use suntan or wind lotions on my baby's skin?
5. Should I let my baby nap outside?
6. How important is it that he play outside?

Restriction and Restriction Devices

1. When should I use a playpen?
2. What's wrong with using a playpen?
3. How much is too much of a playpen?
4. Should I use a harness?
5. Are car seats necessary?
6. My child hates to use a car seat. What should I do?
7. What kind of car seat should I get?
8. Now that she is walking, how should I protect my fragile things from my baby?
9. How should I protect my baby from dangerous things?

Safety

1. What steps should I take to safety proof my home?
2. What are the most frequent accidents that children have?
3. When will I be able to trust my baby to stay away from things that might hurt him?
4. What houseplants are dangerous?
5. What outdoor plants are dangerous?
6. What are some safe outdoor play experiences my child will enjoy?
7. Are mosquito bites dangerous? What about bees? Spiders? Others?

Setting Limits

1. When will I have to start setting limits for my child?
2. I don't want to be mean. Why do I have to set limits for her when she is so little?
3. How do I know he understands the limits I set?

4. Should I give her a reason for the limits I set?
5. How should I enforce the limits I set?
6. What should I do if she doesn't do what I expect her to do?
7. Are there times when it's all right for rules to be broken?

Sex Role Identification and Expectations

1. When will my child know he's a boy (or she's a girl)?
2. Should my girl play with "boys' toys"? Why?
3. Should my boy play with "girls' toys"? Why?
4. My little boy likes to wear nail polish. Is this unusual? Should I let him?
5. My little girl likes to play such rough games. You'd think she was a boy. Should I discourage this?
6. My little boy likes to wear his big sister's clothes. Should I let him?
7. How does a child learn that he is a boy (or she is a girl)?
8. How and when will my child know the difference between men and women?

Siblings

1. How should I prepare my older child for the baby's arrival?
2. How should I start to prepare him?
3. How will my older child feel about the baby?
4. How will I know whether or not he is troubled?
5. Who needs my attention most: my older child or my baby?
6. What are some ways to help my older child understand we still love him?
7. Should we let our older child help care for the baby?
8. Why does my older child have so many accidents when he's near the baby?

Sleeping

1. How much sleep does a baby (child) need?
2. When will she sleep through the night?
3. Can I help her establish or modify a sleep pattern?

4. Does a baby know the difference between night and day? How?
5. Should bedtime rituals be encouraged?
6. Should I put my baby to bed with a bottle?
7. Why has she suddenly started to wake up at night when she used to sleep right through?
8. How many naps does she need? When?
9. Can a baby sleep too much?

Social Development

With adults
1. When will he recognize me?
2. Why is he suddenly afraid of some people he has seen often?
3. Why do new faces frighten him?
4. How aware is he of my moods and feelings?
5. Should I try to conceal my moods and feelings?
6. Does it hurt a baby if he hears us arguing?

With others
7. When will she want to play with other children?
8. When she is with other children she doesn't want to play with them. Why?
9. When other children come to play at our house she is just impossible! Why?

Stimulation

1. Why does my new baby need things to look at?
2. What playthings are appropriate now?
3. Why does my baby need objects to play with?
4. How do I know when a toy is appropriate?
5. What kinds of stimulation are important?

Toilet Training

1. Which comes first, bowel or bladder control?
2. When should I start?

3. How do I know my baby is ready?
4. How do I do it?
5. My child is so active. Will she be harder to train?
6. Can I train my baby around my work schedule?
7. What about the notion of training in twenty-four hours?
8. What if I make a mistake?
9. Should I reward my baby when she "performs"?

Traveling with the Baby

1. What should I know about traveling with my baby?
2. Is a baby easier to travel with at some ages than others?
3. What should I take with me when I travel with my baby?

Questions to Structure Home Visits

I. 0–3 MONTH PERIOD
   A. Standard questions for all parents
      1. The baby's growth and development
         a. What is he doing now?
         b. What new things have you noticed him doing?
         c. Have you noticed him, for example, looking at objects?
      2. The baby's interests
         a. What does she enjoy doing?
         b. What does she enjoy playing with?
            1. How does she play with it?
            2. What does she do with it?
         c. Where does she stay when you are busy?
         d. Where does she enjoy being?
         e. Are there any things she does not like to do?
         f. Are there any objects she does not like to play with?
      3. The baby's environment
         a. Are there things in his crib for him to enjoy?
            1. Are they placed so he can see them?
            2. Do they move easily or make a gentle noise?

Source: Yurchak with others, 1975.

209

4. Parents' questions, interests, and concerns
   a. Do you have any questions about the baby or about what she is doing that you want to talk about?
   b. Do you have any questions about what she will be doing soon?
   c. Do you have any concerns (or worries or complaints) that you want to talk about?
   d. Are there any interesting things that you have observed (or seen her doing) that you want to talk about?

B. Areas of special interest to individual parents
   1. Siblings' feelings about the baby
      a. How does _____ (older sibling) feel about the baby?
      b. How does he show you?
      c. How are you helping him accept all the changes in his life?
   2. Siblings' behavior toward the baby
      a. Sometimes children show us how they feel in ways that seem indirect. Has your older child's behavior changed in any way since the baby's birth?
      b. Some children begin
         1. taking things
         2. demanding more of their parents' time
         3. displaying regressive behavior such as wanting a bottle, soiling their pants, or crying more
         4. hurting the baby, perhaps accidentally
         5. ignoring the baby or pretending he is not there
   3. Sleeping patterns and schedule
      a. How is _____ sleeping?
      b. When does she usually sleep?
      c. Does she fall asleep easily?
      d. Does she wake up easily?

        e. Have you had to make any changes to help her sleep?

    4. Feeding

        a. Is he eating well?

        b. How often does he want to be fed?

        c. Is this convenient (workable) for you?

        d. Are there any questions you have about what or how your baby is eating?

    5. Amount of time spent with the baby

        a. How much time do you spend with your baby?

        b. Does this seem just about right (too much or too little) to you?

        c. What determines the amount of time you will spend together?

        d. Do you have time for your other children? Your husband? Your other responsibilities? Your pleasures?

        e. Do you need help managing your time?

    6. Mother's fatigue

        a. Are you getting enough sleep?

        b. Can you get help caring for your home or your child so you can rest?

            1. When would it be most useful?

            2. Whom might you ask?

        c. Are there some jobs you can let slip for the time being?

II. 3–6 MONTH PERIOD

    A. Standard questions for all parents

        1. The baby's growth and development

            a. What is she doing now?

            b. What new things have you noticed?

            c. Have you noticed her, for example, playing with her hands?

        2. The baby's interests

            a. What does he enjoy doing?

            b. What does he enjoy playing with?

               1. How does he play with it?

2. What does he do with it?
c. Does he play more?
d. Has he become more interested in what he is doing than in what you are doing?
e. Have you noticed that he is not as easily distracted from what he is doing as he used to be?
f. Have you seen him practice (or repeat) a new skill?

3. The baby's environment
   a. Where does she enjoy being?
   b. Where does she like to be while you are working?
   c. Are there interesting objects available for her to explore visually, manually?

4. Safety
   a. Is he more active now than he used to be?
   b. Is his baby seat stable and firmly placed?
   c. Do you ever strap him in?
   d. Have you checked his toys for safety lately?
      1. Are there any pieces that might come off?
      2. Are there any sharp points?
      3. Is the paint nontoxic?

5. Awareness of strange situations (strange person)
   a. Does she seem to be aware of strange people? of strange places?
   b. How do you know? What does she do to make you think so?
   c. Does this worry you?
   d. Does this present a problem to you? How?
   e. Is it more difficult (easier) to leave her than it was the last time we talked?
   f. How often do you leave her with others?

6. Parents' questions, interests, and concerns
   a. Do you have any questions about the baby or about what he is doing that you want to talk about?

            b.   Do you have any questions about what he will be doing soon?

            c.   Do you have any concerns (or worries or complaints) that you want to talk about?

            d.   Are there any interesting things that you have observed (or seen him doing) that you want to talk about?

B.   New areas of interest or concern to individual families (probe as necessary)

   1.   Increase in baby's demands for attention and the possibility of "spoiling" the baby

   2.   Increase in the mother's feeling of need to get away

   3.   Beginning of awareness of strangers

   4.   Persistent scheduling difficulties (sleeping and feeding)

   5.   Advantages and disadvantages of having mother return to work

C.   Areas of continuing concern

   1.   Siblings' behavior toward baby

   2.   Amount of time spent with the baby

   3.   Mother's fatigue and sense of overextension

III.   6–9 MONTH PERIOD

A.   Standard questions for all parents

   1.   The baby's growth and development

            a.   What new things is she doing? (Continue inquiry to include gross and fine motor development.)

            b.   Can she get from one place to another?

            c.   Can she crawl?

            d.   Can she pull herself up?

            e.   Can she cruise?

   2.   The baby's interests

            a.   What does he enjoy doing?

            b.   What does he enjoy playing with?

            c.   What are his favorite toys?

               1.   What does he do with them?

               2.   Have you seen him try to solve problems in different ways?

        3.   Does he use the same behaviors in different situations?

    d.   Where are his favorite places in the house?

    e.   What is his favorite room?

    f.   Where does he spend most of his time?

    g.   Does he like to go outdoors?

    h.   What does he like to do outdoors?

3.   The baby's environment

    a.   Does she get a chance to move about? To explore?

    b.   Does she spend much time in her playpen or crib?

        1.   When?

        2.   What kinds of things does she do?

4.   Safety

    a.   Has he ever pulled things down on himself?

    b.   How does he get hold of an object if he wants it?

    c.   Have you done a safety check of your home this month? (See Massachusetts Safety Council Checklist.)

    d.   Have you safety checked his toys lately?

    e.   Where do you keep your cleaning products?

    f.   Can the area be locked?

    g.   Do you have safety devices on your electric outlets?

5.   Social development

    Strangers

    a.   Is he frightened by strangers?

    b.   Is he frightened by strange situations?

    c.   How do you know?

    d.   Has this changed lately?

    e.   Is it more difficult to leave him than it used to be?

    f.   Does this bother (worry) you?

    g.   What do you do about it?

    Gaining and maintaining attention

h. Does she ask for help? How? When?

i. How does she get attention?

j. What do you do?

k. How much of your attention does she seem to want?

l. How often does she try to get your attention?

m. How much attention do you think she needs?

n. How much attention do you think she should need?

Ability to play social games

o. Does he enjoy playing games?

p. Do you enjoy playing games with him?

q. What kinds of games do you play with him?

r. Who starts the game?

6. Parents' questions, interests, and concerns

a. Do you have any questions you want to talk about?

b. Do you have any concerns (or worries or complaints) that you want to talk about?

c. What about the issue we talked about last time? (Consult record of previous home visit to follow up on issues raised.)

B. New areas of interest or concern to individual families (probe as necessary)

1. Increase in locomobility and its implication for safety and restriction

2. Increase in stranger anxiety

3. Increase of fearfulness in unfamiliar places

C. Areas of continuing concern

1. Amount of time that caretaker must (should) spend with the baby

2. Amount and kind of interactive play that is appropriate for the baby

3. Advantages and disadvantages of having mother return to work

IV. 9–12 MONTH PERIOD
  A. Standard questions for all parents
    1. The baby's growth and development
        a. What new things is she doing?
        b. How does she get from one place to another?
        c. Can she crawl? Stand? Cruise? Walk?
        d. Can she climb on anything?
        e. What does she like to climb on?
        f. Can she go up the steps? Down?
    2. The baby's interests
        a. What does he enjoy doing?
        b. What does he enjoy playing with?
        c. What are his favorite toys? What does he
            do with them?
        d. Does he like to put things into and out of
            other things?
        e. Where are his favorite places in the house?
            Outside?
        f. What is his favorite room?
    3. The baby's environment
        a. Does she get a chance to move about? (to
            explore?)
        b. Does she spend much time in her playpen?
            Her crib?
            1. When? Why do you put her there at
                that time?
            2. What kinds of things does she do?
        c. Does she play alone much?
            1. Where?
            2. How much?
            3. Who decides when she should play
                alone?
            4. Do you think she should be spending
                time alone now? Soon?
            5. What do you do with her when you
                can't be available to her?
    4. Safety
        a. Has he ever pulled things down on himself?

     b. How does he get hold of an object when he wants it?

     c. Have you done a safety check of your home this month?

     d. Where do you keep your cleaning products? Your medicines? Is the area locked?

     e. Do you ever carry medicines in your purse? In your car? Could he get at them if you were not looking?

     f. How long are the cords on your hot appliances (e.g., iron, coffee pot)? Where are the appliances plugged in?

     g. Do you have safety devices on your electric outlets?

     h. Where do you keep matches? Could he get at them?

     i. What do you use on the table while the baby is eating? (plastic? cloth? How easily does it slip or can it be pulled?)

5. Social development

Strangers

     a. Is she frightened by strangers?

     b. Has this changed lately?

     c. Is it more difficult to leave her than it used to be?

Gaining and maintaining attention

     d. How does he gain your attention?

     e. How do you know when he wants your attention?

     f. How much attention do you think he needs?

     g. How much should he need?

Expressing anger

     h. Does she ever get angry?

     i. How do you know if she is angry?

     j. What kinds of situaitons make her angry?

Ability to play social games

     k. Does he enjoy playing social games?

     l. Do you enjoy playing games with him?

      m.   What kinds of games do you play?

      n.   Who starts the games?

      o.   How do you know he wants to play?

6.   Language

      a.   Does she recognize any words?

      b.   How can you tell she understands?

      c.   Does she use any words (sounds) regularly?

      d.   What new words is she using now?

      e.   How does she use sounds?

          1.   To express her desire for something?

          2.   To ask for help?

          3.   To express pleasure?

          4.   To express anger? Frustration?

      f.   Do you talk to her? When? How? How much? Why?

7.   Parents' questions, interests, and concerns

      a.   Do you have any questions you want to ask or to talk about?

      b.   Do you have any concerns (or worries, complaints) that you want to talk about?

B.   New areas of interest or concern to individual families (probe as necessary)

   1.   Need for limits on where child can play and explore safely

   2.   Increase of separation distress

C.   Areas of continuing concern

   1.   Increase in amount and sophistication of locomobility

   2.   Amount of time caretaker must (should) spend with the baby

   3.   Advantages and disadvantages of having mother return to work

V.   12-24 MONTH PERIOD

A.   Standard questions for all parents

   1.   The baby's growth and development

      a.   What new things is he doing?

      b.   How does he get from one place to another?

  c. Does he walk well? Run? Climb? Go up-stairs? Down?

  d. What does he like to climb on?

  e. Does he feed himself? How? What kinds of foods?

2. The baby's interests

  a. What does she enjoy doing?

  b. What are her favorite playthings? (toys?)

  c. What does she do with them?

  d. Where are her favorite places in the house? Outside?

  e. What is her favorite room?

3. The baby's environment

  a. Does he get a chance to move about? (to explore?)

  b. Does he spend much time in his playpen? His crib?

  c. 1. When? Why do you put him there at that time?

    2. What kinds of things does he do?

  d. Does he play alone much?

    1. How much?

    2. Where?

    3. Who decides when he should play alone?

    4. Do you think he should be spending time alone now?

    5. What do you do with him when you can't be available to him?

4. Safety

  a. How does she get hold of an object when she wants it?

  b. Have you done a safety check of your home this month?

  c. Have you safety checked her toys lately?

  d. Where do you keep your cleaning products? Your medicines? Is the area locked?

e. Do you ever carry medicines in your purse? In your car? Could she get at them if you were not looking?

f. How long are the cords on your hot appliances (for example, iron, coffee pot)? Where are the appliances plugged in?

g. Do you have safety devices on your electric outlets?

h. Where do you keep matches? Could she get at them?

i. What do you use on the table while the baby is eating? (plastic? cloth? How easily does it slip or can it be pulled?)

j. Where does she play when you're cooking?

k. Have you checked the labels on her pajamas?

l. How securely fastened are the rugs?

m. Does she ever run about in stocking feet on uncarpeted floors?

5. Social development

a. Is she still frightened by strangers?

Expressing anger and affection

b. Does she ever get angry?

c. How do you know when she is angry?

d. What kinds of situations make her angry?

e. Toward whom is her anger usually directed?

f. Does she show affection?

g. Toward whom?

h. What does she do to show affection?

Ability to play social games

i. Does he enjoy playing games?

j. What kinds of games does he play?

k. Who starts the games?

l. Does he ever begin them himself?

m. How do you know he wants to play?

Gaining and maintaining attention

n. How does she gain your attention?

o. How much of your attention does she seem to want?

p. How often does she try to gain your attention?

q. Are there particular circumstances in which she tries to gain your attention?

Using adults as resources

r. What does he do when he has a problem?

s. How do you know when he wants something?

6. Language

a. Does she recognize any words? Which ones?

b. How can you tell she understands?

c. Can she follow a simple direction?

d. Does she use any words (sounds) regularly?

e. What new words is she using now?

f. What do you do when she talks to you?

g. What do you do when you do not understand her?

7. Imitation

a. Does he imitate anything? What? Who?

b. Does he imitate gestures? Which ones?

c. Does he imitate sounds? Actions? Which ones?

d. Does he ever initiate activities which he has imitated before? Has imitation become a game?

8. Autonomy, independence, and negativism

a. Is it more difficult to get her to do what you want her to do than it used to be?

b. Does she use the word "no" a lot?

c. Does she ever seem to be trying to annoy you? Anyone else? Does this seem to happen at particular times? Under particular circumstances?

d. What do you do when she says "no"? Always?

e. Do you ever give in on an issue?

f. Who usually gives in?

g. Does she dawdle?

        1.   Does this bother you?

        2.   How do you handle it?

    h.   How do you let her know what you want her to do?

    i.   Have you had to say "no" yet? How often?

    j.   What are the things you say "no" to?

    k.   How do you say "no"?

    l.   What does she do when you say "no"?

    m.   If that doesn't work, what do you do?

9.   Parents' questions, interests, and concerns

    a.   Do you have any questions that you want to ask or talk about?

    b.   Do you have any concerns (or worries or complaints) that you want to talk about?

B. New areas of interest or concern to individual families (probe as necessary)

    1.   Increased ability of the baby to compete with older sibling adds new dimension to disputes between children

    2.   Growing ability to control body functions raises issues of bowel and bladder training

    3.   Growth of autonomy and increased sense of independence raises new issues of limits and routines

    4.   Displays of anger and aggressive behavior increase

    5.   Appearance of new and unexplained fears

C. Areas of continuing concern

    1.   Need to balance opportunities to explore with safe exploration

    2.   Need to balance interest in the environment with interest in the mother

    3.   Advantages and disadvantages of having mother return to work

List of Health and Developmental Measures

Table C-1. Health and Developmental Measures Used at Each Diagnostic Assessment.

	Assessment Point		
Type of Assessment	*2 Weeks*	*3½ Months*	*6½ Months*
Developmental examination	None	Bayley Scales of Infant Development Denver Developmental Screening Test BEEP developmental items[a]	Bayley Scales of Infant Development Denver Developmental Screening Test BEEP developmental items[a]
Physical-neurological examination	Physical exam Neurological exam[b]	Physical exam Neurological exam Eye blink test[c]	Physical exam Neurological exam Ewing hearing test
Histories, questionnaires, records[d]	Health history Sleep and Feeding Questionnaire[e]	Health history Hearing and vision history Referral records Sleep and Feeding Questionnaire[e]	Health history Hearing and vision history Referral records Sleep and Feeding Questionnaire[e]

Table C-1. Health and Developmental
Measures Used at Each Diagnostic Assessment, Cont'd.

Type of Assessment	Assessment Point		
	11½ Months (optional)	14½ Months	24 Months
Developmental examination	Selected items from Denver Developmental Screening Test and Bayley Scales of Infant Development	Bayley Scales of Infant Development Harvard Preschool Receptive Language Test Denver Developmental Screening Test	Bayley Scales of Infant Development Denver Developmental Screening Test
Physical-neurological examination	Physical exam Neurological exam Ewing hearing test	Physical exam Neurological exam Eye blink test[c] Vision exam including Sheridan Eye Test	Physical exam Behavioral problems list Neurological exam Allen Card vision screening Ewing hearing test
Histories, questionnaires, records[d]	Health history Hearing and vision history Referral records	Health history Hearing and vision history Referral records	Health history[f]

Table C-1. Health and Developmental
Measures Used at Each Diagnostic Assessment, Cont'd.

Type of Assessment	Assessment Point		
	30 Months[a]	42 Months	Entering Kindergarten
Developmental examination	Stanford-Binet Intelligence Test Denver Developmental Screening Test Harvard Preschool Receptive Language Test Harvard Preschool Abstract Abilities Test	McCarthy Scales of Children's Abilities	McCarthy Scales of Children's Abilities[g]
Physical-neurological examination	Physical exam Neurological exam[b] Allen Card vision screening Ewing hearing test	Physical exam Pediatric Extended Exam at Three (PEET)[h] Vision test Ewing hearing test	Physical exam Pediatric Exam of Educational Readiness (PEER)[h] Hearing exam data Vision exam
Histories, questionnaires, records[d]	Health history Hearing and vision history Referral records	Health history Hearing and vision history Referral records Preschool teacher observations	Health history Hearing and vision history Referral records Parent Questionnaire of Child Functioning

[a]Developmental measure developed by BEEP's staff
[b]Adapted from Prechtl and Beintema (1964)
[c]Developed by Burton White
[d]All measures in this category at all ages were developed by BEEP's staff
[e]Returned by parents in mail after exam; developed by Dan Rosenn, M.D., and BEEP's staff
[f]Interval data gathered by mail at eighteen months
[g]Conducted by independent evaluators outside of BEEP's center
[h]Developed by BEEP's physicians (Blackman, Levine, Markowitz, and Aufseeser, 1983; Levine and Oberklaid, 1977)

Evaluation Data

Table D-1. Demographic Characteristics for
Participant and Comparison Groups at Kindergarten.

	Percentage of Children	
Characteristics	BEEP (N = 132)	Comparison (N = 366)
Sex		
Female	42.4	48.4
Male	57.6	51.6
Birth order		
First	38.6	46.1
Second	38.6	31.7
Third	13.6	12.2
Fourth or later	9.1	10.0
First language at home		
English	85.6	92.9
Spanish	9.8	0.8
Chinese	4.5	3.6
Other	0.0	2.7
Mother's age at child's birth		
More than 35 years	5.7	7.8
21–35 years	86.1	87.2
Less than 21 years	8.2	5.0
Mother's education		
College graduate	52.3	50.5
High school graduate	37.9	42.8
Not high school graduate	9.8	6.7
Father's education		
College graduate	57.6	64.4
High school graduate	31.1	30.2
Not high school graduate	11.3	5.4
Parents in home		
Two	75.0	89.0
One	25.0	11.0

Source: From D. E. Pierson, M. B. Bronson, E. Dromey, J. P. Swartz,
T. Tivnan, and D. K. Walker. "The Impact of Early Education Measured by
Classroom Observations and Teacher Ratings of Children in Kindergarten." *Evaluation Review,* 1983, *7* (2), 191–216. Copyright © 1983 by Sage Publications, Inc.
Reprinted with permission of Sage Publications, Inc.

Table D-2. Results from Fall Kindergarten Observations.

| Variable | Percentages of Children with Concerns | | Odds-Ratios | | |
	BEEP	Comparison	Unadjusted	Adjusted for All Background Variables	Adjusted for Significant Background Variables
Mastery skills					
Tasks completed	5.1	10.9	2.29	2.48	2.05
Task attack strategies	12.7	13.4	1.06	1.28	1.34
Time distracted	9.3	10.3	1.11	1.21	1.10
Social skills					
Time in cooperative play	7.6	18.4	2.75**	3.25**	3.19**
Cooperative strategies	2.5	12.3	5.37**	5.37**	5.37**
Social control of peers	2.5	12.3	5.37**	6.05**	5.53**
Verbal social control of peers	2.5	9.5	4.01*	4.81*	5.87**
Use of time					
Rate of social acts	2.5	16.2	7.39**	8.67***	7.54***
Time in social activities	5.1	12.3	2.61*	2.61*	2.46*
Time in mastery activities	12.7	14.3	1.14	1.04	1.00
Time not involved	1.7	14.8	10.07**	9.39**	9.49**
Overall executive skills	5.9	27.4	5.94***	7.92***	7.32***

Source: From D. E. Pierson, M. B. Bronson, E. Dromey, J. P. Swartz, T. Tivnan, and D. K. Walker. "The Impact of Early Education Measured by Classroom Observations and Teacher Ratings of Children in Kindergarten." *Evaluation Review,* 1983, *7* (2), 191–216. Copyright © 1983 by Sage Publications, Inc. Reprinted with permission of Sage Publications, Inc.

$*p < .05$; $**p < .01$; $***p < .001$

Table D-3. Results from Spring Kindergarten Observations.

| Variable | Percentages of Children with Concerns | | Odds-Ratios | | |
	BEEP	Comparison	Unadjusted	Adjusted for All Background Variables	Adjusted for Significant Background Variables
Mastery skills					
Tasks completed	6.8	10.9	1.68	1.62	1.63
Task attack strategies	7.6	14.8	2.10*	2.64*	2.30*
Time distracted	10.2	14.5	1.51	1.40	1.40
Social skills					
Time in cooperative interaction	11.0	14.3	1.90*	2.18*	2.18*
Cooperative strategies	5.1	14.5	3.16**	3.13*	2.61*
Social control of peers	4.2	10.1	2.53	2.29	2.64
Verbal social control of peers	0.9	8.4	10.70**	17.12**	13.60*
Use of time					
Rate of social acts	4.2	16.5	4.48**	5.05**	4.66**
Time in social activities	1.7	6.4	3.97	3.82	3.71
Time in mastery activities	6.8	14.5	2.34*	2.27*	2.27*
Time not involved	1.7	13.7	9.21**	8.41**	9.03**
Overall executive skills	8.5	24.6	3.53***	3.60***	3.29***

Source: From D. E. Pierson, M. B. Bronson, E. Dromey, J. P. Swartz, T. Tivnan, and D. K. Walker. "The Impact of Early Education Measured by Classroom Observations and Teacher Ratings of Children in Kindergarten." *Evaluation Review,* 1983, 7 (2), 191–216. Copyright © 1983 by Sage Publications, Inc. Reprinted with permission of Sage Publications, Inc.

*p < .05; **p < .01; ***p < .001

Table D-4. Results from Fall and Spring Kindergarten Teacher Ratings.

| Classroom Skill | Percentages of Children with Concerns | | Odds-Ratios | | |
	BEEP	Comparison	Unadjusted	Adjusted for All Background Variables	Adjusted for Significant Background Variables
Fall					
Social	9.9	11.5	1.19	1.43	1.46
Work	18.2	10.7	0.54*	0.63	0.63
Motor	4.5	6.9	1.55	1.34	1.43
Reading	1.6	7.2	4.95*	5.58*	7.77*
Numbers	3.9	2.0	.49	1.13	1.67
Overall kindergarten skills	7.9	9.0	1.30	1.46	1.46
Spring					
Social	7.8	7.9	1.02	1.12	1.02
Work	9.3	5.2	0.54	0.42	0.42**
Motor	5.5	4.6	0.84	0.78	0.73
Reading	15.6	10.3	0.62	0.70	0.63
Numbers	0.8	2.5	3.25	3.19	3.39
Overall kindergarten skills	7.1	6.7	0.77	0.82	0.68

Source: From D. E. Pierson, M. B. Bronson, E. Dromey, J. P. Swartz, T. Tivnan, and D. K. Walker. "The Impact of Early Education Measured by Classroom Observations and Teacher Ratings of Children in Kindergarten." *Evaluation Review,* 1983, *7* (2), 191–216. Copyright © 1983 by Sage Publications, Inc. Reprinted with permission of Sage Publications, Inc.

$*p < .05; **p < .01.$

Table D-5. Demographic Characteristics for
Participant and Comparison Groups at Second Grade.

| | Percentage of Children | |
| | BEEP | Comparison |
Characteristics	(N = 169)	(N = 169)
Sex		
Female	42.6	48.5
Male	57.4	51.5
Birth order		
First	43.8	49.7
Second	37.9	27.2
Third	11.2	11.8
Fourth or later	7.1	11.2
First language at home		
English	87.0	81.7
Spanish	8.9	4.1
Chinese	4.1	1.8
Other	0.0	12.4
Mother's education		
College graduate	59.2	53.8
High school graduate	33.1	37.3
Not high school graduate	8.3	8.9
Father's education		
College graduate	62.7	65.1
High school graduate	29.0	29.0
Not high school graduate	8.3	5.9
Parents in home		
Two	82.8	81.1
One	17.2	18.9

Source: From M. B. Bronson, D. E. Pierson, and T. Tivnan. "The Effects of Early Education on Children's Competence in Elementary School." *Evaluation Review,* 1984, *8* (5), 615–629. Copyright © 1984 by Sage Publications, Inc. Reprinted with permission of Sage Publications, Inc.

Table D-6. Results from Second Grade Observations.

	BEEP (N = 169)		Comparison (N = 169)		
	Mean	(SD)	Mean	(SD)	Significance[a]
Mastery skills					
Tasks completed	84.00	18.00	76.00	23.00	<0.001
Task attack strategies	2.13	0.86	1.82	0.83	<0.001
Time not distracted	94.00	6.00	91.00	12.00	<0.001
Social skills					
Time in cooperative interaction	79.00	20.00	77.00	23.00	NS
Cooperative strategies	0.50	0.41	0.41	0.36	<0.01
Social control of peers	97.00	4.00	96.00	5.00	<0.05
Verbal social control of peers	97.00	5.00	95.00	6.00	NS
Use of time					
Rate of social acts	5.34	1.29	5.34	1.32	NS
Time in social activities	51.00	12.00	51.00	12.00	NS
Time in mastery tasks	54.00	13.00	53.00	13.00	NS
Time involved	98.00	2.00	98.00	3.00	NS

Source: From M. B. Bronson, D. E. Pierson, and T. Tivnan. "The Effects of Early Education on Children's Competence in Elementary School." *Evaluation Review,* 1984, *8* (5), 615–629. Copyright © 1984 by Sage Publications, Inc. Reprinted with permission of Sage Publications, Inc.

[a]Significance is based on *t* tests for matched pairs.

Table D-7. Percentages of Children Who Displayed Difficulties in Meeting Second Grade Performance Standards.

| | Percentages of Children with Concerns[a] | | |
	BEEP (N = 169)	Comparison (N = 169)	Significance[b]
Mastery skills			
Tasks completed	14.2	27.2	<0.01
Task attack strategies	17.8	32.0	<0.001
Time distracted	17.8	29.0	<0.05
Social skills			
Time in cooperative interaction	5.9	8.3	NS
Cooperative strategies	17.8	20.7	NS
Social control of peers	1.8	7.1	<0.05
Verbal social control of peers	3.0	7.1	NS
Use of time			
Rate of social acts	1.8	1.8	NS
Time in social activities	17.2	17.8	NS
Time in mastery tasks	11.2	11.2	NS
Time not involved	1.2	1.8	NS
Problems in mastery skills	11.8	24.9	<0.01
Problems in social skills	1.8	8.3	<0.05
Problems in use of time	1.8	1.2	NS
Overall executive skills	14.2	29.0	<0.01

Source: From M. B. Bronson, D. E. Pierson, and T. Tivnan. "The Effects of Early Education on Children's Competence in Elementary School." *Evaluation Review,* 1984, *8* (5), 615–629. Copyright © 1984 by Sage Publications, Inc. Reprinted with permission of Sage Publications, Inc.

[a]A "concern" is a score below the established criterion in any single category.
[b]McNemar's matched-pairs test.
Note: "Problems" are two or more scores below the criteria in an area.

Early Education
Philosophy Statement

Schools that recognize the value of extending their efforts to the family and to the earliest years of the child's life can enhance the learning of children and the well-being of the community. This conviction is based on the work of the Brookline Early Education Project and on a substantial body of related research on child development.

Clearly, certain conditions in the first five years of life influence health development and success in school. Preventive health care which monitors all areas of the child's development helps reduce the need for later, costly remediation. Consistent opportunities for children to listen to and speak with nurturing adults, especially during the first three years of life, facilitate optimal language and cognitive development. Opportunities orchestrated for the child to practice and master a range of skills — problem solving, perceptual, motor, and social — encourage motivation for self-directed learning and enable children both to esteem themselves and to respect the rights and dignity of others.

Parents are better able to assume responsibility for their child's success in school if they feel confident of their abilities to contribute to their child's learning and to the school and community. Information pertaining to child development plus sup-

Source: Statement adopted by the School Committee of the Public Schools of Brookline, Massachusetts, on April 6, 1981.

235

port for the child rearing role from other adults increase parents' willingness to participate actively.

Especially in these stringent economic times, if some of the school's investments to prepare children for success in school and for responsible adulthood are oriented toward the earliest years and toward building a strong constituency of parents, cost-effective benefits will be realized. Further, if the capabilities of other public and private agencies, such as health care providers, mental health agencies, libraries, day care and nursery schools, colleges and universities, private employers and state agencies, are fully and systematically enlisted by the schools, the resources available to enhance children's learning will be increased despite imminent reductions in tax-based expenditures for public education.

A high quality of education for young children, involving partnership relations between schools and parents as well as full utilization of community resources, is the best insurance policy available to a community that is concerned with realizing a high quality of life for all of its citizens.

References

Adler, M. *The Paideia Proposal: An Educational Manifesto.* New York: Macmillan, 1982.

Ashton, P. T., and Webb, R. B. *Making a Difference: Teachers' Sense of Efficacy and Student Achievement.* New York: Longman, 1986.

Baker, C. *Key Issues in Bilingualism and Bilingual Education.* Philadelphia: Multilingual Matters, 1988.

Baker, K. A., and deKanter, A. *Bilingual Education.* Lexington, Mass.: Lexington Books, 1983.

Barnett, W. S. *The Perry Preschool Project and Its Long-Term Effects: A Benefit-Cost Analysis.* High/Scope Early Childhood Policy Papers, no. 2. Ypsilanti, Mich.: High/Scope Press, 1985.

Barnett, W. S., and Escobar, C. M. "Economic Costs and Benefits of Early Intervention." In S. J. Meisels and J. P. Shonkoff (eds.), *Handbook of Early Childhood Intervention.* New York: Cambridge University Press, 1990.

Bayley, N. *Bayley Scales of Infant Development.* New York: Psychological Corporation, 1969.

Berreuta-Clement, J. R., and others. *Changed Lives: The Effects of the Perry Preschool Project on Youths Through Age 19.* Monographs of the High/Scope Educational Research Foundation, no. 8. Ypsilanti, Mich.: High/Scope Press, 1984.

Bijou, S., and Baer, D. M. *Child Development.* East Norwalk, Conn.: Appleton-Century-Crofts, 1961.

Blackman, J. A., Levine, M. D., Markowitz, M., and Aufseeser, C. L. "The Pediatric Extended Examination at Three:

A System for Diagnostic Clarification of Problematic Three Year Olds." *Journal of Developmental and Behavioral Pediatrics,* 1983, *4,* 143–150.

Bloom, B. *Stability and Change in Human Characteristics.* New York: Wiley, 1964.

Bloom, D. E., and Steen, T. P. "Why Child Care Is Good for Business." *American Demographics,* 1988, *10,* 22–27.

Bowlby, J. *Maternal Care and Mental Health.* Geneva: World Health Organization, 1951.

Bradley, R. H., and Caldwell, B. M. "The Relation of Infants' Home Environment to Achievement Test Performance in First Grade: A Follow-Up Study." *Child Development,* 1984, *55,* 803–809.

Bredekamp, S. (ed.). *Developmentally Appropriate Practice in Early Childhood Programs Serving Children from Birth Through Age 8.* Washington, D.C.: National Association for the Education of Young Children, 1987.

Bridgeman, A. "The Great Preschool Debate: When, What, and Who?" *The School Administrator,* 1988, *45,* 8–11.

Bronfenbrenner, U. *Is Early Intervention Effective? A Report on Longitudinal Evaluations of Preschool Programs.* Vol. 2. Washington, D.C.: U.S. Department of Health, Education, and Welfare, 1974.

Bronfenbrenner, U. *The Ecology of Human Development: Experiments by Nature and Design.* Cambridge, Mass.: Harvard University Press, 1979.

Bronfenbrenner, U. "Ecology of the Family as a Context for Human Development: Research Perspectives." *Developmental Psychology,* 1986, *22,* 723–742.

Bronfenbrenner, U., and Weiss, H. "Beyond Policies Without People: An Ecological Perspective on Child and Family Policy." In E. Zigler, S. Kagan, and E. Klugman (eds.), *Children, Families and Government: Perspectives on American Social Policy.* Cambridge, Mass.: Harvard University Press, 1983.

Bronson, M. B. *Manual for the Bronson Social and Task Skill Profile.* Westport, Conn.: Mediax Interactive Technologies, 1985.

Bronson, M. B., Pierson, D. E., and Tivnan, T. "The Effects of Early Education on Children's Competence in Elementary School." *Evaluation Review,* 1984, *8,* 615–629.

Brown, R. *A First Language: The Early Stages.* Cambridge, Mass.: Harvard University Press, 1973.

Bryk, A. S., Wohlleb, C., Malson, M., and Mathis, M. E. "Evaluation Primer and Related Documents." Unpublished manuscript, Brookline Early Education Project, 1975.

Cahan, E. D. *Past Caring: A History of U.S. Preschool Care and Education for the Poor, 1820–1956.* New York: National Center for Children in Poverty and Columbia University School of Public Health, 1989.

Chamberlin, R. W. "Developmental Assessment and Early Intervention Programs for Young Children: Lessons Learned from Longitudinal Research." *Pediatrics in Review,* 1987, *8,* 237–247.

Children's Defense Fund. *Child Care: The Time Is Now.* Washington, D.C.: Children's Defense Fund, 1987a.

Children's Defense Fund. *A Children's Defense Budget.* Washington, D.C.: Children's Defense Fund, 1987b.

Cicirelli, V., and others. *The Impact of Head Start: An Evaluation of the Effects of Head Start on Children's Cognitive and Affective Development.* Athens, Ohio: Westinghouse Learning Corporation, Ohio University, 1969.

Clarke, A. M., and Clarke, A.D.B. *Early Experience: Myth and Evidence.* New York: Macmillan, 1976.

Clarke-Stewart, A. K. *Child Care in the Family: A Review of Research and Some Propositions for Policy.* Orlando, Fla.: Academic Press, 1977.

Cole, M., and Scribner, S. *Culture and Thought.* New York: Wiley, 1974.

Coleman, J. S., and others. *Equality of Educational Opportunity.* Washington, D.C.: U.S. Government Printing Office, 1966.

Committee for Economic Development. *Investing in Our Children.* New York: Committee for Economic Development, 1985.

Committee for Economic Development. *Children in Need: Investment Strategies for the Economically Disadvantaged.* New York: Committee for Economic Development, 1987.

Cook, T. D., and Campbell, D. T. *Quasi-experimentation: Design and Analysis Issues for Field Studies.* Skokie, Ill.: Rand McNalley, 1979.

Crawford, J. *Bilingual Education: History, Politics, Theory and Practice.* Trenton, N.J.: Crane, 1989.

Crnic, K., Greenberg, M., Robinson, N., and Ragozin, A. "Maternal Stress and Social Support: Effects on the Mother-Infant Relationship from Birth to Eighteen Months." *American Journal of Orthopsychiatry,* 1984, *54,* 224–235.

Cronbach, L. J. *Designing Evaluations of Educational and Social Programs.* San Francisco: Jossey-Bass, 1982.

Darlington, R. B., and others. "Preschool Programs and Later School Competence of Children from Low-Income Families." *Science,* 1980, *208,* 202–204.

Datta, L. "A Report on Evaluation Studies of Project Head Start." Paper presented at the annual meeting of the American Psychological Association, Washington, D.C., Sept. 1969.

Davies, D. (ed.). *Communities and Their Schools.* New York: McGraw-Hill, 1981.

Day, B. D. "What's Happening in Early Childhood Programs Across the United States." In C. Warger (ed.), *A Resource Guide to Public School Early Childhood Programs.* Alexandria, Va.: Association for Supervision and Curriculum Development, 1988.

Dennis, W. "Causes of Retardation Among Institutional Children: Iran." *Journal of Genetic Psychology,* 1960, *96,* 47–59.

Deno, E. N. *Instructional Alternatives for Exceptional Children: Papers Prepared for the Exceptional Children Branch of the National Center for the Improvement of Educational Systems.* Arlington, Va.: Council for Exceptional Children, 1973.

Deutsch, M. *The Disadvantaged Child.* New York: Basic Books, 1967.

de Villiers, P. A., and de Villiers, J. G. *Early Language.* Cambridge, Mass.: Harvard University Press, 1979.

Dougherty, L., Bryk, A. S., and Pierson, D. E. "A Comprehensive Approach to Evaluating Educational Progress." Paper presented at the annual meeting of the American Educational Research Association, Washington, D.C., April 1975.

Dulay, H., and Burt, M. "From Research to Method in Bilingual Education." In J. E. Alatis (ed.), *International Dimensions of Bilingual Education.* Washington, D.C.: Georgetown University Press, 1978.

Educational Research Service. "Kindergarten Programs and Practices in Public Schools." *Principal,* May 1986.

Elkind, D. "Early Childhood Education in Its Own Terms." In S. L. Kagan and E. F. Zigler (eds.), *Early Schooling: The National Debate.* New Haven, Conn.: Yale University Press, 1987.

Elkind, D. "Educating the Very Young: A Call for Clear Thinking." In J. P. Bauch (ed.), *Early Childhood Education in the Schools.* Washington, D.C.: National Education Association, 1988.

Ellwood, D. T. *Poor Support: Poverty in the American Family.* New York: Basic Books, 1988.

Engstrom, L. "The Minnesota Experience with Family-Centered Early Childhood Programs." *Community Education Journal,* 1988, *15,* 16–18.

Epstein, N. *Language, Ethnicity and the Schools: Policy Alternatives for Bilingual-Bicultural Education.* Washington, D.C.: Institute for Educational Leadership, 1977.

Erikson, E. H. *Childhood and Society.* New York: Norton, 1964.

Ewing, I. R., and Ewing, A. W. "The Ascertainment of Deafness in Infancy and Early Childhood." *Journal of Laryngology,* 1944, *59,* 309.

Fathman, A. F., and Precup, L. "Influences of Age and Setting on Second Language Acquisition Oral Proficiency." In K. M. Bailey, M. H. Long, and S. Peck (eds.), *Second Language Acquisition Studies.* Rowley, Mass.: Newbury House, 1983.

Ferb, T. "A Preliminary Study of BEEP Parents' Attitudes Towards Playgroups." Unpublished manuscript, Brookline Early Education Project, 1977.

Fiske, E. B. "Governors' Panel Will Seek Broader Preschool Programs for the Poor." *New York Times,* Feb. 24, 1990, p. 22.

Forman, G., and Kuschner, D. S. *The Child's Construction of Knowledge: Piaget for Teaching Children.* Pacific Grove, Calif.: Brooks/Cole, 1977.

Fort, J. "What BEEP Meant to Parents: A Compilation of Unobtrusive, Interview and Survey Data." Unpublished manuscript, Brookline Early Education Project, 1981.

Fort, J. "Perspectives on Early Education." *Children Today,* 1983, *12,* 25–29.

Frankenburg, W. K., and Dodds, J. B. "The Denver Developmental Screening Test." *Journal of Pediatrics,* 1967, *71,* 181–191.

Fromberg, D. P. "Kindergarten: Current Circumstances Affecting Curriculum." *Teachers College Record,* 1989, *90,* 392–403.

Garcia, E. *Early Childhood Bilingualism.* Albuquerque: University of New Mexico Press, 1983.

Garwood, S. G., Fewell, R. R., and Neisworth, J. T. "Public Law 94–142: You Can Get There from Here!" *Topics in Early Childhood Special Education,* 1988, *8,* 1–11.

Garwood, S. G., and Sheehan, R. *Designing a Comprehensive Early Education System: The Challenge of Public Law 99-457.* Austin, Tex.: Pro-Ed, 1989.

Gilbert, J. P., Light, R. J., and Mosteller, F. "Assessing Social Innovation: An Empirical Base for Policy." In A. K. Lumsdaine and C. A. Bennett (eds.), *Evaluation and Experiment.* Orlando, Fla.: Academic Press, 1975.

Goldfarb, W. "The Effects of Early Institutional Care on Adolescent Personality." *Journal of Experimental Education,* 1943, *12,* 106–129.

Goodlad, J. *A Place Called School: Prospects for the Future.* New York: McGraw-Hill, 1984.

Gordon, E. W. "Evaluation During the Early Years of Head Start." In E. Zigler and J. Valentine (eds.), *Project Head Start: A Legacy of the War on Poverty.* New York: Free Press, 1979.

Gordon, I. *Early Childhood Stimulation Through Parent Education.* Final report to the Children's Bureau, Social Rehabilitation Service. PHS 12-306. Washington, D.C.: U.S. Department of Health, Education, and Welfare, 1969.

Gray, S. W., and Klaus, R. A. "The Early Training Project: The Seventh Year Report." *Child Development,* 1970, *41,* 909–924.

Green, M., and Haggerty, R. J. *Ambulatory Pediatrics III.* Philadelphia: Saunders, 1984.

Gresham, F. M. "Social Skills and Self-Efficacy for Exceptional Children." *Exceptional Children,* 1984, *51,* 253–261.

Grubb, W. N. *Young Children Face the States: Issues and Options for Early Childhood Programs.* Rutgers, N.J.: Center for Policy Research in Education, 1987.

Halpern, R. "Major Social and Demographic Trends Affecting Young Families: Implications for Early Childhood Care and Education." *Young Children,* 1987, *42,* 34–40.

Hamayan, E., and Pfleger, M. *Developing Literacy in English as a Second Language: Guidelines for Teachers of Young Children from Non-Literate Backgrounds.* Washington, D.C.: National Clearinghouse for Bilingual Education, 1987.

Hamburg, D. A. *Fundamental Building Blocks of Early Life.* Annual report. New York: Carnegie Corporation, 1987.

Hanson, M. A. "The Nurse's Role in Early Childhood Education." *Pediatric Nursing,* 1977, *3,* 30–32.

Hanson, M. A., and Levine, M. D. "Early School Health: An Analysis of Its Impact on Primary Care." *Journal of School Health,* 1980, *50* (10), 577–580.

Harter, S. "Effectance Motivation Reconsidered." *Human Development,* 1978, *21,* 34–64.

Hartup, W. W. "Peer Relations." In E. M. Heatherington (ed.), *Handbook of Child Psychology: Socialization, Personality Development, and Social Development.* New York: Wiley, 1983.

Hartup, W. W., and Moore, S. G. "Early Peer Relations: Developmental Significance and Prognostic Implications." *Early Childhood Research Quarterly,* 1990, *5,* 1–17.

Hauser-Cram, P. "Designing Meaningful Evaluations of Early Intervention Services." In S. J. Meisels and J. P. Shonkoff (eds.), *Handbook of Early Childhood Intervention.* New York: Cambridge University Press, 1990.

Hauser-Cram, P., and Pierson, D. E. "The Effects of Participation in an Early Education Project on Parent-Teacher Contacts." Paper presented at the annual meeting of the American Education Research Association, New Orleans, Apr. 1984.

Hauser-Cram, P., and Shonkoff, J. P. "Rethinking the Assessment of Child-Focused Outcomes." In H. B. Weiss and F. H. Jacobs (eds.), *Evaluating Family Programs.* Hawthorne, N.Y.: Aldine, 1988.

Hauser-Cram, P., Upshur, C. C., Krauss, M. W., and Shonkoff, J. P. *Implications of Public Law 99-457 for Early Intervention Services for Infants and Toddlers with Disabilities.* Society for Research in Child Development Policy Report, *3,* no. 3. Washington, D.C.: Society for Research in Child Development, 1988.

Hausman, B., and Weiss, H. B. "State-Sponsored Family Education: The Case for School-Based Services." *Community Education Journal,* 1988, *15,* 12–15.

Hayes, C. D., Palmer, J. L., and Zaslow, M. J. (eds.). *Who Cares for America's Children? Child Care Policy for the 1990s.* Washington, D.C.: National Academy Press, 1990.

Hebb, D. O. *The Organization of Behavior.* New York: Wiley, 1949.

Henderson, A. *The Evidence Continues to Grow: Parent Involvement Improves Student Achievement.* Columbia, Md.: National Committee for Citizens in Education, 1987.

Henshaw, S. K., and others. *Teenage Pregnancy in the United States: The Scope of the Problem and State Responses.* New York: Guttmacher Institute, 1989.

Hohmann, M., Banet, B., and Weikart, D. P. *Young Children in Action: A Manual for Preschool Educators.* Ypsilanti, Mich.: High/Scope Press, 1979.

Hughes, J. M. "Minnesota: A Learning State." *Community Education Journal,* 1989, *16,* 25–28.

Hunt, J. M. *Intelligence and Experience.* New York: Ronald Press, 1961.

Jensen, A. R. "How Much Can We Boost IQ and Scholastic Achievement?" *Harvard Educational Review,* 1969, *39,* 1–123.

Kagan, J. "Perspectives on Continuity." In O. G. Brim and J. Kagan (eds.), *Constancy and Change in Human Development.* Cambridge, Mass.: Harvard University Press, 1980.

Kagan, J., and Moss, H. *Birth to Maturity: A Study of Psychological Development.* New York: Wiley, 1962.

Kamii, C., and DeVries, R. "Piaget for Early Education." In M. C. Day and R. K. Parker (eds.), *The Preschool in Action: Exploring Early Childhood Programs.* (2nd ed.) Newton, Mass.: Allyn & Bacon, 1977.

Katz, L. "Early Education: What Should Young Children Be Doing?" In S. L. Kagan and E. F. Zigler (eds.), *Early Schooling: The National Debate.* New Haven, Conn.: Yale University Press, 1987.

Kronstadt, D., Oberklaid, F., Ferb, T. E., and Swartz, J. P. "Infant Behavior and Maternal Adaptations in the First Six Months of Life." *American Journal of Orthopsychiatry*, 1979, *49*, 454–464.

Kronstadt, D., Palfrey, J. S., Wolman, R., and Hanson, M. *Operations Manual of the Brookline Early Education Project Diagnostic Program from Birth to Age 42 Months.* Brookline, Mass.: Brookline Early Education Project, 1977.

Ladd, G. W., and Price, J. M. "Predicting Children's Social and School Adjustment Following the Transition from Preschool to Kindergarten." *Child Development*, 1987, *58*, 1168–1189.

Lazar, I., and Darlington, R. B. "Lasting Effects of Early Education: A Report from the Consortium for Longitudinal Studies." *Monographs of the Society for Research in Child Development*, 1982, *47*, no. 195.

Levenstein, P. "Cognitive Growth in Preschoolers Through Verbal Interaction with Mothers." *American Journal of Orthopsychiatry*, 1970, *40*, 426–432.

Levine, M. D., and Oberklaid, F. *The Pediatric Extended Examination at Three (PEET).* Brookline, Mass.: Brookline Early Education Project, 1977.

Levine, M. D., Wolman, R., Oberklaid, F., and Pierson, D. E. "The Longitudinal Study of Findings." *American Journal of Diseases of Children*, 1982, *136*, 303–309.

Levine, M. D., and others. "Infants in a Public School System: The Indicators of Early Health and Educational Need." *Pediatrics*, 1977, *60* (suppl.), 579–587.

Levine, M. D., and others. "The Pediatric Examination of Educational Readiness: Validation of an Extended Observation Procedure." *Pediatrics*, 1979, *66*, 341–473.

Lovitt, T. C., and Haring, N. G. (eds.). *Classroom Application of Precision Teaching.* Seattle, Wash.: Special Child Publications, 1979.

McCarthy, D. *McCarthy Scales of Children's Abilities.* New York: Psychological Corporation, 1972.

McGuire, J., and Gottlieb, B. "Social Support Groups Among New Parents: An Experimental Study in Primary Prevention." *Journal of Clinical Child Psychology*, 1979, *8*, 111–116.

McKey, R. H., and others. *The Impact of Head Start on Children, Families and Communities.* Washington, D.C.: CSR, 1985.

Marx, F., Bailey, S., and Francis, J. *Child Care for Children of Adolescent Parents: Findings from a National Survey and Case Studies.* Working Paper, no. 184. Wellesley, Mass.: Wellesley Center for Research on Women, 1988.

Meltzer, L. J., and others. "Evaluation of a Multidimensional Assessment Procedure for Preschool Children." *Developmental and Behavioral Pediatrics,* 1981, *2,* 67–73.

Mercer, J. "A Policy Statement on Assessment Procedures and the Rights of Children." *Harvard Educational Review,* 1974, *44,* 125–141.

Mitchell, A. W., Seligson, M., and Marx, F. *Early Childhood Programs and the Public Schools: Between Promise and Practice.* Dover, Mass.: Auburn House, 1989.

Montessori, M. *The Montessori Method.* New York: Schocken Books, 1964.

Moore, E. K. "Child Care in the Public Schools: Public Accountability and the Black Child." In S. L. Kagan and E. F. Zigler (eds.), *Early Schooling: The National Debate.* New Haven, Conn.: Yale University Press, 1987.

"NAESP's Child Care Survey." *Principal,* May 1988, p. 31.

National Black Child Development Institute. *Child Care in the Public School: Incubator for Inequality?* Washington, D.C.: National Black Child Development Institute, 1985.

National Center for Education Statistics. "Preschool Enrollment: Trends and Implications." Report reprinted from *The Condition of Education.* Washington, D.C.: U.S. Department of Education, 1986.

National Commission on Excellence in Education. *A Nation at Risk: The Imperative for Educational Reform.* A report to the nation and the secretary of education. Washington, D.C.: U.S. Government Printing Office, 1983.

National Governors' Association. *The First Sixty Months: A Handbook of Promising Prevention Programs for Children 0–5 Years of Age.* Washington, D.C.: National Governors' Association, 1987.

Nelson, K. E., Carskaddon, G., and Bonvillian, J. D. "Syntax Acquisition: Impact of Experimental Variation in Adult Verbal Interaction with the Child." *Child Development,* 1973, *44,* 497–504.

Newberger, C., Melnicoe, L., and Newberger, E. "The American Family in Crisis: Implications for Children." *Current Problems in Pediatrics,* 1986, *16,* 671–737.

Nicol, E. "Parents' Views of the Infancy Phase of the Brookline Early Education Project." Unpublished manuscript, Brookline Early Education Project, 1977.

Nicol, E. "Recruiting Methods and Their Effectiveness." Unpublished manuscript, Brookline Early Education Project, 1978.

Nyiti, R. M. "The Development of Conservation in the Meru Children of Tanzania." *Child Development,* 1976, *47,* 1122–1129.

Ogilvie, D., and Shapiro, B. *Manual for Assessing Social Abilities of One- to Six-Year-Old Children.* Cambridge, Mass.: Harvard Preschool Project, Harvard Graduate School of Education, Harvard University, 1969.

Palfrey, J. S., Levine, M. D., and Pierson, D. "Antecedents of Middle Childhood Performance: A Study of Preschool Service Needs." In M. D. Levine and P. Satz (eds.), *Middle Childhood: Development and Dysfunction.* Baltimore, Md.: University Park Press, 1984.

Palfrey, J. S., Levine, M. D., Walker, D. K., and Sullivan, M. "The Emergence of Attention Deficits of Early Childhood: A Prospective Study." *Journal of Developmental and Behavioral Pediatrics,* 1985, *6,* 339–348.

Palfrey, J. S., Walker, D. K., Sullivan, M., and Levine, M. D. "Targeted Early Childhood Programming: The Promise Half Fulfilled." *American Journal of Diseases of Children,* 1987, *141,* 55–59.

Palfrey, J. S., and others. "Selective Hearing Screening for Young Children." *Clinical Pediatrics,* 1980, *19,* 473–477.

Palfrey, J. S., and others. "An Analysis of Observed Attention and Activity Patterns in Preschool Children." *Journal of Pediatrics,* 1981, *98,* 1006–1011.

Pallas, A. M., Natriello, G., and McDill, E. L. "The Changing Nature of the Disadvantaged Population: Current Dimensions and Future Trends." *Educational Researcher,* 1989, *18,* 16–22.

Parker, S., Greer, S., and Zuckerman, B. "Double Jeopardy: The Impact of Poverty on Early Child Development." *The Pediatric Clinics of North America,* 1988, *35,* 1227–1240.

Pendleton, A. "Preschool Enrollment: Trends and Implications." In J. D. Stern and M. F. Williams (eds.), *The Condition of Education.* Washington, D.C.: Center for Education Statistics, 1986.

Pfannenstiel, J. C., and Seltzer, D. A. "New Parents as Teachers: Evaluation of an Early Parent Education Program." *Early Childhood Research Quarterly,* 1989, *4,* 1–18.

Piaget, J. *The Construction of Reality in the Child.* (M. Cook, trans.) New York: Ballantine Books, 1954.

Pierson, D. E., Walker, D. K., and Tivnan, T. "A School-Based Program from Infancy to Kindergarten for Children and Their Parents." *Personnel and Guidance Journal,* 1984, *18,* 448–455.

Pierson, D. E., and others. "The Impact of Early Education Measured by Classroom Observations and Teacher Ratings of Children in Kindergarten." *Evaluation Review,* 1983, *7,* 191–216.

Powell, D. K. *Families and Early Childhood Programs.* Research Monographs of the National Association for the Education of Young Children, *3.* Washington, D.C.: National Association for the Education of Young Children, 1988–1989.

Prechtl, H., and Beintema, D. *The Neurological Examination of the Full-Term Infant.* London: Heineman, 1964.

Provence, S., and Naylor, A. *Working with Disadvantaged Parents and Children: Scientific Issues and Practice.* New Haven, Conn.: Yale University Press, 1983.

Provence, S., Naylor, A., and Patterson, J. *The Challenge of Daycare.* New Haven, Conn.: Yale University Press, 1977.

Radin, N. "The Role of the Father in Cognitive, Academic, and Intellectual Development." In M. Lamb (ed.), *The Role of the Father in Child Development.* New York: Wiley, 1981.

Ramey, C. T., and Campbell, R. A. "Preventive Education for High Risk Children: Cognitive Consequences of the Carolina Abecedarian Project." *American Journal of Mental Deficiency,* 1984, *88,* 515–523.

Ramey, C. T., and Campbell, R. A. "Poverty, Early Childhood Education and Academic Competence: The Abecedarian Experiment." In A. Hudson (ed.), *Children in Poverty.* New York: Cambridge University Press, forthcoming.

Richmond, J. B., Stipek, D. J., and Zigler, E. E. "A Decade of Head Start." In E. Zigler and J. Valentine (eds.), *Project Head Start: A Legacy of the War on Poverty.* New York: Free Press, 1979.

Rivlin, A. M., and Timpane, P. M. *Planned Variation in Education: Should We Give Up or Try Harder?* Washington, D.C.: Brookings Institution, 1975.

Rogers, M. "Bilingual Education for Preschoolers: Some Questions and Answers." Unpublished manuscript, Graduate School of Education, Harvard University, 1975.

Royce, C. K., Darlington, R. B., and Murray, C. K. "Pooled Analyses: Findings Across Studies." In Consortium for Longitudinal Studies (ed.), *As the Twig Is Bent.* Hillsdale, N.J.: Erlbaum, 1983.

Rust, F. O. "Early Childhood in Public Education: Managing Change in a Changing Field." *Teachers College Record,* 1989, *40,* 452–464.

Rutter, M. "Family and School Influences: Meanings, Mechanisms and Implications." In A. R. Nicol (ed.), *Longitudinal Studies in Child Psychology and Psychiatry.* New York: Wiley, 1985.

Salisbury, R. H. *Citizen Participation in the Public Schools.* Lexington, Mass.: Lexington Books, 1980.

Sameroff, A., and Seifer, R. "Familial Risk and Child Competence." *Child Development,* 1983, *54,* 1254–1268.

Sarason, S. B. "Policy, Implementation, and the Problem of Change." In S. L. Kagan and E. F. Zigler (eds.), *Early Schooling: The National Debate.* New Haven, Conn.: Yale University Press, 1987.

Scarr, S. "Testing for Children: Assessment and the Many Determinants of Intellectual Competence." *American Psychologist,* 1981, *36,* 1159–1166.

Schaffer, H. R. *Mothering.* Cambridge, Mass.: Harvard University Press, 1977.

Schlesinger, M. J., and Eisenberg, L. (eds.). *Children in a Changing Health System: Assessments and Proposals for Reform.* Baltimore, Md.: Johns Hopkins University Press, 1989.

Schorr, L. B. *Within Our Reach: Breaking the Cycle of Disadvantage.* New York: Doubleday, 1988.

Schultz, T., and Lombardi, J. "Right from the Start: A Report on the NASBE Task Force on Early Childhood Education." *Young Children,* 1989, *44,* 6–10.

Schweinhart, L. J., and Mazur, E. *Prekindergarten Programs in Urban Schools.* High/Scope Early Childhood Policy Papers, no. 6. Ypsilanti, Mich.: High/Scope Press, 1987.

Schweinhart, L. J., Weikart, D. P., and Larner, M. B. "Consequences of Three Preschool Curriculum Models Through Age 15." *Early Childhood Research Quarterly,* 1986, *1,* 15–45.

Schweinhart, L. J., and others. "Chipping Away at the Mountain: A Progress Report on High/Scope's Voices for Children Project for 1985." Unpublished manuscript, High/Scope Educational Research Foundation, 1986.

Seitz, V., Rosenbaum, L. K., and Apfel, N. H. "Effects of Family Support Intervention: A Ten-Year Follow-Up." *Child Development,* 1985, *56,* 376–391.

Select Panel for the Promotion of Child Health, U.S. Public Health Service. *Better Health for Our Children: A National Strategy.* 4 vols. Washington, D.C.: U.S. Government Printing Office, 1981.

Seliger, H., Krashen, S., and Ladefoged, P. "Maturational Constraints in the Acquisition of Second Language Accent." *Language Sciences,* 1975, *36,* 20–22.

Seppanen, P. S., and Heifetz, J. *Community Education and a Home for Family Support and Education Programs.* Cambridge, Mass.: Harvard Family Research Project, Harvard University, 1988.

Shapiro, J. "Stress, Depression, and Support Group Participation in Mothers of Developmentally Delayed Children." *Family Relations,* 1989, *38,* 169–173.

Shonkoff, J. P., Jarman, F. C., and Kohlenberg, T. M. "Family Transitions, Crises, and Adaptation." *Current Problems in Pediatrics,* 1987, *17* (9).

Siegel, L. "The Predictors of Possible Learning Disabilities in Preterm and Full-Term Children." In T. Field and A. Sostek (eds.), *Infants Born at Risk: Physiological, Perceptual and Cognitive Processes.* Orlando, Fla.: Grune & Stratton, 1983.

Silvern, S. B. "Continuity/Discontinuity Between Home and Early Childhood Education Environment." *Elementary School Journal,* 1988, *89,* 147–159.

Sirotnik, K. "What You See Is What You Get—Consistency, Persistency, and Mediocrity in Classrooms." *Harvard Educational Review,* 1983, *53,* 16–31.

Smith, M. S., and Bissell, J. S. "Report Analysis: The Impact of Head Start." *Harvard Educational Review,* 1970, *40,* 51–104.

Smith, S., Blank, S., and Bond, J. T. *One Program: Two Generations: A Report of the Forum on Children and the Family Support Act.* New York: Foundation for Child Development and the National Center for Children in Poverty, 1990.

Snow, C. "Age Differences in Second Language Acquisition: Research Findings and Folk Psychology." In K. M. Bailey, M. H. Long, and S. Peck (eds.), *Second Language Acquisition Studies.* Rowley, Mass.: Newbury House, 1983.

Spener, D. "Transitional Bilingual Education and the Socialization of Immigrants." *Harvard Educational Review,* 1988, *58,* 133–153.

Spitz, R. A. "Hospitalism: An Inquiry into the Genesis of Psychiatric Conditions in Early Childhood." *Psychoanalytic Study of the Child,* 1945, *1,* 53–74.

Steiner, G. *The Children's Cause.* Washington, D.C.: Brookings Institution, 1976.

Stearns, M. S. *Report on Preschool Programs: The Effects of Preschool Programs on Disadvantaged Children and Their Families.* Washington, D.C.: U.S. Department of Health, Education, and Welfare, 1971.

Swartz, J. P., and Walker, D. K. "The Relationship Between Teacher Ratings of Kindergarten Classroom Skills and Second-Grade Achievement Scores: An Analysis of Gender Difference." *Journal of School Psychology,* 1984, *22,* 209–217.

Terman, L. M., and Merrill, M. A. *Stanford-Binet Intelligence Scale.* Boston: Houghton Mifflin, 1972.

Thomas, A., Chess, S., and Birch, H. *Temperament and Behavior*

Disorder in Children. New York: New York University Press, 1968.

Tivnan, T. "Lessons from the Evaluation of the Brookline Early Education Project." In H. B. Weiss and F. H. Jacobs (eds.), *Evaluating Family Programs.* Hawthorne, N.Y.: Aldine, 1988.

Travers, J. R., and Light, R. J. *Learning from Experience: Evaluating Early Childhood Demonstration Programs.* Washington, D.C.: National Academy Press, 1982.

Upshur, C. C. "Early Intervention as Preventive Intervention." In S. J. Meisels and J. P. Shonkoff (eds.), *Handbook of Early Childhood Intervention.* New York: Cambridge University Press, 1990.

U.S. Department of Education. *The Nation Responds: Recent Efforts to Improve Education.* Washington, D.C.: U.S. Government Printing Office, 1984.

U.S. General Accounting Office. *Early Childhood Education: What Are the Costs of High-Quality Programs?* Washington, D.C.: U.S. General Accounting Office, 1990.

Walker, D. K. *Socioemotional Measures for Preschool and Kindergarten Children.* San Francisco: Jossey-Bass, 1973.

Walker, D. K., and Bryk, A. "The Development of a Kindergarten Assessment Battery for the Evaluation of the Brookline Early Education Project." Unpublished manuscript, Brookline Early Education Project, 1976.

Walker, D. K., Butler, J. A., and Bender, A. "Children's Health Care and the Schools." In M. J. Schlesinger and L. Eisenberg (eds.), *Children in a Changing Health System: Assessments and Proposals for Reform.* Baltimore, Md.: Johns Hopkins University Press, 1989.

Walker, D. K., Ferb, T., and Swartz, J. "Kindergarten Teacher Ratings of School Competence." Unpublished manuscript, Brookline Early Education Project, 1978.

Walker, D. K., Weiskopf, S., and Weiss, S. "Recommendations for a Second Grade Test Battery for Evaluating the Brookline Early Education Project." Unpublished manuscript, Brookline Early Education Project, 1975.

Wandersman, L. "Parent-Infant Support Groups: Matching Programs to Needs and Strengths of Families." In C.F.Z. Boukydis (ed.), *Research on Support for Parents and Infants in the Prenatal Period.* Norwood, N.J.: Ablex, 1987.

Wang, M. C., and Baker, E. T. "Mainstreaming Programs: Design Features and Effects." *Journal of Special Education,* 1985-1986, *19,* 503-521.

Weikart, D. P. "Curriculum Quality in Early Education." In S. L. Kagan and E. F. Zigler, *Early Schooling: The National Debate.* New Haven, Conn.: Yale University Press, 1987.

Weikart, D. P. *Quality Preschool Programs: A Long-Term Social Investment.* New York: The Ford Foundation, 1989.

Weikart, D. P., Epstein, A. S., Schweinhart, L. J., and Bond, J. T. *The Ypsilanti Preschool Curriculum Demonstration Project: Preschool Years and Longitudinal Results.* Monographs of the High/Scope Educational Research Foundation, no. 4. Ypsilanti, Mich.: High/Scope Press, 1978.

Weiss, H. B. "Parent Support and Education: An Analysis of the Brookline Early Education Project." Unpublished doctoral dissertation, Department of Administration, Planning, and Social Policy, Harvard Graduate School of Education, Harvard University, 1979.

Weiss, H. B. "State Family Support and Education Programs: Lessons from the Pioneers." *American Journal of Orthopsychiatry,* 1989, *59,* 32-48.

Weiss, H. B., Yurchak, M. J., and O'Leary, K. "Parent Education and Support: The BEEP Experience." Unpublished manuscript, Brookline Early Education Project, 1977.

Weissbourd, B., and Kagan, S. L. "Family Support Programs: Catalysts for Change." *American Journal of Orthopsychiatry,* 1989, *58,* 20-31.

White, B. L. *Human Infants: Experience and Psychological Development.* Englewood Cliffs, N.J.: Prentice-Hall, 1971.

White, B. L. *Educating the Infant and Toddler.* Lexington, Mass.: Lexington Books, 1988.

White, B. L., and Held, R. "Plasticity of Sensorimotor Development in the Human Infant." In J. F. Rosenblith and W. Allinsmith (eds.), *The Causes of Behavior: Readings in Child Development and Educational Psychology.* (2nd ed.) Newton, Mass: Allyn & Bacon, 1966.

White, B. L., Kaban, B. T., and Attanucci, J. S. *The Origins of Human Competence: Final Report of the Harvard Preschool Project.* Lexington, Mass.: Heath, 1979.

White, B. L., with Kaban, B. T., Attanucci, J., and Shapiro, B. B. *Experience and Environment: Major Influences on the Development of the Young Child.* Vol. 2. Englewood Cliffs, N.J.: Prentice-Hall, 1978.

White, B. L., and Watts, J. C. *Experience and Environment: Major Influences on the Development of the Young Child.* Vol. 1. Englewood Cliffs, N.J.: Prentice-Hall, 1973.

White, R. "Motivation Reconsidered: The Concept of Competence." *Psychology Review,* 1959, *66,* 297-323.

White, S. H. "Some General Outlines of the Matrix of Developmental Changes Between Five and Seven Years." *Bulletin of the Orton Society,* 1970, *20,* 41-57.

Willig, A. C. "A Meta-Analysis of Selected Studies on the Effectiveness of Bilingual Education." *Review of Educational Research,* 1985, *55,* 269-317.

Wolman, R., Yurchak, M. J., and Levine, M. *Manual for the Longitudinal Study of Findings in the Brookline Early Education Project.* Brookline, Mass.: Brookline Early Education Project, 1980.

Yurchak, M. J., with others. *Infant-Toddler Curriculum of the Brookline Early Education Project.* Brookline, Mass.: Brookline Early Education Project, 1975.

Zigler, E. "Project Head Start: Success or Failure?" *Learning,* 1973, *1,* 43-47.

Zigler, E. "Formal Schooling for Four-Year-Olds? No." *American Psychologist,* 1987, *42,* 254-260.

Zigler, E., and Black, K. B. "America's Family Support Movement: Strengths and Limitations." *American Journal of Orthopsychiatry,* 1989, *59,* 6-19.

Zigler, E., and Ennis, P. "Child Care: A New Role for Tomorrow's Schools." *Principal,* 1988, 10-13.

Zigler, E., and Trickett, P. K. "IQ, Social Competence, and Evaluation of Early Childhood Intervention." *American Psychologist,* 1978, *33,* 789-798.

Zigler, E., and Valentine, J. (eds.). *Project Head Start: A Legacy of the War on Poverty.* New York: Free Press, 1979.

Zimiles, H. "Rethinking the Role of Research: New Issues and Lingering Doubts in an Era of Expanding Preschool Education." *Early Childhood Research Quarterly,* 1986, *1,* 189-206.

Index